POISONED
IVY

POISONED IVY

IVY

Benjamin Hart

𝕾𝕯 STEIN AND DAY/*Publishers*/New York

To my mother and father

The real names of all individuals in this book have been used except for
Britain Mills and *Melissa*.

First published in 1984
Copyright © 1984 by Benjamin Hart
All rights reserved, Stein and Day, Incorporated
Designed by Louis A. Ditizio
Printed in the United States of America
STEIN AND DAY/*Publishers*
Scarborough House
Briarcliff Manor, N.Y. 10510

Library of Congress Cataloging in Publication Data

Hart, Benjamin.
   Poisoned ivy.
   1. Dartmouth College.   2. Hart, Benjamin.
3. College students—New Hampshire—Biography.   I. Title.
LD1441.H37   1984   378.742'3   84-40310
ISBN 0-8128-2990-5

CONTENTS

Introduction

I hesitate to write the introduction to this book, because, inevitably, it will be compared with my own *God and Man at Yale*. It is more than this and, I suppose, less. My book, recounting the bias in Yale's teaching, collectivist and agnostic, was on the order of a lawyer's brief, full of quotations from textbooks, sample statements from professors, quotations from their letters to the student newspaper. There is almost none of this in the book about Dartmouth by Benjamin Hart. He documents the existence of a bias, but he does so in nonsystematic fashion, and I hasten to say that I'm glad of this, because lawyers' briefs are, on the whole, tedious reading.

Hart's book doesn't concern itself with a comprehensive indictment of Dartmouth's curricular bias. It does more. It describes the way in which the liberal mind works when its basic assumptions come under attack. Hart describes a peculiar "ethos" that has come to pervade the academic establishment, an ethos that the Dartmouth administration and faculty have tried relentlessly to inflict on their students. This ethos was made clear when Dartmouth's president declared that mere disagreement with Dartmouth's Affirmative Action (read "reverse discrimination") policies is by definition "racist"; when Dartmouth proclaimed itself the center for the Nuclear Freeze movement in the Ivy League; when the official college chaplain wrote a letter to all Dartmouth students defending the merits of the active homosexual life; when Dartmouth elected to award an honorary degree to left-wing Shirley MacLaine, while ignoring the Nobel Prize-winning, free-market economist Milton Friedman, who lived just ten miles up the road; when the Dartmouth faculty formally denounced the election of Ronald Reagan in a vote; and when Dartmouth's administration did everything in its power to purge the traditional Indian symbol from Dartmouth neckties, jackets, and notebooks, because, as the students were told by college deans, the Indian symbol is "racist and offensive." Offensive to whom? Offensive to liberals. It's all in accordance with some egalitarian theory.

But *Poisoned Ivy* is not a political treatise; it is an undergraduate's account of his years at Dartmouth. It is not the narrative of a poet, although there is poetry in some of the passages here. Benjamin Hart is, above all, fiercely enthusiastic about life. Some of the very best passages in the book engage us in football, wild parties at his fraternity, cramming for final exams. There are moments when one hopes there will not recur one more drinking scene, although here one must remind oneself that the purpose of reading this book is to take comprehensive account of what life is like on a college campus. The writing is not always even, but it is always engaging. Indeed, the book is rich with nostalgia. The author's sense of sight and smell are marked; the reader feels the tang of Hanover, New Hampshire, and the smell of winter and fall. The author has extraordinary recall when he reiterates what he heard during his undergraduate years. Monsignor Nolan could go into publication from just talking to Hart. In fact, he has. And what he said was splendid, and splendidly said.

I mean to convey that *Poisoned Ivy* has some of almost everything, and a great deal of some things. They are very interesting to me, and I expect they will prove very interesting to many people. It is absurd to suppose that the audience will be limited to a Dartmouth audience. Although Dartmouth is in some ways unique in the sense that, well, the White House is unique, or the Bohemian Grove, or the slums of Manila. The phenomena on which Hart spends his time are phenomena one would almost certainly see elsewhere in American colleges and universities. The antireligious bias of religion departments is hardly unique to Dartmouth. The legendary intolerance of professional liberals one wishes were restricted to Dartmouth and the Smithsonian, but unhappily it is everywhere evident. So what Hart describes will prove interesting to everyone interested in the kind of experiences young people have in college today. And I believe today, as strongly as I believed when I wrote my first book, that a knowledge of what young men and women are reading, and saying, and listening to, is social intelligence of the very first rank.

What is, I suppose, almost entirely unique is the experience of Dartmouth with its competition newspaper, the now-famous *Dartmouth Review.* The author was there when it occurred to a very remarkable and colorful young man—I speak of Keeney Jones—to retaliate against the firing of a student conservative (who accidentally was elected editor-in-chief of the official Dartmouth paper) by founding an opposition paper. What came of that experience, as a result of the combination of high spirit and institutional stuffiness, was a weekly newspaper that has driven some otherwise composed Americans quite literally insane.

Syndicated columnist Patrick Buchanan, recently defending *The Dartmouth Review,* remarked that—following an age when students used American flags as loin cloths, when streaking nude at commencement was almost part of the official program, when a national moratorium was declared in protest of democratically-arrived-at decisions, when shrines were built to Ho Chi Minh while his troops were killing American boys—to object to the irreverence of *The Dartmouth Review* is to betray an imbalance of critical judgment. Some of what has appeared in *The Dartmouth Review* I would not myself have published. On the other hand, I would not myself publish some of the material I myself wrote and published.

oh, ten years ago. Not because the thought was necessarily wrong, but because age brings on evolving perspectives.

The Dartmouth Review is primarily distinguishable by its high spirit. And that high spirit is illuminated by the context in which it was born. If you think back on it, the effort of the president of Dartmouth to erase the historical association of the college with the Indian is really—is it not—a venture in misguided evangelism? Moreover, the humorless insensitivity of that drive moves the iconoclastic spirit. When an entire auditorium full of Dartmouth students and alumni go wild with pleasure at an arrant display of the Indian symbol, what, really, are they engaged in? Retroactive genocide? When Affirmative Action evolves into separatist, sealed-off living quarters and fraternities for black students, officially sanctioned by the college, the rhetoric of desegregation runs into problems with reality that beg exploration. And such exploration is being done by *The Dartmouth Review,* some of it more tastefully than some other; in fact, some of it reads like a right-wing *National Lampoon.* But always in what I have seen there is, I think, an observable integrity of spirit, in the absence of which these words would have been written by someone else. Surely it is only on a campus where the cause militant of its president has become the elimination of the Indian symbol, that on Election Night in November 1980 a dissident student faction would hold a formal black tie evening event and greet Ronald Reagan with a cheer, on the grounds that, no doubt, he will give Dartmouth back its Indian.

The spirit, as I say, is there. Hart's love of Dartmouth as an institution with all her tradition shines through. And we meet some wonderful characters, the portraiture wonderfully done. Benjamin Hart majored in English literature and is concerned with language and poetry. He is also concerned with politics, sociology, and modern culture. At twenty-four, he is off to a fine start and has written a book that handsomely repays the time spent reading it.

William F. Buckley, Jr.

Prologue

The colonial government of Virginia, according to Benjamin Franklin, set up a fund for the purpose of educating a half-dozen young Indians at William and Mary College. The government promised to see that the students would be well provided for and instructed in the learning of white people. "It is one of the Indian rules of politeness," wrote Franklin, "not to answer a public proposition the same day that it is made; they think it would be treating it as a light matter, and that they show it respect by taking some time to consider it, as of a matter important." The Indian spokesman, therefore, did not answer until the following day. He began then by expressing his genuine gratitude toward the Virginian government for making the offer:

> For we know that you highly esteem the kind of learning taught in these colleges, and that the maintenance of our young men, while with you, would be very expensive to you. We are convinc'd, therefore, that you mean to do us good by your proposal; and we thank you heartily. But you, who are wise, must know that different nations have different conceptions of things; and you will, therefore, not take it amiss if our idea of this kind of education happens not to be the same as yours. We have had some experience of it; several of our young people were formerly brought up at colleges of the Northern Provinces; they were instructed in all your sciences; but, when they came back to us, they were bad runners, ignorant of every means of living in the woods, unable to bear

either cold or hunger, knew neither how to build a cabin, take deer, or kill an enemy, spoke our language imperfectly, were therefore neither fit for hunters, warriors, nor counselors; they were totally good for nothing. We are, however, not less oblig'd by your kind offer, tho' we decline accepting it; and, to show our grateful sense of it, if the gentlemen of Virginia will send us a dozen of their sons, we will take great care of their education, instruct them in all we know, and make *Men* of them.

WELCOME
TO THE ZOO

ONE bright New England morn-
ing late in spring term, a senior was delivering copies of *The
Dartmouth Review* to the various administration offices of Dartmouth College. On the way out of one of the buildings, he was
confronted by a middle-aged, upper-level college official who,
completely unprovoked, attempted to push the senior through a
plate-glass door, punched him in the face, kicked him in the leg,
and, while the student tried to restrain him by using a headlock, bit
the student on the chest. The student hadn't punched back; he
thought any violence on his part would result in his expulsion. By
the time a group of college employees ran out of their offices and
subdued the administrator, the senior's sweatshirt was soaked with
blood from the four-inch wound.

The student, after receiving treatment for the bite wound and a
tetanus shot at the college infirmary, filed assault charges against
Samuel Smith, the administrator who had attacked him and who
happened to be black. "It's obvious," commented an editorial in
the *Manchester Union Leader*, "that Dartmouth College administrator Samuel Smith's bite is worse than his bark."

Hanover District Special Justice John I. Boswell refused Smith's *nolo contendere* plea, found him guilty of assault, fined him $250, and put him on three months' probation. The college administration suspended Smith for ten days and, as the *New Republic* put it, "instructed [him] to keep his teeth to himself."

This strange incident did not end there. Three days after the assault, the Dartmouth faculty assembled and voted 113-5 to censure, not the assailant, but the newspaper the senior was distributing, *The Dartmouth Review*. The faculty attacking the newspaper at the meeting were, by and large, militants of every description. They routinely employed the terms "racist" and "sexist" to characterize the students associated with the *Review*.

"It's about time these racists were run out of town," said William Cole, professor of music.

Professor Cole was a kind of guru for the militant black community. He often took up class time talking about questions of race, even though it had nothing to do with the subject of the course. The *Review* once published an article criticizing how Cole conducted his classes. Commenting on the article, Cole said, "You c*ck-s*ck*rs f*ck with everybody. You have f*cked with the last person."

Cole employed similar language at the faculty meeting in his support of a resolution censuring the *Review* for the "offensive content" of its articles.

All but five members of the faculty supported Cole. A number of the speakers said the assault on the student was justified, given "the outrageous material published in his newspaper."

"In the final analysis, the votes of the faculty were not directed against the students who work on the newspaper. It was a public affirmation of our concern for minority issues," said religion professor Charles Stinson, a friend of the student, and more calm in outlook than others in attendance.

But the faculty, by supporting the censure resolution, in effect supported the assailant, Samuel Smith. And, to the surprise of the student, the Dartmouth administration took the side of the faculty:

"The Dartmouth Review," commented Robert Graham, Jr., director of the college news service, "was becoming a baneful influence on campus." The meeting led one to believe that students working for the publication were legitimate targets for assault.

Others, however, disagreed with the Dartmouth faculty. *The Dartmouth Review,* wrote columnist Patrick Buchanan, "is among the best written, best read of the dissenting campus journals that now dot the Ivy League." The paper has been praised by George Will, Hodding Carter, William Simon, Jack Kemp, and other luminaries. Even a generally hostile report in the *New Republic* observes that *The Dartmouth Review* is avidly read in the community, and has achieved a national reputation far beyond the regular student paper, *The Dartmouth.* The *New Republic* article concludes that "the *Review* has succeeded where countless tenured professors have failed—in instigating animated discussions in the Dartmouth community about freedom of the press, affirmative action, women's rights, and journalistic ethics."

Before going on with this story, I ought to let you in on a few facts that I do not think are disqualifying. The victim of the assault, the "bitee," happened to be me. My father is Jeffrey Hart, an English professor at the college, an editor of *National Review,* a syndicated columnist, and a former speech writer for Ronald Reagan. He once said, "Fifteen years ago I went to a faculty meeting and fell asleep. When I woke up I thought I must have died and gone to Hell. I never went to another one."

After I was attacked by Smith, but before going to the infirmary for treatment, I walked over to my father's office. He was correcting the page proofs of his new book on the Fifties entitled *When the Going Was Good.* I was bleeding badly from the chest wound.

"Dad," I said, "I've just been bitten by a college administrator."

"You're kidding," he said laughing, never looking up. He continued to work on his book.

"Really!" I said. "Look at this."

He raised his eyes and saw my bloody sweatshirt.

"My God!" he said. "You're not joking."

My father was, understandably, surprised. But not that surprised. He knew how deeply many on the Dartmouth faculty and in the administration hated *The Dartmouth Review*. In an official college bulletin, the paper had been called "blasphemous." It was a strange term to use, but in a way accurate, because the *Review* had ridiculed, lampooned, and deeply offended every liberal piety left over from the Sixties—pieties that, although abandoned elsewhere, were still deeply entrenched in the academic establishment. Actually, my father's attitude toward the biting incident was dispassionate. No one was crippled, and the attack was, after all, an interesting academic phenomenon.

The issue was this: In the spring of 1980, a group of students, including me, began publishing a weekly newspaper called *The Dartmouth Review*. In its short existence, the paper had taken off like a missile, which regularly landed in the center of the Dartmouth administration, housed in Parkhurst Hall. Every week, as it exploded, the bureaucrats ran for cover. The paper achieved national notoriety, through coverage by *Time*, *Newsweek*, *The Nation*, *The New York Times*, the *Los Angeles Times*, and almost every other major newspaper. Its editors appeared on network talk shows. It supported Ronald Reagan for president, while the establishment student newspaper, *The Dartmouth*, backed John Anderson and, in an editorial, likened Reagan to Hitler.

The *Review* criticized severely the cafeteria-style course selection at Dartmouth. We found it peculiar that there was a non-Western but no Western course requirement. It was possible, for example, to survive at Dartmouth without ever having read a word of Shakespeare, Dante, or Homer. The *Review* criticized the obviously political academic departments—Black Studies, Urban Studies, Native American Studies, Women's Studies—and favored a renewed emphasis on the classics, which had passed the test of time. All this stood squarely athwart the ten-year direction of Dartmouth President John Kemeny's administration. The *Review* had become an item of grave concern, not only to the militants on the faculty but to formulators of college policy in Parkhurst Hall.

To paraphrase what Marlow said in Conrad's *Heart of Darkness*, the biting incident, and the response to it by the Dartmouth faculty, "opened my eyes." I suppose it was the intellectual dishonesty that struck a nerve. Imagine, for a moment, that the administrator had been white and the student he attacked was a black editor of a Trotskyite publication. The moral indignation on the part of the faculty certainly would have cut in the other direction. Or think of it in another way: When student dissenters of the Sixties were burning American flags, taking over administration buildings, and destroying private property, we got only silence from the academic establishment. Where was the faculty outrage? I suspect there is a political agenda behind this selective indignation, especially since, at an earlier meeting, the Dartmouth faculty, in a formal vote, denounced the election of Ronald Reagan—a peculiar item of business for educators.

It was the visual impact, the absurd appearance of many on the faculty at this gathering, that for me said it all. Some wore leather jackets or ponchos. Burlap bags, funny-looking shoes, blue jeans, and beards seemed to be the uniform. I saw no equivalent at this meeting of, say, a Lionel Trilling or Edmund Wilson, great literary critics of the Fifties. It wasn't so much that the Dartmouth faculty lacked style—it had declared war on style. The entire scene represented a spiritual and moral decay that began to take hold in the early Seventies, when a certain political ethos, originating in the Sixties, became institutionalized—when flag burning, gay rights, and appeasement were incarnated in George McGovern, the 1972 nominee of the largest American political party. Antipatriotism became fashionable, even respectable. Patriotism became akin to fascism. We heard over and over again about the "lessons of Vietnam."

Poisoned Ivy

Today, the nation is in the process of rejecting McGovernism. Ronald Reagan is president, and surveys show that the age group within which he is most popular is between eighteen and twenty-four. The college establishment, though, has become the last refuge for the defeated protesters of the Vietnam era. And where these academic holdouts from the Sixties could not exercise their political will over the rest of the country, they are attempting today to impose it on the college student.

The tragedy, it seems to me, is that Dartmouth has the raw potential to be the best liberal arts college in the country. It has the physical assets, both of architecture and nature. It can select the very best students for admission. The faculty is supposedly the best money can buy, and there are certainly a number on it who are more than competent in their respective fields. There is tremendous wealth concentrated at the roots of Dartmouth—a great capitalist accumulation: the Georgian architecture, Baker Library with its towering spire, Memorial Stadium; statesmen, entrepreneurs, scholars, and men of substance make up its alumni; Daniel Webster and Robert Frost walked these corridors and studied in these rooms. I remember reading about a great Dartmouth halfback of the Forties named Frost, who was shot down over Italy during World War II. There was no intellectual or heroic equivalent to these men on the Dartmouth faculty of my time. If style is an enhancement of life, an attempt to rise above humdrum existence, then Samuel Smith, Bill Cole, and their 113 supporters on the Dartmouth faculty had made a profound refusal.

With the stylistic decay at Dartmouth, there also occurred a loss of authority. As an institution, Dartmouth, over the last decade or so, has not exercised educational leadership. Its overall influence has been, if anything, destructive. Openly hostile toward American values, Dartmouth took on a decidedly third world aspect. It downplayed the intellectual foundation of Western man and prompted, instead, an intensely political "special interest" curriculum that satisfied the demands of militant groups. Without the great stories, songs, and speculations that have survived the centuries, what Matthew Arnold called the best that has been thought and said, we are emotionally and culturally impoverished. We know not where we are nor whence we came.

Dartmouth became the center of the Nuclear Freeze movement for the Ivy League. The religious impulse in students was undermined by the official college chaplains, who encouraged instead a desire for "social justice," which meant redistribution of income at home and the approbation of Marxist revolutionary movements abroad. Homosexual activity was officially sanctioned, even funded, by the college, using student tuition money. And, as I found out, anyone who objected risked finding himself on the receiving end of violence at the hands—and teeth—of a representative of academic officialdom.

Dartmouth, of course, was not unique. It was not even the worst offender. But it is a good example of how the American university has dissipated its energy and squandered its intellectual and spiritual capital. That meeting of the Dartmouth faculty struck me generally as an applicable metaphor for the corruption and apparent hatred of distinction that have invaded many of our elite institutions. The other islands of what we might call Sixties Leftism include portions of the major media and entertainment worlds, and the largely anonymous clergy at the middle bureaucratic levels of the American Catholic and Protestant churches. As the nation at large has tended to the right, college faculties have, if anything, become harder left, self-consciously embattled enclaves.

These conclusions were the culmination of four years of experience with Dartmouth's academic officialdom. But my purpose here is not to promote an ideology or worldview. I want only to tell the reader what happened—what I saw. It was my total Dartmouth experience, beginning with my first day as a freshman, and including what I observed in the administration, the classroom, campus social life, and even what I saw on the athletic fields, that crystallized my views on education, politics, religion, and America.

THE FIRST DAY

WHEN I arrived in the fall of 1977 with my bags at South Fayerweather dormitory, I was conscious of the pale September sunlight on the bare walls of my room. All my friends were going to other colleges, so today was a beginning as horrifying as the first day of first grade. My sense of isolation was not eased when I walked outside for a moment and looked across the Green through a row of old elms to Parkhurst Hall, where the president, John George Kemeny, had his office, and beyond to the hills where some trees had already begun to turn brilliant shades of red and yellow, amid the green of the pines. The mild chill in the breeze was a reminder that the first frost had arrived the night before.

I went back inside to unpack. My roommate had not yet arrived. What would he be like? I knew his name and searched through the freshman book for his picture. He looked like a decent enough guy, with a round baby face and bowl-style haircut. I certainly would have felt a lot better had he been there. Did he like sports, or was he more of an intellectual? I studied his freshman book picture. Not having refined features, he did not look like an intellectual, so I put up my poster of Bjorn Borg hitting his two-fisted backhand. Well, I thought, maybe I'll see him after lunch.

How did I get lunch? Since my father was a Dartmouth professor, I had grown up across the river in Vermont and was familiar with the surrounding area, but I had no idea how Dartmouth students went about getting fed. I had never needed to know before.

The loneliness remained. As I sat on the cold tile floor, the radiator began to rattle. The problem of lunch remained. The need for an upperclassman's advice grew desperate. But I didn't know any upperclassmen, any more than I knew any freshmen. I began to wish even more fervently for the appearance of my roommate.

Like every freshman, I felt both excitement and apprehension. I was about to start my college adventure at Dartmouth, in the cold and still hills of northern New Hampshire. I remembered how, when I was a child, my grandfather, who had graduated with the class of 1921, would take me to football games and teach me all the Dartmouth songs. I remembered how my father, a member of the class of 1951, once introduced me to the Dartmouth Indian. I was ten years old. The tall, savage-looking man shook my hand and then lifted me onto his shoulders so that I might see over the heads of what appeared to me to be enormous and frightening monsters —players standing on the sidelines. I remembered how the Dartmouth Indian, with a big green "D" emblazoned on his chest, would hammer on a huge drum and let out high-pitched war cries, and how this would inspire the crowd and the team. As far as I knew when I was ten, Dartmouth had never lost a home football game. I thought perhaps it had something to do with that savage, yet somehow dignified, creature standing on the sidelines in his loincloth, moccasins, war paint, and feathers.

Now here I was as a Dartmouth freshman. I sensed that the place had changed, but could not immediately understand how. I was soon to learn that the simple purity of life in Hanover had become far more complex. The most obvious sign of change was that the Indian no longer stood on the sidelines. He was no longer seen on the football uniforms, nor could one find Indian neckties in the shops of Hanover. Murals portraying the founding of Dartmouth College and the education of the Indians—Dartmouth's first students—by its founder, Eleazar Wheelock, were covered over. Dartmouth songs that had been sung for generation after generation but that made either direct or indirect references to the Indian, could no longer be found in the freshman book.

The Indian symbol, it was claimed, offended some Indians who attended the college. We were told by top administrators that even though Dartmouth was founded for the purpose of educating Indians, the Indian was no longer appropriate as a symbol for a modern institution.

This was the *new* Dartmouth, a Dartmouth that my grandfather never would have understood. I knew that Dartmouth had changed a great deal during the previous six years under the leadership of President John Kemeny. But, I was told in mailings sent to me before I arrived, that all was for the best. So I was happy at the prospect of attending the *new* Dartmouth.

I remembered a time, perhaps six years earlier, when I was standing with my grandfather on the Green. It was Dartmouth Night—the night before the first home football game, against Princeton. Most of the town attended the pep rally to hear rousing speeches by the coaches and players and to watch the traditional bonfire. That year the bonfire was ninety railroad ties, about fifty feet, high. It is the job of every freshman to help build the bonfire, making it taller than the year before. The flame roared, its fiery tongue lashing upward toward the stars, and sparks flew perhaps two hundred feet into the sky, as the intense heat drove the crowd back to a safer and definitely more comfortable distance. It was an awesome sight, and I was confident there was nothing quite like it at any other school in the country. The faces of the crowd and the magnificent eighteenth-century buildings were lighted by the ascending blaze. The smoke surged upward, obscuring a bland moon, and a mob of freshmen ran around the perimeter of the fire, most of them half-naked, with feathers, headbands, and maybe a touch of war paint, yelling war whoops and singing along as the band played fight songs in anticipation of a victory the following day. Towering above the trees, surveying the whole scene, amid the white and brick colonial buildings was Baker Tower, built during the Twenties, a time many thought of as Dartmouth's golden age, under the presidency of Ernest Martin Hopkins, a businessman and Protestant lay preacher from Boston. Baker Tower, the glow from the fire illuminating its huge Big Ben-style clock, looked down on the Ivy League from the New Hampshire woods as if to remind Harvard, Yale, and Princeton that, in terms of pure physical beauty, they had nothing to compare with the towering spire in Hanover.

I looked at my grandfather for a moment, his face reflecting the orange of the bonfire. He must have seen this exact scene countless times before. Not much had changed since he was a freshman, I thought. But then he leaned over and asked me, "Do you see that building over there?" He pointed to the Hopkins Center, a modern building that stood out among its surroundings. I remembered wondering why anyone would build such a thing, much less put it in the middle of campus. It made about as much sense as acne on Princess Grace. A modern art center, it was a turquoise blue polyglot, with pipe railings, industrial plate glass, ramps, and a flat roof. It was a modern piece of junk that would stand forever as a monument to America's ugliest decade.

"That will be the ruin of Dartmouth," my grandfather said.

He was right. Built during the late Sixties, the Hopkins Center was a symptom of an infection that had begun to take hold at Dartmouth. Like all infections, this one, too, would spread. By the mid-Seventies, similar buildings were scattered all over campus. My grandfather, a retired architect, hated that building. He knew it represented a conscious attack on Dartmouth's organic origins. He understood its implied philosophical and political statement, its sharp break with the past.

I decided to get up off the floor and look out the window. In every doorway stood small groups of upperclassmen meeting their friends. From window to window, greetings were joyously shouted. I stood there watching a scene that must have occurred in exactly the same way for generations and would occur again for generations to come. It gave me a sense of communion with the past, a feeling that I had become part of something important. I walked outside and stood for a moment on the steps of Dartmouth Hall, where I could get a good view of Baker Tower. The weather vane at the top of the spire, a sculpture portraying a meeting between Eleazar Wheelock and Big Chief Occum at the founding of Dartmouth, was almost invisible in the halo of morning sunlight glistening off the clock beneath it. Considering its reference to the Indian, I wondered why administrators had not removed it. I suspected it was because no dean had a tall enough ladder. The scene as a whole gave me my first sense of the transitoriness and insignificance of these campus figures, except as part of a two-hundred-year succession. As I watched the flood of new arrivals stopping by all the dorm windows, hailing familiar faces, again a gloom came over me.

I returned to my room, and thought nothing could better express my sense of isolation than the Bjorn Borg poster hanging crookedly in an otherwise-bare room. Suddenly the poster seemed juvenile. As I unpacked my crates and boxes, I concluded that almost all my possessions looked juvenile in contrast to the academic grandeur of Dartmouth. I found a baseball mit, a football, a poster of Walter Payton running for a touchdown. I decided to store this testimony to my immaturity in the closet. I wondered what it would be like to study here, where my dad was a well-known professor. I wondered what my peers might think. I wondered what my circle of friends would be like, what fraternity I would join, if any. My interests, I thought, were pretty standard, so I imagined everything would be fine, once I met some freshmen.

I unpacked my books. One by one I took them out and flipped through them. I thought my collection would probably impress many of my classmates. There were Homer, Dante, Shakespeare,

27

Chaucer, and Yeats. All this was pure affectation since I had not read much Shakespeare or Yeats, and I had not read any Homer, Dante, or Chaucer. I felt a little silly, but I decided to put these books on the shelves along with Plato, Aristotle, Aquinas, Rabelais, Voltaire, Diderot, T. S. Eliot, Bernard Shaw, G. K. Chesterton, each of whom was a closed book to me. It occurred to me how really little I had read in my life. This was something of an embarrassment, since my father's field was English and he had quite a reputation as a literary critic.

The Baker bells boomed the noon hour, and I was no nearer to solving the problem of lunch than before. Maybe I should just wait for my roommate to arrive, I thought, two heads allegedly being better than one. But he might not arrive for hours, perhaps not until tomorrow! It became apparent that I must venture out into the corridor for help.

When I opened the door, I was met by a freshman lugging his trunk up the stairs.

"You must be Jeff Kemp," I said.

"That's right. And you must be Ben Hart."

"Yup," I said. "Let me help you get your stuff into the room, and then maybe we can figure out what to do about getting some lunch."

"We're supposed to go over to Thayer Dining Hall," he said. "I've got a map of the campus."

I was struck immediately by the resourcefulness of Jeff Kemp, who looked exactly like his freshman book picture. He was a stocky two hundred pounds. His voice had the strange quality of being husky and, at the same time, high-pitched. It was a voice I had heard from only one other man—his father, Jack, whom I had seen the previous week on the "CBS Evening News" promoting the Kemp-Roth tax cut program. (I, of course, had no way of knowing at the time that Jack Kemp's plan would one day become the centerpiece for President Reagan's economic policies.) Jeff's voice would be good for delivering public addresses or barking out football signals as the Dartmouth quarterback.

We lugged Jeff's bags into the room and put them in the middle of the floor.

"I see you like tennis," Jeff commented, looking at the Bjorn Borg poster, which by that time had fallen off the wall.

"I heard you were recruited to play football."

"I played at a small high school in Bethesda, Maryland. I don't know how I'll stack up against players coming from the bigger schools, though. I don't even know who they've got."

"Your father was all-pro for the Buffalo Bills," I said.

"You're a football fan," said Jeff.

"Absolutely," I said. "Do you have plans for the pros?"

"You don't go to Dartmouth expecting to play pro ball," said Jeff.

We began unpacking Jeff's boxes. Out came footballs, cleats, a baseball, and some sports posters. His belongings did not look so different from mine.

"Let's get some lunch," he said. "I told Dave Shula I would meet him outside the dining hall at one o'clock."

Everyone knew who Dave Shula was, even before he set foot on campus. He was the son of Miami Dolphins coach Don Shula, probably the most respected football mind in the pro game. The athletic department had already made a big deal over the fact that the sons of both Jack Kemp and Don Shula would be playing football for Dartmouth. Suddenly I felt less self-conscious about who I was. My father was only a professor and an editor of a small magazine.

Dave Shula was waiting for us outside Thayer. He had blond hair and looked a lot like his dad, although his features were more angular. His manner was methodical; he preferred not to waste time or engage in small talk. He was very polite, though, and did not rush someone like me, who was less disciplined about time.

"Dave," Jeff called. "Sorry we're late. I want you to meet Ben Hart, my roommate."

After finishing the formalities and waiting in line to purchase our meal contracts, we went to the main dining area to eat. Both Jeff and Dave were glad to find a table with people they knew, and I was glad to have the opportunity to meet more freshmen. We sat down with our trays of food—onion soup, spaghetti, milk, soda, and apple pie. Dave took the seat to my right, Jeff sat across from me. I nearly choked on my spaghetti when I saw what had just sat down next to Jeff. He was the most enormous creature I had ever seen. On his tray were thirteen glasses of milk—I counted them—eight sodas, three pies, a large bowl of onion soup, and a mountain of spaghetti. I saw the pack of shoulder muscle move under his sweatshirt as he picked up his tray and went back for seconds. He wore a wide, leather weight lifter's belt and had closely cropped hair, almost a crew cut. He would be a fearsome sight to a defensive player facing him from across the line of scrimmage.

"Ken," Dave said. The gigantic one looked up from his refilled plate. "I'd like you to meet Ben Hart, Kemper's roommate." I was soon to discover that a lot of people called Jeff "Kemper." "Ken Cook is an offensive tackle on the team," he said to me. Dave had assumed something of the role of student politician.

"Hello," Ken said.

Dave, who seemed to know everyone at the table, directed my eyes two seats down from Ken. "I want you to meet Buddy Teevens," he said to me. "He might be the starting quarterback on the varsity this year. He's only a junior, so he has another year of eligibility to play. Buddy, this is Ben Hart, Kemper's roommate."

All the players seemed to know each other, even though it was only their first or second day in Hanover. They had met their coaches at the gym earlier that day. At most schools, football teams arrive weeks before the other students in order to begin practice. But Ivy League rules prohibit organized football practice for incoming freshman players prior to the start of the academic year.

"Good to meet you, Ben," Buddy said in a friendly way.

Buddy was shorter than the rest but ruggedly built. He had sandy blond hair and an obvious Boston accent. Most striking was the intensity that lit up his green eyes. Buddy had the information on

30

how to get along, and as inexperienced freshmen we were all eager to listen. He ran through the names of the other characters sitting at the table.

"That guy there in the Hawaiian shirt and beads is Mike Lempress. He's from San Francisco."

"Hey man . . . how's it goin'? The weather's not so good here, but that's the way it is . . . guess it'll do. Not many girls either . . . might be a rough four years." There was no doubt he was a Californian—laid-back, talkative, and a little spaced.

"That's Joe, Bob, Freddy, and Frank," Buddy said.

"Are you guys ready for those placement tests tomorrow?" Jeff asked.

"My God," yelled Joe. "Do we have tests before classes even start?" Joe's face lost all color at the thought.

"You didn't know that?" Jeff asked. "How else are they supposed to know what sections to put us in?"

"They wouldn't want to put someone who has had calculus in with someone who hasn't," Dave said. "That wouldn't be fair."

"Well, if you want my advice on all this," said Buddy, "I'd say it's best to flunk all these placement tests. Unless you score high enough to get credit for the course, the tests don't count for anything. If you do badly, or decide not to take them at all, you won't be put in with all the tools."

"Tools?" Freddy asked.

"It's a Dartmouth term for know-it-all," said Joe. "I'll bet Freddy's a real Black and Decker."

"Anyway," Buddy said, "you have a better chance of getting good grades if you don't get placed in an advanced math or language section. It's always better to start low and work your way up, than find yourself at a level above your ability. Remember, an 'A' is an 'A' and an 'E' is an 'E' no matter what course you take. An 'A' is good, and an 'E' gets your ass sent down Route 91."

The information and advice continued. When Buddy stopped talking, one or another of the freshmen at the table would pass on some secondhand tidbit of legendary character, gleaned from an

31

anonymous source. "Someone told me the economics department has some of the worst professors at the college." Or, "Apparently, there is one professor who's so bad people take his course just to see if anyone can really be that bad." Or, "His lecture notes are supposedly so ancient that once students saw a page fall off the podium and shatter as it hit the floor." Or, "There is supposed to be a guy teaching French who is a brilliant wild man."

"That's John Rassias. He was written up in *Time*. They say he does all kinds of things in class—climbs walls, breaks windows, swings off balconies—anything to make a point stick. He sure gets results."

"They say freshmen can't get dates."

"Speak for yourself," said Mike.

"A monastic life isn't my idea of college, let me tell you," said Joe.

People from all corners of the table volunteered information. Amazingly, most of what was said proved to be true, even the part about dates. Only recently had Dartmouth started admitting women, and they were still far outnumbered by the men. I sat there and absorbed all of what was said, and I thought to myself that the difference between going to Dartmouth and another school might be greater than I had supposed.

Later that night I met all my new acquaintances in front of Massachusetts row where floodlights illuminated a large party. Ken Cook, the giant lineman, was there holding an enormous beer stein that looked more like a vat than something you would drink out of. I wished my head towered above the mob the way his did, as I had a hard time seeing who was there.

"Hey man, what's shakin'?" It was the Californian, Mike Lempress. He had dark hair and wore a white V-neck sweater, bell-bottoms, and flip-flop sandals. To everyone's surprise, he was surrounded by a mob of very enthusiastic girls. "Hey, Shu . . . man . . . Kemper, Buddy, Ben, Freddy . . . good to see you dudes. I'm really fired up about this place. It's not like San Fran, man, but I'll take it

for four years." The girls giggled. Mike looked exactly like Joe
Namath, with a dimple right smack in the middle of his chin.

"Hello, Mike."

"Hello, Lemp."

"Glad you could make it, Lemp." Mike Lempress had already
become known as "The Lemp."

A group of upperclassmen had noticed our group—freshmen
were not supposed to be noticed. Lemp was a little on the loud side
and seemed to have the ability to draw attention to himself. If a
freshman drew attention to himself, he risked being labeled uppity.
It was not good to be an uppity freshman. One upperclassman
walked over to where we were standing. He had on a green letter-
man's sweater with a big white "D" on his chest. He looked at me.

"I think you and this flower child here just volunteered to play in
our chug-off," he said.

"What's a chug-off?"

I soon found out that it was a drinking game involving two
teams organized into two separate lines. Each team member would
hold two beers. At the shout of "Go!" the first man in each line
would chug his first beer. When he was finished, the next in line
would chug. After each in line had chugged, the first in line would
slurp down his second beer, and so forth. Spillage, as it was called,
was unacceptable. Anyone who spilled beer, even a drop, would
have to chug the remainder of the beer, refill his cup, and chug
again. The first team to finish won. The losing team, of course,
would have to chug again, the theory behind that being that the
losing team needed the practice.

In my first chug-off, I found myself on a team of freshmen pitted
against a team of upperclassmen from Phi Delta Chi fraternity. The
winners of last year's annual fraternity chug-off, they chugged ten
beers in 9.2 seconds—official time—an Ivy League record. They
didn't just drink the beer; they inhaled it. They didn't simply pour
the beers into their mouths; they wrapped their lips completely
around the rim of the cup and then squeezed the thing with their
hands like a tube of toothpaste, crushing the plastic so that the

33

liquid would shoot down their throats, which they had trained to open like a trap door.

Needless to say, we lost, and I had my share of spillage. It was not long before I was quite drunk. Despite the loss, the laughter of the crowd was invigorating. The Lemp was a complete wreck by the end of the evening. Someone said that he had consumed eighteen beers in two hours. I heard Lemp singing an old Dartmouth fight song that he must have learned that evening: "Dartmouth's in town again, run girls run. Dartmouth's in town again, fun girls fun. . . ." He staggered over to the grass in order to lie down.

An amorphous band of freshmen had begun to take shape. That first day had brought us together. Something more than juxtaposition at a table in Thayer Dining Hall had given us confidence in each other. Kemp, Lemp, Dave, Joe, Freddy, Frank, and I would all, later on, join Buddy's fraternity, the famous and awful Beta Theta Pi. That night Californians were discovering that Easterners were not the cold aristocratic snobs of Ivy repute. Easterners found that being from the Midwest did not mean being a bore. All were pleased to find that athletic prowess counted in their favor, as long as they did not desire stardom too quickly, or worse, too visibly. Although no one ever missed an opportunity to criticize another's strange customs and accent, everyone tried to acknowledge the good fellowship and merit in these new faces.

I looked at my watch. "It's two in the morning!" Jeff had long since gone off to bed.

"I think it's time to hit the sack," said Lemp—the effects of the alcohol had begun to wear off. "Are you leaving, Ben?"

"Yes," I answered. "I want to get to bed before sunrise."

Still, on my way back to my dorm, I stopped and stood for awhile, rapt in submission to this grand beneficence of wood and stone, this sequestered hill overlooking a single winding valley that was bathed in moonshine and that sheltered me at the end of this day, which I would probably remember until my last hour.

I loved Dartmouth. I couldn't wait to find my niche in this two-hundred-year-old bastion of continuity. Men like Daniel

Webster, Robert Frost, and Nelson Rockefeller had walked these same paths, along with other men who, although not famous, were nonetheless, as much a part of this place as the long list of renowned alumni.

For an hour I looked across the campus, forgetting the world. Afterward I returned to South Fayerweather dorm, to find my own name written in Old English letters on the door of my room. It felt good to walk in and find Jeff sound asleep in his bed, sensing that even though I had met him only today I had a friend for life. It was pleasant to climb into my bed for the first time and to pull my own blankets over my tired body to protect it from the cool September breeze coming through the open window. But it was my greatest satisfaction to look over at my book case, its titles and authors lit by the moon. I looked forward to consuming them all during my next four years. For that purpose, and that alone, was this small college built. "That is what we do here," I had heard a professor say. I had entered a new world, sensed its magic, and heard the whisper of a great Western tradition beckoning me onward.

TEAMING UP

ON the Saturday before classes began, the morning was spent meeting the president of the college, John Kemeny, and I must say that my conversation with one of the president's aides left a deeper impression on me than did the president himself. President Kemeny was not in good physical shape. His complexion was pasty, as if he had not ventured outdoors since taking office. He was a chain-smoker and had a chronic cough. He had trouble walking up a flight of stairs without stopping for breath, and, according to his secretary, he almost never arrived at work before eleven in the morning.

One other peculiar thing about him: during his entire ten years as Dartmouth president, he delivered only twenty-eight speeches to the student body. That just about covered his convocation and graduation obligations and possibly one other address during the year. In the past, Dartmouth presidents had spoken to the student body about once a week. Ernest Martin Hopkins, for example, spoke almost every day at morning chapel, which all students were then required to attend. As a result, he had an important influence on what the students thought and talked about. George Champion of the class of 1926 and the chairman of Chase Manhattan Bank once said, "President Hopkins was like a father to me. He once said that if I wasn't an asset to my family, my community, and country when I left Hanover, Dartmouth had failed." Kemeny, on the other hand, was about as available as a solar eclipse. Many students didn't know what he looked like, and most hardly ever thought about him. He didn't like to go out for lunch, preferring to have his sandwich brought in from a local restaurant. Kemeny's work took place behind the scenes, out of public view. It was as if he did not want people to know what he was doing. He kept his work and his plans to himself and sent out proxies to answer questions and fend off the curious. Kemeny tried to change Dartmouth from the inside out, and people were beginning to object.

But for all John Kemeny's peculiarities, he must be given credit for making Dartmouth's mathematics department one of the best in the country. He went to Princeton and later became an assistant there to Albert Einstein. President Dickey brought him to Dartmouth to add prestige to the mathematics department and to oversee the building of the Kewitt computer center. As a matter of fact, it was John Kemeny who invented BASIC, a widely used computer language.

A gifted mathematician, however, does not necessarily a good president make. As almost everyone who has spoken even once with a mathematician can tell you, the mathematical head often has blinders attached to it. When life doesn't fit neatly into a theory, it's not life's fault. It's like trying to fit a suit into a suitcase that is too small, taking out a pair of scissors and cutting off the sleeves and legs, and then wondering why the suit is so funny-looking. That's exactly what John Kemeny tried to do at Dartmouth—fit life into a theory. But his theory was too small.

On a Sunday evening early in the fall, the student body gathered in the enormous Rupert C. Thompson Hockey Arena to hear the annual address of welcome and exhortation by President Kemeny. Kemeny had come under a good deal of criticism from the alumni about the repeated poor performance of the football team. Everyone knew it was a conscious effort on the part of Kemeny to scale down the importance of athletics, especially men's athletics. Alumni contributions were not up to snuff, and the students awaited their president's explanation.

Kemeny was sitting in a chair to the left of the speakers' podium waiting for Ralph Manuel, dean of the college, to finish his introduction. President Kemeny made it a point never to bring cigarettes to a convocation address, having been told by his aides that it would be deleterious to his image if the students saw him chain-smoking, especially during a speech on college athletics. The abstention left him in obvious discomfort. One could hear the phlegm rattling in the deep regions of his throat. When it was his turn to speak, Kemeny stood up, using the chair he had been sitting on for support, shuffled across the floor to the microphone, and delivered his address to the students:

> . . . I certainly do not concede that concentrating all your energies on the soundness of the body has anything whatsoever to do with achieving a sound mind. I will concede the first statement ["a sound mind and a sound body"] because if you're going to abuse the human body, a deterioration of the mind is likely to follow.

President Kemeny paused for a moment to take a few deep breaths. He put his hand to his lips, as if forgetting that he did not have a cigarette. He looked at his fingers and then put his palm to his mouth again to muffle a series of coughs. The coughs began softly, then escalated, until I thought the violence of the convulsions might cause him to become sick right then and there. He was able to pull himself together and, damp-eyed, continued.

> I have not detected a close correlation between physical achievement and intellectual achievement. Indeed I might go as far as to detect a negative correlation between the two.

39

Poisoned Ivy

He paused a moment; his sides heaved several times. He fumbled with his papers, then went on.

> America is famous as a country in which physical fitness is greatly prized; there are enormous campaigns reminding us of the importance of physical fitness. My regret is that they are not accompanied in anything like the same measure by organized campaigns for mental fitness. Indeed the danger signs are up all around the nation, and I will mention a few of them. Each of them points in the direction that the importance of the body over the mind is out of proportion in our country today.

I looked over at Jeff Kemp and Dave Shula. I knew they were optimistic about their football careers at Dartmouth. Now their faces indicated considerable consternation. I saw several members of the football coaching staff, including head coach Joe Yukica, and wondered what must be going through their minds. They must have had questions as to what president Kemeny's speech foretold about the future of Dartmouth football—but not many questions. Kemeny's rousing welcome continued:

> The human brain is a remarkable instrument. In the age of computers, it's very popular to write articles exploring the superiority of machines. I have had occasion to write more than once on the other side of the particular debate. Take into account that the computer today is a million times faster in its processes than the human brain, and yet it is true that there are many tasks ordinary human beings carry out without difficulty that today's computers cannot do, or do so badly that we can far excell them in these tasks. One wonders how it is possible, how one can give away a factor of one million in speed and yet out-perform these magnificent monsters . . .

I felt relieved that a computer still couldn't write *The Divine*

40

Comedy, feel a strong belief in God one moment and doubt the next, or enjoy taking a pretty girl out for dinner.

The bells boomed out Dartmouth's alma mater from the tower of Baker Library as the undergraduates filed out of Thompson Arena and down the gravel walkways past the football stadium, toward the center of campus, finally arriving either at the quiet of their own rooms or at a fraternity party on Webster Avenue.

The president's speech seemed to have little impact on the other students. Nothing Kemeny said provoked much comment one way or another. As for me, I came to the conclusion that physical fitness was a better addiction than cigarettes. The main topics of conversation that evening were how the Boston Red Sox would fare against the New York Yankees in the upcoming three-game series, or what was going on in the fraternities that night.

From out of the darkness I heard a yell, "Ben! Wait up!"

I turned and saw someone running up behind me. It was too dark to see who it was.

"It's me, Greg Fossedal. You remember, we met yesterday at Aquinas House. You were watching the Red Sox game on TV."

"Sure," I said, "you were with that Jones fellow. I think he and I are taking Latin together."

Greg had a slightly amused look on his face. He was an enormous lumbering individual of Norwegian descent, weighing perhaps 235 pounds. When he walked he leaned forward in an exaggerated way, his neatly pressed trousers bulging around the calf area.

"I'm supposed to meet that Jones fellow at the Hanover Inn for a few drinks. We'd like to have you join us for our evening wine." He said this as if it were a nightly ritual.

We arrived at the Hanover Inn, which was situated at the corner where Wheelock and Main streets intersect. It faced Baker Library, which was on the other side of the Green. We entered the bar area and found a vacant table.

"What will you have this evening, Mr. Fossedal?" asked the waitress.

41

"After listening to that convocation address . . . I'll have a liter of white wine and a gin and tonic," answered Greg, with a big grin.

The waitress looked distressed, then smiled as she took down the order. Her blue eyes looked at me.

"What will you have, Sir?"

"A glass of burgundy, please," I said.

The waitress, in her white evening gown, was pretty. Light from the candles glistened off her red hair.

"I want you to meet that Jones fellow," said Greg, with a muffled chuckle. "Mike Jones."

"What an ordinary name," I said.

"His full name is Michael Keenan Jones. Some of us just call him Keeney, and he's not ordinary at all," said Greg. "His mother told me that the moment Keeney was born she knew that something was odd. He landed in this world grinning. It was as if, from the very start, he knew this place was an amusement park."

"I'm looking forward to meeting him."

"He said he might bring his friend along. Anthony Desiré."

"What's Anthony Desiré like?" I asked.

"A very bright fellow, sharp of wit, but somewhat eccentric."

"Where's he from?" I asked.

"He grew up in Washington, D.C., and was educated by Jesuits. He's one of Dartmouth's brightest track prospects. He specializes in the middle distances."

The waitress carried our overloaded drink tray from the bar to our table. While Greg lined up his gin and tonic and liter of white wine, and polished off both in short order, two subdeans, seated nearby, seemed to be getting apoplectic, which may have given Greg a bigger lift than the alcohol.

Looking out a window that separated the bar from the lobby, Greg suddenly exclaimed, "Oh good! Here comes Keeney—and there's Anthony." As he stood up to greet the newcomers, he put on a pair of Vuarnet sunglasses.

"Greetings!" said a tall, slender black fellow, putting out his hand to shake mine. "My name is Anthony Desiré."

42

"Ben Hart," I said. "It's good to meet you."

Anthony took off his raccoon coat. He was wearing a white sports jacket with a red-and-white, candy-striped shirt unbuttoned at the collar.

"This is Michael Jones," said Anthony. "Some know him as Keeney Jones, or M. K. Jones, or M. Keenan Jones."

"What name are you going by this evening?" Greg asked.

"Keeney is fine, or just Mr. Jones. Whichever makes you more uncomfortable."

Jones was wearing a blue-and-white-striped seersucker jacket, white flannel trousers rolled up at the cuffs, loafers and white socks, a necktie with a picture of Uncle Sam saying "We Want You," and two buttons on his lapel, one of which read "Nixon in 1980," and the other with a picture of a B-52 bomber, under which was written "DROP IT." His cheeks were red, and he had an impish grin, as if he had just done something completely irresponsible. He was pulling behind him, on a leash, a baby blue foam-rubber shark. The shark's name, I learned, was Chesterton. Jones ordered a strawberry daiquiri, threw his Sherlock Holmes hat on a rack, exposing his blond curls, and sat down between Anthony and Greg.

"Hello, Ben," said Keeney. "I believe I saw you at Aquinas House the other day, watching TV, or was it at the liberation theology Mass, with the electric guitars and the sermons against American support of the Shah?"

I knew immediately that he was talking about Father Joe, a trendy Jesuit who had recently come to Dartmouth from Boston, allegedly because he was attuned to our generation.

"It couldn't have been at that Mass," I said. "I prefer Monsignor Nolan. He still talks about God and the sacraments. Strange thing, though, his Masses are packed anyway."

"I overslept the real Mass," Jones said, "so I was forced to go to what they call the folk liturgy. You know Father Joe. . . ." Keeney chuckled, "He threw out all those buzz words about not being *ethnocentric* or *divisive*, and he mentioned something about *inter-*

43

personal relationships, which struck me as redundant. I simply do not understand the reason for putting the prefix *inter* on the word *personal.* And if something is *interpersonal,* doesn't that make it a *relationship?* Now I must say that I'm extremely *ethnocentric,* which I suppose is *divisive.* But didn't Christ say he was going to separate the wheat from the chaff and the goats from the sheep? Sounds *divisive* to me. Oh well, Father Joe's sermon didn't apply to anything I was doing, so I tuned out and read my *National Review* until he finished."

"Waitress! Uhh . . . waitress!" called Anthony.

The red-haired girl walked over. Anthony smiled at her, exposing what seemed to be an inordinate number of teeth.

"What can I get you?" she asked.

"I'll have a Gibson, up, when you get a chance."

"Certainly," she said.

Greg had just finished a second liter of white wine, to the shock of those at nearby tables, especially the two subdeans. Greg held his beverage well, and spoke clearly.

"What did you think of President Kemeny's speech this evening?" he asked Anthony.

"It doesn't look good for sports," Anthony said. "I think the man hates football and hockey more than track. You can tell he hates anything that has the tint of macho."

"Kemeny probably doesn't know the track team exists," said Keeney. "He'll get rid of football first, if he can. That would be a much louder political statement."

"What Kemeny hates most are the alumni," said Anthony. "They are much too plebian for him. That's why he's put such an effort into getting government grants for the college. If he can get the government to finance this place, he can proceed with his own private agenda. But, as long as Dartmouth runs on alumni contributions, the alumni will be a problem for him. If he gets the chance, he'll give it to them where it hurts, he'll cut back on football."

As the evening went on, I could feel three good friendships developing: with Greg, with Anthony, and with Michael Keenan

44

Jones. I could never figure out whether Jones was in spirit the oldest or youngest student to attend Dartmouth College; he was only seventeen, but he used to say, "I can't wait until I'm forty-five and extremely fat."

I ordered another glass of wine; Jones decided to get another strawberry daiquiri; Greg asked for a vodka martini "shaken, not stirred"; Anthony told a few ethnic jokes, one of which went something like this:

"There was a very urbane black gentleman on a train reading the *Wall Street Journal*. Dressed in a Brooks Brothers suit, with gold tie pin, it was obvious he had risen high on the corporate ladder; perhaps he was the chairman of a major bank. Sitting across from him was a lower-class Southern woman. She was growing increasingly enraged while watching the suave black man flip through the stock price quotations. Before getting off the train, she walked up to him, stared him straight in the face, and screamed 'Nigger! Nigger! Nigger!' At which point the black man looked around and asked, 'Where? Where? Where?'"

Greg and I winced. Anthony, naturally, laughed uproariously.

After a while we decided to walk over to Webster Avenue to see what was happening at the fraternities. Jones paid the bill.

"Isn't it a little early?" asked Keeney. "I mean, the women are still doing whatever it is they do with themselves before going to the parties."

"It's not too early to get some beers," Greg said. "Let's go over to the Beta house before it gets too crowded."

The wine was humming in my head as I tried to listen to the somehow distant conversation of my newfound friends. The bells chimed in Baker Tower. President Kemeny's sour speech earlier that evening seemed foreign to all this.

We arrived at the Beta house. The place was so packed with people that I found it difficult to move. The New Wave group "Blondie" blasted from Beta's eight-speaker stereo system. People were dancing outside because there was no room in the building. The booze was flowing and people were laughing, but Keeney

45

found the party extremely distasteful. He could not stand the closeness of the big crowd, the smell of stale beer and sweaty bodies. What Jones hated most, however, was the loud music; you could not hear the person talking to you, which may not have been altogether a bad thing. Keeney saw the entire scene as barbaric, Philistine, and beneath the dignity of the Ivy League. Although Jones always defended the fraternities against attacks by the administration, which he saw as even more Philistine, he thought that these social clubs ought to be a bit more cultured, sophisticated, elegant.

I saw Jeff Kemp wrestling with someone in the middle of the floor. Several people in the corner of the room had completely passed out.

"This is our culture," I heard Jones say, "the leaders of tomorrow's America." He pointed to a young gentleman getting sick out the window, or booting, as it was called in current jargon.

Downstairs, on the slime-coated floor of the basement, one could find what was known to the administration in Parkhurst Hall as a horror show. Mike Lempress had chugged his tenth straight beer and had some notion of breaking the all-time Dartmouth record of thirty-three. He failed, but not from want of trying.

Buddy Teevens, the starting Dartmouth quarterback, had convinced a freshman to place a beer cup on his head, the idea being that Buddy would try and knock the plastic cup off by throwing a beer keg at it. It turned out that Buddy was better at throwing footballs than kegs—much better. Buddy missed and the poor freshman spent the rest of the night in the clinic, a not-uncommon consequence of the sport popularly known as William Tell.

While I was talking to one of the frat brothers from Alpha Delta, he suddenly looked ill. His face turned distinctly greenish as he ran to the garbage can. From out of his stomach came a section from a golf ball, which he had swallowed earlier that afternoon while playing beer golf. Beer golf was another popular sport in which, for every stroke one loses to the opponent, one must chug a beer. After

46

his trip to the garbage can, the young scholar returned, and we continued our conversation.

Anthony had met a pretty blonde-haired girl named Judy from Colby Sawyer, a nearby women's college. Judy was charmed by Anthony, and neither had been seen for quite some time.

Greg and I stayed at Beta until about three, drinking beer and talking with some of the house brothers, but I could not hear much of what was said over the blast of the eight speakers. The enormous Ken Cook was entertaining a group of Smith girls by smashing beer cans with his fist. The girls had traveled to Dartmouth from Smith College for the weekend. They were quite impressed by Ken and giggled a lot. But a smallish fellow, by the name of Charlie, stole the show when he used his forehead to crush an unopened can of beer. He stood the can on its end and smashed his head squarely on its top. As the metal sides of the container burst, beer flew all over the room. Life in the fraternity basement, despite its lack of class, had a certain primitive charm. I decided I would probably join the house in spring; most of the people there knew how to have a good time.

Keeney, Anthony, Greg, and I spent many idyllic afternoons at the Hanover Inn drinking white wine, burgundy, gin fizzes, strawberry daiquiries, Margueritas, martinis, Gibsons, or whatever struck our fancy. If the weather was nice, we would lunch on the inn's outdoor terrace, sitting there until dusk and sometimes well into the evening.

Some resented our group, accusing us of being cliquish. If that meant preferring the company of some to the company of others, we were cliquish.

Greg, Jones, and I often discussed literature and life. A major theme with Greg was injustice. He sympathized with the powerless. Bullying was central to his conception of human evil. I remember his raging when he heard that Karen Blank, a dean who sat on the college disciplinary committee, lectured a student for an hour immediately after he had been kicked out of school. The

47

student couldn't walk out or talk back because he hoped that someday the committee would readmit him.

"That lecture," said Greg, "was gratuitous. It was a form of bullying. The dean had no right to abuse her power by inflicting it on a student helpless before her."

To hear Greg's thoughts about Karen Blank and her Committee on Standing and Conduct, as it was called, one might conclude that his sentiments were liberal. But by no stretch of the imagination would he be considered a liberal by the Establishment at Dartmouth, mainly because his criticisms were directed toward them.

Administrators disapproved of Greg, as did many on the faculty, for his firm conviction that books are the best teachers. This belief had more to it than might at first glance appear, for, in essence, it was an attack upon the elective system, which has been taken for granted in higher education for the better part of a century.

"The elective system is, in fact, no system at all," Greg once said. "Classes are taught and students are free to go through the course catalogue and choose what they think they might like best."

"You don't think the freedom is a good thing?" I asked.

"Absolutely not. A freshman has no idea in what direction he wants to go because he knows so little when he first gets here. Unless someone puts him on the right track and tells him who the best writers, artists, scientists, and thinkers are, how is he supposed to find out? Ignorance does not make a person free, and the hit-or-miss style of course selection does no one any good."

"The only thing many students will get out of Dartmouth is a college diploma," Jones interjected.

"The college," said Greg, "should decide what students ought to study. Ignorance in students is excusable, but in professors with Ph.D.s, it is not. What is the faculty for if they can't distinguish between the important and the unimportant?"

We talked a lot about Dartmouth and how it could be improved. We acknowledged that there were many brilliant individual courses at Dartmouth. But there was no core curriculum, no requirements other than one English composition class, a language, and a non-Western course. There was no agreed-upon set of books that everyone had to read. We didn't know exactly what books ought to be included in such a curriculum, but we thought they should reflect the consensus of history. As Samuel Johnson once wrote in his great essay on Shakespeare:

> To works . . . of which excellence is not absolute and definite, but gradual and comparative; to works not raised upon principles demonstrative and scientific, but appealing wholly to observation and experience, no other test can be applied than the length of duration and continuance of esteem.

Homer, Virgil, Plato, Aristotle, Dante, and Shakespeare pass this test. Other works do, too.

"Such a curriculum would make intelligent conversation possible among students," Jones said. "If students read Lucretius, they would know atheism and materialism are not new ideas."

"A great-books requirement would give students a sense of where they came from," said Greg. It was not a welcome notion with the faculty, as it meant many professors would have to reeducate themselves.

The decision by Dartmouth to drop just such a curriculum was part of the Sixties notion that we must not be judgmental. "All things have merit, and it's pretty arrogant for us to decide what's worth reading," said one professor. "We don't have the right to make judgments about anything, especially after what we did in Vietnam," said another. So the dropping of requirements was, in essence, part of the philosophy of cultural relativism that swept the college campuses.

But Greg made an even broader interpretation of this trend in education. He said, "It represents a conscious attack on Western values. What it says is that our nation and our civilization are no longer worth preserving."

His conclusion seemed far-fetched to some, and to others it sounded authoritarian and dogmatic. To me it appeared to be true.

Poisoned Ivy

The conversations begun on the terrace and at the Hanover Inn bar ranged from the most profound to the most trivial of subjects. We discussed people we despised and those we admired. Friends do not need to agree about everything, but they must have the same heroes and consider the same people fools. Friends do not judge each other; they judge the world, and by similar standards.

Most of what I remember that term took place at the Hanover Inn. When the weather was good, we sat out on the terrace. Otherwise, we ate and drank in the shadow of an old wooden clock ticking away the hours in the Coffee Shop. "B.K." (Before Kemeny), the Coffee Shop was called the "Bible and Drum," but Kemeny apparently ordered the name changed because it was allegedly offensive to the Jews and native Americans, although I never met a Jew or Indian who could explain why. The whole idea struck me as odd, because the Jews had written the Bible, and it didn't seem that Indians had cornered the market on drums.

Jones and I often went to Mass together. Jones seemed to spend an awful lot of time in the confessional. Whatever he said to Monsignor Nolan through the grille, his confessions must have been memorable, as the silver-haired priest always emerged from the booth afterward with an amused look on his face.

Before I knew it, classes were over, and I had to take my final exams. For one week, I was a model student. I forbade anyone to enter my room. I lived on iced black coffee and peanut butter sandwiches. I crammed my head with neglected texts. To my surprise, I survived the exam period.

In fact, I did okay.

A Stale Whiff from the Sixties

I remember walking early one morning at the beginning of winter term with Greg and Keeney. Keeney and I were on our way to Latin class, and Greg was going to Professor Charlie Wood's Intellectual History of the Middle Ages. The campus was white with new-fallen snow, and the pale January sunlight made long shadows of the surrounding elm trees, the branches of which had long since lost their leaves. There was a nip in the air, and students ran from building to building to escape the cold.

"The problem with modern education is that you never know how ignorant some people are," Keeney said. "It's not that students are stupid. In fact, many have a worldly surface. But suddenly the crust breaks and you find yourself in a bottomless pit of chaos. You find that they have taken nothing but education courses along with some psychology and sociology, urban studies, or something like that. You find that they have taken no history, philosophy, or literature, and don't know anything of the experience of Western Man. Many students here think that Dante was a painter."

From inside his woolen scarf, Greg said, "We're producing

51

mostly middle-management people. They'll do a nice job in a government agency, writing pamphlets on world hunger."

I opened the day's edition of *The Dartmouth* and found that both Leonard Reiser, the college provost, and Margaret Bonz, in charge of Affirmative Action, "expressed disappointment that no black has been appointed to the faculty of Arts and Sciences over the past two years."

"Our situation has not improved, it has deteriorated," said a memo from Reiser. The provost reassured the reporter from the daily student paper, however, that "the college has already begun to increase black appointments. Last November the board of trustees added a provision to the Dartmouth Affirmative Action program that permits the college in "exceptional cases" to bypass certain Affirmative Action regulations in making faculty appointments."

Provost Reiser explained to *The Dartmouth* that "the goal of the new provision is to allow the college to make more senior faculty appointments of women and minorities." Reiser went on to tell us, "Department chairmen are working harder today to try and recruit minority candidates."

Winter term could probably best be summed up as a period of black rage. There were daily demonstrations in front of Parkhurst Hall against college investments in corporations that do business with South Africa. The pages of the daily student paper provided a kind of megaphone for grievances expressed by black leaders on campus. *The Dartmouth* reported, "Nature does not prepare men for the roles of master and *racist*. It requires training. . . ." Afro-American president Jimmy Defrantz railed on to an enchanted mob, mostly white and upperclass:

. . . To make women and men deny other men and women, men must be carefully taught to hate, and the lessons learned by one generation must be relearned by the next. The lessons of hatred are still being taught today. The mentality that originally allowed slavery to exist is being kept alive and well.

Parkhurst Hall had decided that the problem had gotten out of hand. Administrators launched an all-out war against *racism* and *sexism* on the campus. An ad hoc Committee for the Faculty on Equal Opportunity was formed to report on incidents of discrimination at the college. *The Dartmouth* gave the following account of their first meeting:

> As the result of the Committee on Equal Opportunity's (C.E.O.) meeting with the Gay Student Association, the C.E.O. is discussing the adoption of a written amendment that would prohibit sexual preferences as a mode of discrimination in the hiring of employees. . . .
>
> Barbara Smith, a committee member and counselor at the college infirmary, told the C.E.O. that "the Gay Students Association would like to see Dartmouth adopt a policy such as that of Cornell University, which states that [bias with regard to] sexual preference is a form of discrimination."

Professor Richard Sterling is a full professor in the government department and "chairperson" of the Committee on Equal Opportunity. He cleared up all confusion with regard to the purpose of the C.E.O. when he explained to a group of reporters that "Dartmouth is a highly segregated campus, in the sense that groups live in solitude when the opportunity to pursue diversity is at its peak in undergraduate years. How many have had the opportunity to talk with native Americans? . . . There is a mutual fear of discussing issues that might bring racist views out into the open." Professor Sterling went on: "One student related an incident in which she met with a professor to discuss a problem. In the course of the conversation, the professor said that he was not *'overly fond of blacks.'*"

I thought about Sterling's statement for a moment, and concluded that I could not think of a single person, white or black, of whom I was *overly fond*. Not being overly fond of a person with minority status was officially condemned by Professor Sterling as *racist*. I wondered if not being *overly fond of* a woman would mean that I was *sexist*. I later found that this was not the case. In fact, experience soon proved the opposite to be true. If you seemed overly fond of a woman, you risked an appearance before Karen Blank's Committee on Standing and Conduct for *sexual harassment*.

According to a memo that was circulated among all college employees, *"sexual harassment* is deemed by the college to be a form of sex discrimination, and, therefore, any *sexual harassment* of employees and students at the college will constitute a violation of the college's *nondiscrimination* policy. . . . This policy and the mechanism for redress will be called to the attention of all members of the Dartmouth College Community annually."

"There is nothing wrong with birds of a feather flocking together," explained Professor Sterling. Extending this fowl analogy, he added "except when they act as vultures to the other flocks."

At this point a translation might be of some use. What Professor Sterling meant to say was there is nothing wrong with the Afro-American Society, a *sui generis* black organization that is completely supported by student tuition money, but the fraternities cannot be tolerated. Professor Sterling was at the forefront of a move to abolish the Greek-letter societies, which he saw as *racist, sexist, elitist* organizations that encouraged alcohol abuse, and more esoteric arts, like "mooning."

"When the distance-keeping and segregation inhibit students from *delighting in the diversity*," Sterling said, "the situation is pitiful." Yet for most Greek-letter societies, beer, wine, whiskey, and gin were diverse enough.

The attacks on the fraternities by the Kemeny administration and many faculty members were relentless. Parkhurst Hall followed Professor Sterling's lead and also condemned the fraternities as *sexist* and *racist*.

54

These charges would put anyone on the defensive. But the terms were, in fact, irrelevant. The fraternities were crawling with young men and women, white people, black people, brown people, short people, tall people, communists, fascists, Republicans, Democrats—a motley selection of the human race. Perhaps they did encourage alcohol abuse, but the fraternities, far from being too exclusive, most certainly were not exclusive enough. More should have been done to keep out the riff-raff—people who wandered in off the street. That is, Jones's criticisms were more on the mark. There was a certain inelegance and lack of sophistication about the Greek-letter societies.

The following column, which I reprint in part, appeared in the opinion page of *The Dartmouth*. It was written by an undergraduate named Monty Brower and expresses the philosophy that governed Dartmouth officialdom:

> The fraternities are racist institutions. They institutionalize the White majority at the College, a majority that is insensitive to the legitimate concerns of the minorities. *Racism* in fraternities is not personal; we see it in their inability to understand problems and issues facing the minorities. The very fact that the fraternities cannot see why they are *racist* is a reflection of this lack of understanding as well as the collapse of the College as a community. . . .
>
> Throughout their long history at Dartmouth the fraternities have done so much more to divide the community than any other institution. Because of the fraternities, we have no community at the College. . . .
>
> The purpose of this College is to instill an *ethos* into its students, so that no matter what they do, they will have some idea that an education is the means to a serving society, instead of just a ticket to a fat salary.
>
> If the College is to be successful in creating an *ethos* in the students, it must regain its sense of common higher purpose. The fraternities work against this *ethos*. They must be abolished in order to save it.

Poisoned Ivy

It was not long before I found that Brower's *ethos* was alive and well at Dartmouth. The fraternities spent the year fighting for their lives against this *ethos*. At this point, despite their often déclassé behavior, it became clear that the fraternities must be saved, for they were the last refuge on the campus from the suffocation of this new kind of moral *ethos*, more Philistine and barbaric than anything that took place in the basement of Beta house.

While Professor Sterling and the Committee on Equal Opportunity (C.E.O.) met with members of the Gay Students Association, leaders of minority groups and militant feminists, women who wore bras, skirts, and lipstick did not count as a minority. These women liked men, for example, and could often be found at fraternity parties, as long as it was not too late, when decorum tends to deteriorate. These women would probably not even be outraged if asked out on a dinner date. These women were not a good model for the *ethos*.

For the approved view, you might read Judy Ornstein in the pages of *The Dartmouth*. "So the fraternities are trying to clean up their act? I invite anyone who believes this to walk down Webster Avenue and look at Sigma Nu's snow sculpture."

Sigma Nu had a long-standing tradition of building a set of round breasts for the Winter Carnival snow sculpture competition. In February of 1979, however, with the threatened abolition of fraternities, the titular artists simply piled up two mounds of snow, adding no detail, and leaving the exhibit open to interpretation. Much more offensive things could be found in the Hopkins Center's gallery of modern art. Any woman who thought that Sigma Nu's snow sculpture was funny did not understand the *ethos*. On this occasion Ms. Ornstein saw the opportunity to gain a moral victory, not to mention the approval of Professor Sterling's Committee on Equal Opportunity and the establishment in Parkhurst Hall:

People can say that Sigma Nu's breasts "are all in fun," or a joke, or a tradition; however, I and many other people find them demean-

56

ing. As a woman who values her intelligence and other aspects of her personality, can I be blamed for suspecting that the sculpture expresses what the brothers of Sigma Nu really perceive to be the most important attribute of women?

I think this is clearly a case of the fraternity failing to change as the college community changes. If such intransigence continues it might well be the death of fraternities.

Clearly, Sigma Nu never considered making a snow sculpture of a woman's personality.

Under threat of probation, Sigma Nu redesigned their sculpture, transforming the two piles of snow into twin pyramids, still salacious, but cubist. This, of course, did not exactly fall in line with the *ethos* either. The fraternities had already been judged the root cause of every social problem at the college. It did not matter that nearly sixty percent of the student population belonged to one of these clubs.

There were daily protests in front of Parkhurst Hall by black militants and members of The Dartmouth Radical Union. Both groups, incidentally, along with the Gay Students Association, were funded by the college. Black leader Jimmy Defrantz stood on the Parkhurst steps with his fuzzy moustache, his Afro comb stuck in his Afro, his long trench coat, and his Cuban shades, surrounded by his friends with their portable tape decks, their tight pants, and their funky shoes. Standing next to Defrantz was a slim, blonde-haired woman with a corn-row hairdo, who must have spent an hour in front of the mirror. She wore a purple bandanna as a headband to go with her skin-tight purple pants and Gucci shoes.

And there was Keeney Jones, with his foam-rubber shark, Chesterton, listening to Defrantz's demands. "We want an admissions policy aiming at attaining a black student population representative of the nation as a whole. . . ." Defrantz screamed over a megaphone to an ecstatic mob. "We want an increase in the number of blacks hired as faculty. . . . We want a program of *true* support for black students at Dartmouth. We believe the college bears an unavoidable moral and political responsibility to end investment [in corporations that do business with South Africa]. We support complete economic sanctions against South Africa, sponsored by the United Nations."

It was warm for January, just below freezing, hardly cold enough to prevent a demonstration, although it looked as if the breeze blowing in from the West might bring flurries. Keeney always showed up at these rallies, looking deliberately outrageous, wearing his "Nixon in 1980" and "I Love Ron" buttons. You could see his breath rise from behind his blue woolen scarf. The contingent of deans, subdeans, and faculty members who always attended such functions to demonstrate their virtue, looked at Keeney disapprovingly; not attuned to the *ethos*, he was obviously a misfit in the new Dartmouth.

TAKE AN INDIAN TO LUNCH

AFTER dinner one night, Keeney, Greg, and I walked to Thompson Arena for Dartmouth's hockey game against Brown. A victory would assure Dartmouth the Ivy League title and a place in the Eastern playoffs. More than six thousand people attended—standing room only. Excitement reverberated through the building. A kind of static electricity filled the air. The nervous anticipation was of the sort one might find at the Rose Bowl. The ice was empty, as the two teams waited in their dressing rooms. The scoreboard counted down toward zero, and silence descended over the mob. All eyes focused on the two gates from which the players would emerge. Dartmouth was ranked among the top five in the country at that point in the season, and in Hanover the support for the team was rabid. Ten, nine, eight, seven, six, five, four, three, two, one, bang! The gates flew open and the forty-five players from the two teams charged onto the ice. The sudden roar from the crowd was deafening, like a gasoline fire. One instant dead silence, and the next, everything was out of control. The band played the Dartmouth fight song. The fans cheered and sang as several players unleashed titanic slap shots from the blue line for practice. Others waved to their friends in the stands.

The fraternity house blocks were in rare form that night. Fifty brothers from Theta Delta Chi sat directly behind Brown's All-American goalie, Mark Holden, faces pressed up against the glass and screaming insults and banging the panels loose with their fists.

"Hey, Sieve! You better be wearing a lot of padding tonight, 'cause you're going to spit rubber."

"Who taught you how to stop pucks? Truman Capote?"

The crowd began to chant, "BUDDY! BUDDY! BUDDY!" and Eugene "Buddy" Teevens, who that fall had shattered almost every Dartmouth passing record on the football field, raised his stick in the air. He was what hockey aficionados know as an "enforcer." A thunderous roar went up. The crowd well knew that Buddy was also on the verge of setting hockey records for time spent in the penalty box. You could see the fear on the opposing players' faces as Buddy skated by. Fist clenched in the air, he sneered. This was not a sport for genteel tastes. It was a North American spectacle, more violent than football, if only because the rules are less defined. Apparent cheap shots often fall in that gray area not fully covered by the rules. Cuts, stitches, bruises, missing teeth, fractures, torn ligaments, and destroyed knee cartilage were injuries generally thought to be accoutrements of the game.

Five gladiators from each team positioned themselves for the opening face-off, protected by a suit of leather and plastic armor, and carrying a stick that could be used either as a weapon or tool. Dartmouth won the face-off, and this typified the action of the game. The Brown skaters could not move the puck into the Dartmouth zone without being hammered to the ice by Green defensemen. The thud of bodies checked against the boards was heard loud and clear in the top row of seats. The Green attackmen shelled the Brown goalie relentlessly with thirteen shots to Brown's three in the first period, and Dartmouth scored two goals in eight seconds. It was through the heroic effort of their goalie that Brown trailed only 2-0 after the first twenty minutes of play.

When the two teams skated onto the ice for the second period, the mob sat in stunned dead silence for a brief instant. Two of the skaters were not dressed to play hockey; instead they wore feathers, war paint, a loin cloth, and a big green "D" emblazoned on their chests. *They were dressed like Indians!* The symbol that had been outlawed by John Kemeny was back. In the flesh.

Suddenly, the dam burst, and in a flood of emotion the mob cheered as I had never heard it. The band played. Hats, gloves, scarves, fluttered onto the ice. All one could hear were happy people and the thunderous roar of joy and life, as they cheered, "DARTMOUTH INDIANS! I-N-D-I-A-N-S! DARTMOUTH INDIANS! SCALP 'EM!"

Despite warnings over the public address system to the mob to quiet down so the game could resume, people rose to their feet, held each other arm in arm, and sang the college alma mater, "MEN OF DARTMOUTH SET A WATCH LEST THE OLD TRADITIONS FAIL. . . ." Dartmouth shut out Brown 5-0 and went on to the semifinals in the N.C.A.A. tournament, finishing third in the nation.

The atmosphere of joy that gripped the town that evening was like nothing I had ever witnessed before. Fraternity parties on Webster Avenue lasted until the early hours. Bands played, booze flowed, people sang and danced. Even Keeney Jones, who did not particularly like hockey, and who thought fraternity parties barbaric orgies unbecoming to the Ivy League, could not help but be caught up in the happiness that permeated the campus. Jones's objection to the fraternities was not a moral one; it was purely stylistic. Anyway, the entire evening was certainly an affront to the *ethos*.

I woke up at 2 P.M. the following afternoon with a splitting headache and five hours late for class. I got dressed, put on my blue down parka, wool hat, mittens, and rubber boots, and walked outside to greet the cold. It was not snowing yet, but it looked as though it might. I ambled over to the mailboxes to find out what *The Dartmouth* had to say about the hockey game. On the way I passed a few people who were talking about the skaters who had dressed up as Indians.

61

Poisoned Ivy

"Did you see today's paper?" one student asked.

"No," said another, "I haven't picked up my mail yet."

"There's a picture of Shaun Teevens, Buddy's little brother, dressed up like an Indian."

"That was Buddy's little brother?"

"You didn't know that? The entire campus is talking about it."

"I should have known, but I didn't recognize him with the war paint and feathers. He's always been a great fan of the Dartmouth Indian."

"They say Shaun is a better skater than his brother."

"He's a good guy. I don't think I've heard him say a nasty thing to anyone."

"Sounds a lot like Buddy."

"They're rugged Boston Irishmen. They might, of course, get drunk on Saturday night and inadvertently break someone's nose. But they are sincerely sorry the next day."

The two students, like many others, were great admirers of the Teevens tradition, which dates back to their father's days as an undergraduate. Mr. Teevens had played football and hockey for Dartmouth, graduating with the class of '53. Because of bad health, Mr. Teevens was unable to attend many of the games Buddy and Shaun played. He had been in and out of the hospital for a number of years, and had recently had a heart attack. It was particularly sad because the Teevens family was so close.

On the front page of *The Dartmouth* was a picture of Shaun Teevens skating in full Indian garb. There were scores of stories about the event. President John Kemeny called the incident "horrendous" and "in the worst possible taste." "The administration," he said, "would undertake an investigation into the incident."

William Cook, professor of Black Studies, whose shaved head had been featured on the cover of a recent issue of the *Alumni Magazine*, recommended that the students involved be given "the strongest possible disciplinary penalty." Would scalping them do?

Robert Z. Norman, professor of mathematics, proposed "very strong disciplinary penalties for the students."

It seemed a little odd that, in the face of obvious widespread support for the Indian skaters at the game, the newspaper contained no comments defending them; odd, too, despite the fact that many students knew that the front-page photo was of Teevens, administrators were completely unable to identify the Indian skaters.

Now, it is true that administrators and faculty members were not the only ones to use this occasion to score moral points. There were a few students, the type who normally do not attend sports events, who found fault with the mass approval of the Teevens stunt. Michael Boldt from the class of '79 summarized his own complaints with this letter to *The Dartmouth*:

> The resurgence of the Indian cheer at Sunday's varsity hockey game has to be one of the most disturbing incidents to come to light since the beginning of the fraternity controversy. . . .
>
> What is disturbing about Sunday's gesture in particular is that it indicates a far more basic imperceptiveness and hollowness of values on the part of many Dartmouth students.
>
> If some who cheered feel that their cheering was simply an act of personal expression, they are seriously deluding themselves. As the Indian symbol and the survival of the fraternities have become closely linked over the past few months, anything involving the symbol has clearly become not just a "personal" matter (if it ever was that) but a political one as well.

Outside Parkhurst Hall Jimmy Defrantz organized the brothers of Alpha Phi Alpha, an all-black fraternity, and therefore the only truly racist house on campus, and the Afro-American Society, another all-black organization that is funded completely by student tuition money, and announced their grievances to a delighted mob in which gays, hippies, yippies (nostalgic for more of the Sixties), and feminists predominated. There was the usual contingent of faculty members, deans, subdeans, and other administrators. Defrantz, looking as if he had just stepped out of the pages of *Jet*, complained about the "incredible abuse laid on blacks at Dartmouth."

I took a long look at the slim black woman standing next to me with her corn-row hairstyle, gold hoop earrings, bright red leather high-heeled boots that came up to the knee, and Calvin Klein jeans. She turned, looked at me for a moment, and said, "We recognize that this country is the most oppressive in the world." Her tone was very matter of fact. I nodded politely; after all, look what we were doing to the Indians. She looked back to Defrantz.

"We plan to submit a list of demands to President Kemeny and Dean Ralph Manuel, outlining the steps which the college must take to reverse its hypocritical stance," Defrantz said. "We want the black student population to reflect the Afro-American population in this nation as a whole. . . . We want divestiture of college stock in companies dealing with South Africa."

A red-haired girl with designer jeans, a white form-fitting sweater, fur boots to go with her fur collar, and an almost perfect Greta Garbo face spoke up. "I think the minority groups have been very badly treated in this country. What kind of community outreach programs can I get into? Is there some committee I can be on? Or some sort of encounter group? I want to get involved. I'm so confused . . . I just don't know what to do."

"You can help us burn the whole fuckin' thing down," said this huge black man dressed completely in jet black leather from head to toe. He looked at the red-haired girl and said, "this whole fuckin' thing has got to go, man. We're not interested in reform. . . . We can build somethin' else. . . ."

Karen Blank, dean of freshmen and chairperson of the College Committee on Standing and Conduct said, "We have to listen to *them*." She was talking with the little red-haired girl about how to get more *involved*.

Right up where Defrantz was speaking were more deans, eating it up. They looked so *right* standing there, wearing "NO NUKE" buttons and nodding their heads rhythmically to every demand.

These souls from the administration had an average salary of $30,000. Their function here at Dartmouth was to stay *attuned*.

I was with Greg and Anthony when we met Shaun Teevens that afternoon walking down Main Street. He had on two warm-up jackets, a scarf, no hat, blue jeans, and a pair of Converse sneakers. As he walked, his head hung down and his hands were in his pockets.

He looked up in time to see us coming, and in his tough Boston accent asked how we were doing.

"Just fine," I answered. "That was a great thing you did at the hockey game."

"Thanks," said Shaun, "I thought it might contribute to the school spirit."

"It really did," said Greg. "Some alumni I talked with said it was one of the most inspiring moments of their lives."

"I never really understood the old Dartmouth until I heard the cheers when you skated onto the ice," said Anthony. "I never knew how much a symbol can mean."

"I think that deep down, under all that moral indignation, even the administrators like what you did," said Greg.

"I don't think so," said Shaun. "I'm going before the Committee on Standing and Conduct tomorrow. You know—Karen Blank. Anything might happen. I'm not even sure what they're charging me with. They won't say."

"Can't you appeal to the college handbook where it says 'freedom of dissent will always be protected by the college'?" asked Anthony.

"I think that rule only applies to certain cases," Shaun said. "I was told by Dean Blank that it does not apply when you are offending someone."

That evening I met Jones for dinner at Five Olde Nugget Alley, one of the local restaurants. I told him about meeting Teevens on

Main Street, and about his going before the Committee on Standing and Conduct.

"They'll use him as an example for others," Jones said.

Jones always had a particularly keen grasp of how the Dartmouth establishment looked at those outside the *ethos*. Their invincible virtue stemmed from the fact that they thought of almost nothing but minorities. The grievances of blacks, Indians, Hispanics, and a certain type of woman took priority over everything else, especially over the protection of Shaun Teevens's right to express enthusiasm for the Dartmouth hockey team.

Richard Jaegar, associate director of admissions, expressed the official view of Dartmouth's admission policy to a reporter from *The Dartmouth*. He tried to explain why his office had not done a better job of recruiting blacks, Indians, and women. "A lot of other schools are competing for the same minority students," he said. "Everyone is vying for their share." But a number of officials charged that it was Teevens's "*racist* act" that caused a drop in minority applicants.

On February 28, after a manhunt by campus police that spanned several days, Dean Ralph Manuel announced that "the students who were involved [the Indian skaters] voluntarily came into my office and confessed." The Dartmouth administration had finally caught the blasphemers.

"They came into my office to apologize to those members of the community they had offended, and were on their way to the proctor's office," said Ralph Manuel. "I have no knowledge of the charges to be brought against the students."

The dean of the college had no idea what charges would be brought against the Indian skaters, yet President Kemeny called the incident "horrendous," Black Studies professor William Cook had called for the "strongest possible disciplinary penalty," and math professor Robert Norman had publicly advocated "very strong disciplinary penalties for the students." Not one person in the administration would say, or even seemed to know, what charges would be brought against the Indian skaters.

The following day, *The Dartmouth* ran a story saying that the

Committee on Standing and Conduct had suspended the Indian skaters from school. There was no explanation given.

Early that same morning I ran into a young lady named Mary. Her expression reflected a lifetime of moral superiority. She felt that most of the college should receive the same punishment as Teevens: "It seems unfortunate," she said, "that the two Indian skaters are going to bear the rap alone for the insensitivity demonstrated in Thompson Arena last Sunday when two thousand people or so [more like five thousand] were also guilty, as seen by their participation in the Indian Cheer."

Wow! I thought. I had never heard the *ethos* put in better terms. Suddenly I was very happy that the president of Dartmouth was John Kemeny and not Mary. Perhaps they could have spliced together a few hockey films and nabbed at least another thousand students for cheering "Wah-Hoo-Wah!" Possibly a few faculty members and administrators to boot. This would be Dartmouth's version of Robespierre's Committee for Public Safety. It would deter others from ever cheering again. All that would be left of the college would be two hundred robots and the *ethos*.

So after a voluntary confession and apology to the community, Shaun Teevens found himself suspended from school with one week left in the term. Under these circumstances, one receives no credit for academic work completed, and no refund of paid tuition. He simply had to pack his bags and leave. No more hockey, no more football, no more fun in the basement of Beta house, and, if it was any consolation, no more fatuous discussions with the dean. The entire Dartmouth educational structure had crashed down on Teevens.

It was early in March and the term was drawing to a close. Jones and I were taking a course in modern Christianity. Jones, to the professor's discomfort, referred to this class as "three heretics a week." We both had term papers due. I was writing on Kirkegaard and he was doing something on Hegel. It was customary, at term paper time, to make frequent trips to Dunkin' Donuts, which was open all night and located about ten miles outside of town in a

67

place called West Lebanon. It was a clean well-lighted place with a pleasant atmosphere and a friendly, vibrant little waitress who always made us feel welcome.

It was three in the morning when Jones and I decided to drive to the doughnut shop and finish our work at the counter, eating and drinking coffee. There, at that time of night, one could get a feeling for life as it actually exists in rural New Hampshire.

"Hello, Ben. Hello, Michael," the waitress would say with a New Hampshire accent. "We have some good clam chowder tonight."

"That sounds fine," I said.

"Some coffee?" asked the waitress.

"Sure." I answered.

"Me too," said Jones.

There were farmers, night watchmen, truck drivers, and town bums sitting in a line at the counter and shooting the breeze about this and that. I didn't notice him at first, but sitting down at the end of the counter, talking to a school bus driver, was Shaun Teevens.

"Hey Shaun!" I called to him. He looked up.

"Ben, Keeney, what are you guys doing down here?"

"Jones and I have to finish up our term papers. What's happening with you?"

Shaun excused himself to the bus driver and sat next to us.

"I wanted to get out of Hanover," said Shaun. "I really love Dartmouth. No place in the world I'd rather spend time. But, if you ask me, I think the people who run the college are a little nuts."

"Are you actually kicked out of school?" I asked.

"I was," said Shaun. "But alumni groups raised a lot of money and were ready to launch a lawsuit against the college for violation of my First Amendment rights. Kemeny backed down on suspending me, and instead he's put me on a very strange disciplinary program."

"What do you have to do?" I asked.

"Brace yourself," said Shaun. "I've been ordered to conduct public seminars, wherever I can get students to listen, about the evil of the Indian symbol. In addition, I've been commanded to take an Indian to lunch once a week for a year."

68

"It hardly seems flattering to the Indians to be used as part of a weekly punishment," Jones remarked.

"A different Indian each week?" I asked.

"Yup," said Shaun.

"That will be difficult statistically," Jones said, "given the fact that there are only forty Indians to go around."

"Yeah," Shaun agreed. "It'd be easier if they all looked alike. I don't mind eating lunch with the Indians. The thing that really threw me, was the hearing the C.C.S.C. gave me," said Shaun. "Have you heard of Karen Blank? She's one of the principal moralizers on the committee. I tried to explain to her why I dressed up as an Indian. I told her that the hockey game was very important and that I thought it would help school spirit. I had no intention of offending anyone."

"What did she say to that?" I asked.

"She never heard me," said Shaun. "She just would not listen to anything I said."

"But what did she say you had done wrong?" I asked.

"It wasn't clear," said Shaun. "In fact, they never defined the charges against me. What Blank seemed to say was that physical violence . . ."

"Like beating someone up?" Jones cut in.

". . . That's right," Shaun answered. "Physical violence was the same as something she called *emotional violence*."

"What's that?" I asked.

"Well, she went on about how I was perpetuating *stereotypes* and how this offended some members of the community. She kept on using phrases like *toleration, stereotypic attitudes,* and *awareness*."

"I saw her statement on the decision in *The Dartmouth,*" Jones said. "It was absolutely unintelligible."

The following is part of Karen Blank's statement defending her committee's recommendation to suspend Teevens:

> . . . The members of the Committee suspended the skaters because we believe that they have violated the rights of Native American

69

students who had come to this College expecting to *thrive* and *grow* as individuals without having to live with *stereotypic attitudes* imposed on them. When they (the Indians) received their letter of acceptance to Dartmouth, they were not told that, because of their backgrounds, they would be the victims of *emotional violence*. The long deliberated decision to suspend represented an institutional stance that such *victimization is not tolerated.* [Emphasis added.]

Teevens finished his doughnuts and coffee and told the locals goodbye. He put on his winter parka over his Dartmouth hockey sweatshirt and walked out the door into the cold night air.

"That's a great kid there," the bus driver said.

"Sure is," said the night watchman. "They must be teachin' the right things on that campus."

The performance of the Dartmouth administration was so peculiar that it drew the attention of the national media. William F. Buckley, Jr., wrote his famous column entitled "Take an Indian to Lunch," in which he said that ordering students to forget about the Indian symbol was like telling them "to go for a full minute without thinking of a purple cow. From time to time students think about the Indian and its proscription makes it all the easier to think about."

Buckley continues:

> My guess is that the students who have gotten into so much trouble at Dartmouth, that their story is being told in the national press, have no hostility whatever of a racial kind against the American Indian, any more than—let us say—one naturally supposed that Al Jolson was anti-black because he sang in black-face. But they are being treated by the Dartmouth authorities as though they had conspired the massacre of Wounded Knee. . . .

Buckley went on to recall a little-known incident in the early life of President Kemeny. ". . . When he was a student at Princeton, the bullies cornered him one night and shaved off one end of his little mustache, thus ineluctably sentencing the remaining half to perdition. But it isn't only young people who are bullies."

As a result of President Kemeny's decision to ease the punishment of the Indian skaters, enraged minority students elected to destroy the traditional Winter Carnival snow sculpture. A forty-foot-high gold prospector carved in ice once stood proudly at the center of the Green. But a group of morally indignant protestors used ice axes and cans of red and black spray paint to ruin weeks of hard labor. The Dartmouth snow sculpture was another old Dartmouth tradition under attack—it was never clear to me what the basis of this attack was. I only knew that there were those who, for whatever reason, hated the snow sculpture. There were others, Shaun Teevens for instance, who liked that particular tradition and who liked being outdoors with friends working on something that everyone could enjoy.

"We won't calm down. This is only the beginning. We'll fight for our respect because we don't want to be denied an education," screamed Martha Wharton of the Afro-American Society to a delighted mob that included blacks, native Americans, feminists, hippies, yippies, deans, subdeans, more administrators, and faculty members, including Professor Dick Sterling and his crew from the Committee on Equal Opportunity, who felt guilt and *concern.* "I've always expressed my concern for the underprivileged," said the pretty little red-haired girl as she leaned forward in her pink pants suit, fur collar, and "ABORTION NOW!" button.

Afros, ponytails, goatees, leather jackets, funny-looking shoes, Trotsky glasses, foul smells, guitars, pot fumes, couples of all sexual peculiarities making out, women nursing babies. It was all there. They had all come out of the hills for this one. It looked like the Sixties revisited, except for one thing. There were no placards. They had simply forgotten them. Instead of a protest, it looked like a commune.

71

Poisoned Ivy

A young woman of Latin descent—she was extremely short and wore a headband and some kind of peasant dress—nudged my arm, looked up at me, and said, "We're Maoist utopians and we're prepared to fight to the death." I smiled politely.

"We are not sorry that we defaced the snow sculpture," Martha Wharton screamed. "It stood for a Dartmouth tradition that black students and native American students have not been a part of. The memory of that [ruined snow sculpture] will be burned on every student's mind. All minority groups are glad to see it happen because someone finally made a statement that everyone can see."

No one got into any trouble with Karen Blank's Committee on Standing and Conduct, or with Dick Sterling and his Committee on Equal Opportunity for destroying the Winter Carnival snow sculpture. Members of the Committee on Equal Opportunity poured their hearts out over the causes of blacks, native Americans, Latinos, feminists, and homosexuals. Do you think they would do as much for the lower-class whites, the Irishmen from South Boston, or the Teevens family, with nine children, struggling to put three of them through college, while the father lies dying in the hospital? . . . Fat chance, Sahib.

That evening Keeney, David, Anthony, and I ate dinner at Thayer Dining Hall. The common topic of conversation was the protest earlier that day. Many students seemed to be sympathetic to the militants demands, probably because it was dangerous, politically and perhaps physically, not to be. If one took issue with what was said, one risked being labeled *insensitive*. Like Shaun Teevens, one would lose the respect of the Nice People, and worst of all, the vast majority of administrators would look upon one as a boat rocker or, worse yet, a snow sculptor.

Oh, one other thing. President Kemeny decided to cancel classes on the last day of the term for the purpose of holding a moratorium. This was a *consciousness raising* event designed to foster *racial awareness* and encourage people to "dialogue" about the *insensitivity* of the campus "bigots." These bigots were members of fraternities, Wasps or the Wasplike, and anyone who did not think day and night about issues of race. Such people were not always overtly racist; racism is usually implicit—"institutionalized," as Defrantz liked to say. On the day of Kemeny's moratorium, faculty and administrators were supposed to hold seminars and group discussions on race relations. Black, Latino, feminist, radical, and self-proclaimed homosexual leaders were given Webster Auditorium, complete with microphones and loud speakers. Hysterical speeches about the evils of the white man, unless he was homosexual, could be heard across the campus. You see, while we're on the subject of race, we might as well broaden the moratorium theme to the topic of *tolerance* of the *oppressed* in general. Women, or, more accurately, a certain kind of woman who is closer to Liz Holtzman than, say, Margaret Thatcher, are among the *oppressed*. And, by *gays*, they don't mean a Plato, but rather a kind of homosexual who spends much of his time flaunting his gayness. So the harangues and demands went on. Deans, subdeans, registrars, and clerks all turned out for the event. They listened, patted each other on the back, proclaimed their own virtue, and demonstrated to all the *concerned* an ability to *relate*.

AN UNSENTIMENTAL EDUCATION

ONE day I thought I would take the advice of Professor Charles Stinson and sit in on a Women's Studies class.

"It might help broaden your perspective, which is Euro-and-ethnocentric," said Stinson, an academic advisor and friend of mine.

Professor Sally McConnell from Cornell University was that month's guest lecturer, and she spoke to us on "The Sexual (re)Production of Meaning." In attendance were fourteen female students, one other male, and a number of Women's Studies professors. McConnell began her talk by accusing men of having "stolen the power of naming."

"Language today demonstrates the power of sexist semantics," she said.

Her thesis was this: Men, because they tend to dominate conversation [which is not my experience], have also dominated the language. She called this "linguistic imperialism," because women are forced to use male words and, therefore, are unable to express themselves properly. The example she cited was a man asking a woman to have sex. When the woman answers "No," the man often interprets this to mean "Yes"; she is then raped, according to McConnell. I thought, What about encyclopedia salesmen who are told no?

I asked McConnell if she meant physically raped. McConnell replied, "Sometimes, but usually she has been raped by the language, or the reinterpretation of language in the mind of the man, which is just as bad." How do you punish language rapists? Cut off their vocabulary?

I found McConnell's lecture to be representative of what goes on in the so-called "Studies" departments—Women's Studies, Black Studies, Native American Studies, and so on. Advocates of such programs say they are needed because certain minorities, including women, have been neglected by history as part of a conscious, or unconscious, effort on the part of the white male to dominate the culture. I was unaware that Jane Austen, Emily Bronte, Edna Millay, and Dorothy Day, allegedly all women, had been neglected. I read their works in the English courses I'd taken, and I'm quite confident they did not need Affirmative Action to make it into the syllabus. It seems to me that Martin Luther King, Jr., is a figure in American history, not black history. We even have a national holiday for him, although not for Jefferson or Lincoln. Who's been neglected here?

The idea behind these programs, of course, is political. The stated purpose behind Dartmouth's Women's Studies program, according to its own charter, for example, was "to introduce students to feminist scholarship, make it an integral part of the Dartmouth curriculum, and create an intellectual atmosphere to make it legitimate."

The program, according to its own evaluation of itself, established three goals: "(1) destruction of false axioms, logic, and conclusions; (2) reconstruction of reality, the addition to the record of the facts of women's lives; and (3) the construction of integrative theories, ideas, and frameworks for investigating women's experience, and the introduction of these into the classroom."

76

In an article in *Signs*, the national Women's Studies quarterly, Maryssa Navarro, a Dartmouth history and Women's Studies professor, and a self-proclaimed Marxist, wrote that "Because feminist scholarship has its roots in the women's liberation movement, its examination of social institutions, artistic paradigms, and academic assumptions have a strong militant quality. In general, for feminist scholars, empirical knowledge is not an end in itself, but a means of denouncing sexual inequalities in order to redress them."

According to the course description of Women's Studies 1, the subject "is not *about* women in society, it is itself a force in the evolution of women's roles."

But Women's Studies was not enough. Some colleges and universities across the country have begun instituting Men's Studies programs. *Wait*, you say, weren't Women's Studies programs started to combat discrimination by men? Before you imagine set battles between Men's Studies students and their female equivalents, put your fears to rest. The purpose of Men's Studies was to reinforce the message of Women's Studies.

Professor Harry Brod, who teaches Men's Studies at the University of Southern California, explains, "Men certainly have not been oppressed the way women have been. But they are repressed, which is the price society makes them pay for being in the privileged group. Men have the power and the dominant position, but at the price of their emotional and personal lives.

"This is another step in the antisexist women's movement," says Brod, "in supporting both women's rights and in recognizing the disadvantages of being the privileged group." So the worst thing to do to women is give them privileges, thus clobber them with disadvantages? Does this hold up well under scrutiny?

As of this writing, Men's Studies programs exist, or are being contemplated, at Brooklyn College, the University of Oregon, Berkeley, Rutgers, Wellesley, and Dartmouth.

The same kind of specialized ideological messages follow in the Black and Native American Studies curricula. What I could never understand was why any student would pay more than $10,000 a year to take Women's Studies when they could be reading Plato,

77

Aristotle, Dante, and Shakespeare. The answer might be found in the hostile attitudes expressed by an important segment of the American academic community toward the great works of history, and in particular Western history.

From under the rubble of the Sixties emerged a peculiar self-defeating style of literary criticism. This came into vogue at the same time as the anti-Western curriculum. Literary criticism has its roots in journalism. Its purpose was to make literature more available to the reader. Good criticism, according to Samuel Johnson, was grounded in "common sense," and spoke to the layman, avoiding the tendency to be esoteric and exclusive.

A lot of what is being done today, however, especially by the younger professors, has nothing to do with journalism. Its vocabulary is specialized, often coming at us in a private technical jargon that it might require, say, a professor to explain. It tends to be hostile, not only toward the reader but also toward the work upon which the critic is commenting. The idea behind this type of criticism is to "demythologize literature" and to remove it from its privileged status in academic life, I suppose, ultimately taking it off the reading lists altogether. In this academic demolition derby, the poem or story becomes irrelevant and the critic primary. The literary work is merely a stage upon which the critic performs. A number of critics, in fact, prefer not to deal with major works at all because the literature can detract from the criticism. Like musicals about musicals and movies about movie-making, the obvious outcome is critiques of critiques published in, of course, "The New York Review of Each Other's Books."

Lou Renza, a Dartmouth English professor, for example, wrote an eight-hundred-page complex structural analysis of Sarah Orne Jewitt's short story "White Heron," a minor story by a minor writer. The point was not to shed light on the literature. The point was Renza's analysis. Perhaps it was a virtuoso performance. "Mental masturbation," is what some students called it.

Structuralism, semiotics, deconstructionism—the academic fads flow in succession, representing aggression against literature.

Semiotics has to do with reducing the poem or story to sounds or "signs." Structuralism attempts to draw various contrasts, parallels, and oppositions and show how they all turn against each other. Deconstructionism attempts to make the literary work self-destruct. The language becomes "self-emptying," something like a cistern. Needless to say, this kind of criticism has nothing to do with making it easier for the reader to understand the poem. In fact, skip the poem altogether: it's a performance by the critic, the whole point of which is to inflate the critic and degrade the author who, in the case of Shakespeare, is not around to defend himself.

All this is an assault on language, logic, and ultimately Western culture. Anything you see can be "deconstructed," from a Greek tragedy to a snow sculpture, although I don't recall Marx ever being deconstructed. Shakespeare and the telephone directory are both brilliant or inane, depending on the criteria one sets. There are also the less intellectually ambitious forms of criticism. We have the Marxist, feminist, and ethnocultural perspectives on literature, in which certain moral criteria are established to determine the quality of the work. *Huckleberry Finn,* with its once-prevalent racial stereotypes, is out, while "politically correct" poems on female genitalia are in.

Dartmouth English professor Brenda Silver tells her class every year that Ernest Hemingway is "a bad writer," because of his negative view of women. But, if education is merely political, as in the case of the Studies departments, then it might be better to read Malcolm X than *The Tempest.* From a moral point of view it might be better to read *The New York Times* than Machiavelli (though I doubt it). But this has nothing to do with the quality of writing, only its attitude. "Academic Stalinism," is what Greg Fossedal called it.

But we don't read great books to agree with them. We read them because in the judgment of millions of readers over hundreds of years these books are better than their competitors. The longer a work endures, the more esteem it has. This is why Shakespeare is preferable to a Harlequin romance. He states things better. The purpose of reading literature is not to make one more up to date with moral or political trends. It is to make one wise.

But, just as the Dartmouth administration bullied Shaun Teevens, the intellectual community uses technical and moral theories to bully the great works, attempting to demonstrate how quality is subjective, so that it can substitute its own reading list (usually political in content and anti-Western) for the traditional curriculum. It's certainly true that determining the quality of work is problematical. I really don't know if Bob Dylan's ballads are literature or not. Is Hunter Thompson literature? Is Ken Kesey? Perhaps. But the *Iliad* has been literature for 3,000 years. Maybe the Beatles will gain the status of Mozart. Time will tell, but the smart money's not on the Beatles.

There were a number of excellent courses and professors at Dartmouth. The *ethos* did not pervade every classroom. There was Professor Norman Doenges, for example, who taught me Latin. He gave me an understanding of grammar and syntax. I began, in fact, to think of these things often outside the classroom as so basic to the human mind that, if they are not studied, systematic thought is impossible. I had studied some German before, but Latin was more attractive to me. It had something elegant about it, like a mathematical idiom, which I learned from Professor Sleznic in the mathematics department.

Professor David Wykes taught me English composition in a course that came under the heading of English 5. English 5 was perhaps the most valuable course I took during my four years at Dartmouth even though I would never receive a lower grade.

It was my good fortune to have Professor Wykes, a hawk-faced surly fellow who was unpopular with many students. He had done his graduate work at Oxford and spoke in a cold aristocratic tone that intimidated many of my classmates. He criticized every sentence that I wrote so severely that I winced at the prospect of having him read my essays at all, although his many negative comments made his rare compliments even more valuable.

I had a problem, for example, with what he called "dangling modifiers." In one of my early essays I wrote, "Reading about Milton's Satan, the poem really comes to life."

Professor Wykes photocopied the page and gave copies to every student in the class. My writing mistake was an example of what not to do, and we examined my error for the better part of half an hour.

I took a class in Shakespeare given by Professor Peter Saccio, a thin Italian who was an extremely dramatic lecturer and sometimes sported a cape. His course heavily influenced my decision to choose English literature as my major area of study. He horrified the class one day when he broke down in tears at the end of a lecture on *King Lear*. At first the students just sat, riveted to their seats, not knowing how to react. After a moment several people in the front row regained their senses and helped the sobbing Shakespearean away from the podium and out of the room, ten minutes before the class was to end.

Professor Saccio spoke of Shakespeare's other tragedies: *Macbeth, Othello,* and *Hamlet.* He distinguished each one by describing the passion of the obsessed hero. After Saccio's lectures I thought that I understood and felt the plays, and somehow knew that never in my life would I encounter a poet who better expressed the wide range of human emotions.

Mathematics I completely failed to understand; it was a weakness I never made an attempt to overcome. And since I was free under the pick-and-choose system to ignore physics, chemistry, and biology—to my later regret—I chose the easiest sciences to fulfill the requirements. Not that these "gut" courses, as the students called them, were without merit. In fact, the two science courses I took had great power over me. I learned about the Big Bang and Darwin's theory of evolution, and got some idea about the nature of the cosmos we live in. But I did none of the hard work and painful research that sooner or later this lonely discipline demands. I took some good philosophy courses, where I read Plato and Aristotle, discovered Descartes and Kant. I also took a superb religion course with Professor Stinson. We spent the entire term reading the works of Thomas Aquinas. Ten weeks, however, was not time enough to do more than scratch the surface of his theology.-

My intellectual adventures outside literature, however, were too superficial for me to remember with pride. What I do remember is wishing later that the administration had concerned itself more with the discipline of my mind and less with the discipline of ice skaters.

I recall watching commencement at the end of my sophomore year. Anthony, Greg, and Keeney Jones were there, as was Jones's foam-rubber shark, which drew perplexed stares from the parents of graduating seniors. It would be at least two years before any of us would put on caps and gowns. We listened to speeches by President Kemeny, the valedictorian, recipients of honorary degrees, and important alumni, who, unmindful of the new *ethos*, sported Indian neckties. It was a brilliant day, and a cool breeze blew from the north. The ceremony took place at the foot of Baker Tower, which for me put things in perspective. In its shadow, all social distinctions, prejudices, and vulgarities from the year past seemed to shrink. To size.

I don't believe there were ever happier faces than those of the seniors when the dean of the college, Ralph Manuel, shook their hands and gave them their diplomas. But the scene was also sad in a way. While these graduates might, on occasion, cross paths with their college pals, never again would they have identical interests and obligations. I wish I had known then that this period in my life would be remembered with tears as a time when I did not have any concern other than keeping my social commitments and making sure that I was not thrown out of school for neglecting my assignments, or, worse, dressing up as an Indian. How unsympathetically in later life we criticize the unproductive ways of youth, the irresponsible but virtuous moments in the life of an undergraduate.

THE APPOSITE SEX

IN the fall of 1979, I decided to move into a large single room in Richardson, one of the largest and best dorms on campus. The rooms were spacious, with fireplaces and high ceilings; my grandfather, had lived in Richardson his entire undergraduate years. My father had lived in a dorm called Wheeler. The rivalry between the two dorms was ferocious. Wheeler was next to Richardson, and at night one perpetually heard drunken freshmen screaming out of their windows.

"Hey Wheeler! Do you hear me Wheeler?" they would yell. Wheeler was like a person. "You really suck, Wheeler!"

"Richardson!" someone would yell from across the way. "Your mother wears army boots!"

Actually, what was said was far cruder. This is a censored book.

The Richardson-Wheeler rivalry was the oldest and most famous at Dartmouth. Richardson, in particular, was a bastion of Dartmouth tradition and one of the last two remaining all-male dorms on campus. For as long as anyone could remember, the two dorms dominated all intramural competition. This was, in part, because of their large size, but mainly because of the residents' tremendous enthusiasm, which had somehow been passed on through the generations. There was a tradition of spirit there, and one could often hear the refrain "Richardson pride!" before an important intramural football game.

It was a Friday evening late in November. There would be a party at Beta later that night. I knew where Jeff Kemp, Mike Lempress, and Shaun Teevens would spend their evening—in the fraternity basement drinking beer, singing along with old Beatles tunes blasting at full volume through the eight speakers. At Dartmouth, parties always began at ten o'clock and lasted until the unrespectable hours of the morning. When Beta threw a party, everyone knew it, because everyone could hear it.

At about six, I did some laundry. Around seven I thought it might be a good idea to shave, even though there was not much sign of growth. It had been a number of days since I had inflicted that terrible razor on my skin.

I hated shaving, and it did not help matters when I badly cut myself. With a careless flick of my fingers, the steel blade sliced a straight line just above my upper lip. Blood dripped everywhere. I was in a bad state, until a pretty young lady who was strolling down the hallway happened to glance through the open door.

"That looks pretty bad," she said. "I have some Kleenex. Put some on the cut. It'll help stop the bleeding."

"Thanks," I said, my humiliation apparent.

"You do look silly with that clump of Kleenex across your lip."

"What's your name," I asked.

"Melissa."

"Pretty name," I said, unable to think of anything else.

"You're Ben Hart. We were introduced at a Beta party last term." She paused for a moment and looked at me. "You don't recognize me, do you?"

"Oh sure I do, now." I didn't really, although her voice was vaguely familiar; it was upper class—Eastern seaboard and rather high-pitched, without being irritating. She was tall and thin, with lovely strawberry blonde hair that swirled around her cheeks.

84

"Do you have any rubbing alcohol?" she asked.

"Yes. In the medicine cabinet."

"I'm going to put some on that cut before it gets infected."

"Yeow!" The stinging pain shot from my lip through my entire body.

"Be more careful when you shave then. I have to go now. I'm expecting a call from home. Maybe we should get together—go to a movie or something."

"Okay," I said. "I'll give you a call. Are you going to the party at Beta tonight?"

"No, I usually don't have a good time at those things. Too much of a mob scene."

"I know what you mean."

"What's your major?" Melissa asked.

"English," I said. "What's yours?"

"Philosophy," she answered, "but I'm also a pre-med. I'm taking organic chemistry this term."

"Sounds awful," I said. "Where are you from?"

"Originally, I'm from the Boston area, but my family just moved out to San Diego. I've got to go," said Melissa. "Please give me a call."

"I will," I said. "See you soon."

She smiled as she left. I liked her big green eyes. I wanted to give her a call, but the term would end in a week or so, and I didn't know when I'd get a chance. What a way to meet a girl, I thought, standing there with a mustache of tissue and blood clinging to my upper lip.

At ten o'clock the wound was under control, and it was time to go over to Beta. I walked out into the cool November night. No snow had fallen yet, but the ground was frozen. The moon had risen above the old elms just across the way. Laughter and voices could be heard from all corners of the campus. There was life in the passageways of the college as people converged on the party.

When I approached Beta, I saw that Webster Avenue was more than just alive. There was an atmosphere of chaotic energy—

85

energy that had been building up for an entire week, waiting to be released in explosive fashion on Friday night. Beta was in full swing. From inside the house echoed music and voices. People were coming and going. Their variously colored sweaters, trousers, dresses, jackets, blouses, and shoes blended together. It promised to be a splendid evening, and some romantic speculation rose within me at the sound of female voices.

When I walked in, I immediately spotted Britain Mills. Britain was very beautiful, and she made the young men around her uneasy. The pale wall-lights shimmered off her long blonde hair, which she liked to brush back so that it ran like a river down her spine. She had on a bright red dress, low cut and sleeveless; it hung to just below the knee, showing her sinewy but appealing calf muscles.

Britain was in her element. She ordered one freshman to get her a drink. Then, seeing a group of boys, she would smile at them from twenty feet away, breeze along, stop and wheel, and press indiscriminately against these hapless members of the opposite sex. She would say, "What's up, Jim?" or "Hello, Bill," talk with them for a minute, then simply desert them, completely conscious of what she had done to their night.

I saw Jeff Kemp standing against the wall with a beer in his hand. He was wearing a brand-new cowboy hat, boots, and blue jeans. A big wad of chewing tobacco made his cheek stick out. He was unaffected by the presence of Britain Mills. He looked over at me.

"Hey, Hart," he said. "Where have you been all night, and what happened to your lip?"

"A little accident," I said.

"You get into a fight or something?"

"No, actually, I cut myself shaving."

"Better say you got into a fight," said Jeff.

"How does it feel to have the football season over with?" I asked.

"It didn't feel like a season to me," said Jeff. "I never got into a game. But Buddy really kicked ass out there."

"I still can't believe Dartmouth won the Ivy League title," I said.

"We were picked by the sportswriters to finish last," said Jeff. "But we have a tradition to uphold. Dartmouth has won more Ivy League titles than anyone."

"Buddy really came through against Brown," I said.

"I'll say he did. He showed everyone that he's a better quarterback than their guy, Mark Wipple."

"Everyone said Wipple would be All-Ivy this year. He was the starter at Brown for three years. Dave Shula's been doing a hell of a job catching the ball," I said.

"Sure has," said Jeff.

"Howard Cosell showed some of Shula's great receptions on 'Monday Night Football' half-time highlights."

"Dave'll break all the records before he's through here," Jeff said. "What do you say we hit the basement?"

"Sounds good to me. I hope they have beer on."

"Of course they do," said Jeff. "Beta's never out of beer."

When we arrived downstairs, a mob was cheering a couple of sophomores who were the last remaining contestants in the legendary "shot-a-minute" contest, in which the object is to drink one shot of beer every minute. The last man standing wins. It is perfectly fine and within the rules to boot, lose lunch, or yawn in technicolor, as the jargon goes. It's even all right to pass out for a moment, as long as one can still get a shot of beer down one's throat, somehow, every minute. Friends of contestants were on hand with buckets of ice water to revive their man should he go down too soon.

I looked for a moment at the huge line of people waiting to get a beer, at the end of which was that pathetic-looking freshman who had been sent here twenty minutes ago to get a beer for Britain. He hadn't made any progress, and didn't look as if he was going anywhere for quite some time, as people kept pushing him out of the way.

"Here you go, Ben." It was Jeff. He had just put a cold beer in my hand.

87

"Thanks," I said.

"What?" he asked. He could not hear me over the roar of the crowd. The runner-up of the "shot-a-minute" contest had just hit the floor, face down, felled like a tree, SMACK! He hadn't even used his hands to break his fall. I think he broke his nose, which was bleeding badly. A couple of brothers picked up the hapless gentleman and rushed him to the college infirmary. He had tossed 183 shots of beer down his throat. Later that night, when some girls expressed their desire to play, the game was stopped.

"There's Buddy," said Jeff, pointing to a stocky fellow with sandy blond hair. Buddy was hanging upside down from a pipe, like a bat. From this position he was holding court with five or six girls. He had on his green-and-white football jersey, number five.

"Hey Ben!" Buddy yelled. He signaled for me to come over.

"Great game last week against Princeton," I said.

"Thanks," he said, still hanging upside down from the pipe. "Kemper tells me you're thinking of joining Beta."

"I think I want to in the spring," I said.

"Hell of a group of guys in this house," said Buddy.

"I can see that," I said, as I looked over at Mike Lempress, who was face down in a puddle of beer.

The scene upstairs was different. People there were dressed well, and their behavior was more genteel, in an effort to make a good impression on the opposite sex. But Britain seemed especially bored with the men. How many lines she must have heard that evening. New men, who may have showed mild promise when first introduced, had managed to bore her in a matter of minutes. She would just stand there, freezing them with upward glances and giving languid answers to their inane questions.

A very waspy young gentleman of medium height and blond hair appeared. Evidently he was Britain's date for the evening. He was holding a half-empty plastic cup of beer, and looked very distressed. His name, I learned later, was Woody. He played fourth string end for Dartmouth.

"Where have you been all evening?" Britain asked.

"What do you care?" he answered.

"What do you mean by that? I thought you were going to get me a drink. I had to send some freshman downstairs because you never appeared. He never made it back either. I've been waiting an hour."

"You looked to me like you were having a great time, so I went downstairs to watch the shot-a-minute contest. I had five or six beers and then came back."

"Well, I wasn't having a good time. It's been miserable, and you haven't been a very good date."

"I thought you were tired of having me around when you had a dozen other men to impress."

"I think you ought to apologize for leaving me all alone like this."

Woody did not apologize. Britain looked angry and went toward the closet to get her coat. She was going to walk home alone. On her way out of the room she caught her arm on a nail protruding from the doorway, and cut herself. Drops of blood dripped onto her dress.

"Oh no!" she screamed. "Now look what you've made me do. I've ruined my best clothes . . . blood stains all over . . . and I'll have a scar on my arm . . . Ohhhh . . . awful, awful, awful."

Her face was red with rage, and tears streamed down her cheeks. All conversation stopped. Everyone stared at Britain's injured arm and then looked with pity at Woody.

Woody, at first, froze with panic, but then ran into the bathroom to get a towel. He wrapped it around her arm to stop the blood. Someone brought some Band-Aids. The cut was taken care of. But as far as Britain was concerned, the incident definitely took care of Woody.

I joined Beta during spring term of my sophomore year. I had never felt any compelling need to be in a fraternity house, except that I had begun to lose track of friends I had made freshman year, people like Jeff Kemp and Mike Lempress. They were members of Beta, and I knew that Shaun Teevens planned on joining, too. Shaun was still on probation for the "Indian skater incident" and was not allowed to participate in any college-connected social activity. Whatever Parkhurst Hall thought, however, did not carry much weight in Beta House, and all the brothers were glad Shaun chose Beta over Heorot, a raucus fraternity full of hockey players.

Since the shaving incident, I had become a casual acquaintance of Melissa's, and often saw her at Mass. One Sunday I decided to ask her to lunch. It would be our first date. That day her strawberry blonde hair looked especially startling, offset by a white dress. Melissa always took care to look her best on Sunday. Not usually highly visible, she was not, at first sight, especially beautiful. Her legs were long and gangly, and her body showed some of the problems of youth. But she had the potential to become, in a year or two, a stunning beauty. She accepted my invitation to lunch.

Melissa and I had a lot in common. She liked to ski and play tennis, and was a believing Catholic. It was easy to spend the afternoon with her. She never put anyone on the defensive, and she had a kind heart. I think she began to feel something toward me, although she seemed reluctant to show it. I liked the guarded sweetness of her smile and her warm innocent eyes. I began taking her out regularly, to dances, movies, and restaurants.

Later that spring I decided I would take her to the Parker House, a very good restaurant in Woodstock, Vermont. It was not cheap but had the reputation of serving the best food north of Boston. So I decided to empty my rather meager checking account.

Melissa had on a ruffled blue blouse with buttons part way down the front and a long white skirt that matched her high-heeled shoes.

Our waiter looked like the later Orson Welles. He was enormously fat, had a dark mustache and beard, and wore a tuxedo.

"Would you like to see a wine list?" he asked, with a French accent.

"What do you recommend in red wine?" I asked.

"The Châteauneuf du Pape is very good."

"That will be fine," I said.

Melissa seemed very pleased to be there. Between dinner and dessert a band began to play.

"Maybe you'll dance with me," she said, the candlelight glowing off her cheeks.

The band played Frank Sinatra's "Come Fly With Me." I enjoyed holding Melissa in my arms, her body pressed close to mine.

After a few dances, we went back to the table for dessert.

"Do women ever go after men?" I asked her.

"No. The men are always there, and if the girl is good looking enough, she only has to blink or smile at them. It's instinctive, completely unconscious."

"Can't a man make a girl fall for him?"

"Some men can, but only the ones who don't care."

I turned that fact over in my mind for a moment.

"Of course, it doesn't help to be indifferent if the fellow doesn't have what it takes," Melissa added.

"That's very tough on the man," I said.

"It's worse for the girl. An ugly girl can smile and blink all she wants. It won't do her any good."

"What about an ugly man?"

"It doesn't matter as much, as long as he has interesting things to say or is thought to be in some way exciting. Men age much better than women."

"That's why it's important to find a girl who's fun to be with. What if I married someone who looked great, then turned out to be a bitch?" I said. "Where would we be in fifteen years, when the wrinkles begin to appear? I suppose it's best to find someone who is both beautiful and intelligent."

"It's seldom you find beauty and intelligence in the same person," Melissa said. "When you do, you'll spend the rest of your life afraid of the explosion that might someday erupt."

"Other people spend their lives trying to find that little spark that would set off the explosion," I said. "Then it's like a kid trying to light a fire with a wet match in the rain . . . only the wet match is

91

intelligence that was never cultivated, and the rain is beauty she has lost. The explosion never comes because there is no fire. There is not even a small spark. Everything is wet because there never was any spark."

"And suddenly the marriage goes sour, lives are ruined, and existence doesn't seem such a good thing after all," Melissa said.

We finished dinner, and I drove her back to her dormitory. I enjoyed walking her up the path to her front door. I enjoyed putting my arm around her, and I enjoyed kissing her goodnight. It was midnight, and the moon hovered delicately over Dartmouth Hall.

MAN
AND
GOD . . .

DARTMOUTH, for some strange reason, engaged in a vigorous campaign to encourage students to study abroad. I could understand this if the purpose was to master a foreign language. But I didn't see the point of studying English in England and philosophy in Scotland, unless one simply wanted to see those countries. In which case it would be better to go there unencumbered with course requirements. These programs proliferated under the presidency of John Kemeny, conveniently removing students from the campus. The college, in its view, functioned better without the interference of either alumni or students. They couldn't send alumni abroad, but they could send students.

I have to admit, however, that my main bias against the foreign study approach stemmed from the fact that Melissa went on two consecutive overseas programs and was away for more than a year. This took the wind out of the sails of any romantic relationship because we began to lose contact, as she hopped from Scotland to France to China.

Early in September, I met Michael Keenan Jones at Chase Field. He was watching football practice, wearing a green vee-neck sweater, a Dartmouth Indian bow tie, khaki trousers, and loafers.

"Looks like Kemp might have a shot at quarterback this year," I said.

"They say it's between Jeff and this fellow McLaughlin," replied Jones.

It was a brilliant autumn day. The team had finished a two-week period of double practice sessions, and spirits were high in anticipation of the opening game against Princeton.

Phwump. Kemp had just completed a pass to split-end Dave Shula. *Phwump.* McLaughlin completed one to tight-end Mike Lempress. Crunch, crack, thump—flesh and bone met plastic and leather. *Phwump, phwump, phwump,* more passes completed. Perspiration, deep breathing, yells, and grunts: these were the smells and sounds of the practice field. The sun was bright, and the air was crisp and clear.

Jones was interested in the practice, but not as much as I was. Something of a football fanatic, I had encouraged Jones to take a look at the team. He thought football a curious spectacle.

Jones's major preoccupation was the campus uproar over a column he had written entitled "Short Term Cuts Tee Time," which had appeared in the previous day's edition of *The Dartmouth.* He was thrilled that there were seven letters denouncing him on the editorial page.

"Keeney, I see your column got quite a response."

"SHHHHH! Not so loud," he took out a pair of sunglasses and put them on.

"What's the matter?" I asked.

"Better not say Keeney in public," he said, sliding the sunglasses down his nose. "The campus is in a state of hysteria. I'll have to go underground for a few days."

"But everyone knows who you are," I said.

"Everyone knows me as Michael, not many know me as Keeney. I'd like it to stay that way," he said.

Jones's column had described campus figure Howard Hawkins,

a throwback to the Sixties. Hawkins first arrived on campus in the fall of 1971, but as of 1980 had not yet graduated. More suited to Berkeley than Dartmouth, he had long hair, a beard, and a bad smell because he rarely bathed or washed his clothes. He spent all his time thinking about South Africa's apartheid system and was still waiting for a Marxist revolution to overthrow the government there. He organized protests and showed leftist propaganda films in the student center. He wasn't such a bad guy, although he was out of place in 1980. For better or worse, America was out of Vietnam, and most students couldn't have cared less about South Africa. As far as they were concerned, that nation had complex problems it would somehow have to deal with.

The administration, however, loved Howard. They kept him around and funded most of his activities. They institutionalized Howard's views in something called the Tucker Foundation, a multimillion dollar left-wing organization funded in part by student tuition money. Howard no longer had to fight the Establishment. All *his* people were *in* the Establishment and desperately wanted to help him. But Howard did not know that and, because of this, was a slightly pathetic anachronism.

Howard often spent his lunch hour picketing Parkhurst Hall. This made the deans and other administrators feel good. They decided to hire him to help run a new leftist academic program called the Alternative River Community. No one had ever criticized Howard before, because it was not considered *nice* to do so.

Jones violated the *ethos* by making fun of Howard. Jones said things that many students thought but would not dare say. Jones's column also made fun of President Kemeny's brainchild, the short nine-week term. This was a double no-no. It was considered in extremely poor taste by *nice* people. Jones wrote:

> G. K. Chesterton once said, "anything worth doing is worth doing badly." I submit that this quote sums up the Dartmouth experience. The nine-week term is the temporal equivalent of war, to misquote President Carter on his energy program. Students are

95

asked to do too much in too little time for too much money. President Eisenhower used to play golf, while occupying the most important office in the world. The current Kemeny Plan leaves no room for men like Eisenhower.

Instead we find Howard Hawkins '75, who has not yet graduated. He found no room in the eight-week term for his version of golf . . . social activism. He decided to extend his stay. Like Nixon, Hawkins's slogan is "four more years!" Nixon, though, had the good sense to leave when his time was up.

Again, like Nixon, Hawkins works in many locations—the Alternative River Community, Foley House (a leftist organization on campus) and the far-left Tucker Foundation. He is also in charge of the Liberation Film Series at the Common Ground Center. . . .

In a queer turn of events, the Common Ground, which is supposed to be the student center, is actually a staging ground for perverted theater. There is as much call for lesbian theater in Hanover as there is for Tab at Phi Delt on sink night.

. . . Back at the Common Ground Student Center, after the latest showing of Howard Hawkins's Liberation Film Series, our student government met to consider matters of gravity. In a twist of Lord Acton's observation that absolute power corrupts, we find here that the absolute absence of power corrupts just as badly. No doubt it was the news of South Africa's invasion of Afghanistan that prompted our student government to single out that country as the target for divestment.

At last, finally ensconced in my room, attired in smoking jacket and ascot, I played my favorite song: Leon Redbone's "Big Chief Buffalo Nickel" and reflected on one man's experience at Dartmouth. I thought, "Hell, my golf game's been ruined here. I find my time is wasted being pestered by nickel philosophers peddling worn-out ideas. Who is to say golf isn't more important than drivel?"

Perhaps if there was more time in the course of a Dartmouth

term, Howard Hawkins could have done his extracurricular work during the normal four years, and maybe I could find some time to play golf.

Jones, of course, had copies of all the letters denouncing him. He mentioned something about framing the best ones. This particular social commentary was one of his early efforts. His writing would become more polished, but the basic style was there. What people never understood about Jones is that he liked to shock and appall. It was the letters to the editor that, for Jones, made writing worthwhile.

"Read this one," Jones said, pulling a crumpled edition of the newspaper out of his pocket. It was written by Donald Rosenthal. He's a writer for the *Alumni Magazine,* and he's threatening to become macho."

Because I am not very strong, I rarely feel incensed enough to punch someone in the nose. But this is a public warning to Keeney Jones: Keeney, I'm going to be in the newspaper offices several times this week and if I see you there I'm going to make you eat your last column. I think it's sad enough that someone professes the beliefs that you claim to, but to do it publicly is simply in bad taste.

Jones pointed out another letter written by Joel Getzendanner of the class of 1980:

At first I was mildly amused by Mr. Jones's column "Short Term Cuts Tee Time." It then began to dawn on me that this might not be an absurdist parody of the conservative reactionary spirit. I was surprised to discover that "Keeney Jones" was not a pseudonym for an aspiring satirist, but was an actual flesh-and-blood news editor who was weaned at one of the country's finer preparatory academies. . . .

97

Poisoned Ivy

In yet another letter, Steven Godchaux '81, gives his views:

> I address this letter to Keeney Jones, whose political stance defies any rational rebuttal. A more appropriate response is what follows:
>
> May the bluebird of happiness discharge upon your penny loafers. May the fleas of a thousand camels wreak havoc upon your Brooks Brothers boxer shorts. May Ronald Reagan be the lifeguard at your little sister's swimming party. May all your children someday drop their croquet mallets and join the Peace Corps. And finally . . . the most hopeful of all . . . may an unruly mob of campus blacks, gays, and native Americans ignore you and your tripe.

"I like the last letter best of all," Jones said. "The last sentence doesn't make much sense to me, but I think this fellow has some talent."

"I guess you don't mind the heat you're getting."

"Are you kidding? The *ethos* has been such a suffocating force on campus that people worry all the time about what they say and do. Officialdom has been asleep for a long time. It's time someone gave it a kick. People are responding now! The whole structure is shaking like a jelly fish."

I don't know what my four years at Dartmouth would have been like if it had not been for Michael Keenan Jones. He was a continual presence, even when he wasn't taking courses. He seemed to give life to the place. He liked to ridicule those who held what he called "approved views." Jones understood the philosophy of correctness that permeated campus life. For many it overpowered the urge to do something really original or to become a genuine character. It was not considered good taste to like Jones's columns, but everyone read them. It was considered poor form to be seen enjoying his company, but everyone, if pressed, admitted that he was at least amusing. In most circles he was considered a social liability. But I knew that sometime later in life when my class would come back to Hanover, perhaps for their twenty-fifth reunion, the same people who hated him in their younger more self-righteous days, would say, "Do you remember that extraordinary fellow? I wonder what became of him?"

That fall I decided to move off campus. Professor Bernard Segal, of the Sociology Department, rented out an apartment suitable for two students. The rent was a lot cheaper than a dorm room, and the location was good, a quarter mile from where my classes met. The apartment was, in fact, the third floor of Professor Segal's large brown Victorian house. It had two bedrooms and a bath. It was here that I got to know a student named Richard Shoup, who became a major influence on my life.

Rich was quiet. Not that he didn't like to talk: he loved conversation; he was just not socially flashy. I don't believe he ever set foot inside a fraternity house; not because he was morally opposed to the clubs, but he had absolutely no urge to see what went on there.

He was short, perhaps five-feet-six, dressed conservatively, had brown hair that he wore short and parted on the side, and had a pair of round wire-rimmed glasses that he was seldom without.

Rich's career at Dartmouth was unusual in that he arrived an Episcopalian and left a Catholic. When he converted, all hell broke loose back home. His parents temporarily disowned him, and, because he was cut off from them financially, he was forced to take two years off from college. While he worked to make enough money to come back to school, he taught himself Latin, Greek, and Hebrew, and gained as thorough an understanding of scripture as I have ever seen in someone his age. His parents had wanted him to major in economics as a practical background for business administration. But this was before the break. He was never much interested in economics, so he decided to major in classics. He spent most of his days reading Virgil, Catullus, Ovid, Aristotle, and Plato, in the original. And every Sunday he would play the organ at Mass. He also spent a good deal of time reading theology at Aquinas House and talking to Monsignor Nolan.

Poisoned Ivy

I should say here that I was raised a Catholic. While my temperament was not particularly religious, I did occasionally go to church with my parents. I had never been inclined to think much about God or religion, but simply accepted Christianity's fundamental dogmas as true. So, I suppose I would be considered an orthodox Christian. It seemed to me that existence was a good thing, and I was very glad to have been born. Life, it seemed to me, was not only a pleasure but a kind of weird privilege, and I thought it appropriate to thank Whoever it was Who was responsible.

I did know something of Professor Bernard Segal before I moved into the upstairs floor of his home. I remembered reading about his trip to Cuba with Marxist Women's Studies professor Maryssa Navarro. Upon his return, he told a reporter from *The Dartmouth,* "I've never been anywhere in Latin America where both the people and I seemed to be so free of fear." Segal went on, "I observed a kind of political and social openness that means freedom," adding, "at the same time, there are obvious limitations on formal and public expression of ideas." Sounds a bit like Dartmouth. When a reporter asked him if he thought he might have been fed a lot of propaganda, Segal responded, "I've been propagandized before. I know the difference between propaganda and the things I see and feel." When a reporter asked Segal what he thought about Castro having such close ties with the Soviet Union, he replied, "I'm no great fan of the Soviets. But if I were a Cuban, given the choice between American investment and styles of development, and what Cuba has gotten from Moscow, Moscow wins hands down." I wondered if Havana University had a Women's Studies Program.

Once when I ran into him on Main Street and we walked together for a bit, I said I was puzzled by his notion of freedom because I knew that Cuba had more political prisoners per capita than any other country in the world.

"That's not true," he said. "America does."

"How so?" I asked. "I feel free to say anything I please."

"That's because you're in an affluent class," he said. "Crimes are

100

committed by those less fortunate than you, by people in lower classes. They are the victims of an oppressive economic system."

I think it fair to say that Professor Segal was active in most of the left-wing causes on campus, but he lacked the raw energy to be a really outspoken soldier of the Left. Nevertheless, it was clear where he stood politically. His special interest was Latin America. He seemed to know a great deal about Nicaragua, El Salvador, Guatemala, Costa Rica, Colombia. He was intensely interested in the politics of those countries and involved himself in the "Stop American Aid to El Salvador" movement that was becoming a lively issue on campuses across the nation. The idea was to equate American interest in El Salvador with American involvement in Vietnam.

I knew Professor Segal's basic political stands before I moved into his house, because some months earlier he was the featured speaker at a panel discussion on El Salvador. Well, actually, it was more of a presentation than a discussion, since the three other speakers were either brought in by, or were members of, the Dartmouth Radical Union.

On the podium, the bespectacled Professor Segal answered questions with great authority. Unfortunately, his brown shoes, brown corduroys, brown shirt, and brown hair swept to the side, made him look more like an authority on the Thousand-Year Reich than on Latin America. The message of the panelists was that the antigovernment opposition in El Salvador had "massive popular support." The opposition of which they spoke, those who wanted to "feed the poor" and "restore social justice," were guerrillas, armed and trained by the Club Med of the academic left, Cuba. (As it turned out, the guerrillas did not have "massive popular support." The election that followed proved that. Despite threats from the Left that anyone who voted in the morning would be dead in the afternoon, two-thirds of the eligible voters turned out and the Left took a terrific political defeat.)

I, on the other hand, had been an outspoken Reagan supporter, and, in fact, had worked for him in the fall and winter of 1979 and

1980 against George Bush in the New Hampshire primary. Evidently, Segal failed to make this connection when showing me the apartment, because it was a terrific shock for him when, on receiving my first rent payment, he discovered he had rented his home to the political equivalent of Charles Manson.

I had accumulated quite a load of campaign paraphernalia: posters, buttons, literature, and other inspirational material. I hung most of it on the wall of my apartment in Professor Segal's house. I was the same "pest" who had organized "Students for Reagan." Also on the wall, next to my huge Reagan poster, were life-sized pictures of Babe Ruth, Humphrey Bogart, and Ernest Hemingway, none of whom would have been comfortable with Professor Segal, had they met.

Across the hall from my room was Rich Shoup's. Rich was apolitical. But he was overtly religious, in a quiet sort of way. He never lectured others about religion, but whenever I had questions about doctrine, he would have an answer.

He did pray a lot. A set of rosary beads hung on his bedpost. If outside the room he was quiet about religion, the inside of his room looked like a shrine. He had a statue of the Virgin Mary and a picture of Saint Francis of Assisi hung on the wall. Clearly, Rich Shoup was not an ordinary Dartmouth student.

I took an immediate liking to Rich. He was extremely bright, pleasant, and easy to get along with.

Professor Segal never did get accustomed to the way the upstairs of his house looked, a cross between the Vatican and the Reagan ranch. I think he originally allowed me to stay so he could show his colleagues how "open-minded" he was. But gradually, he seemed to become bitter about the arrangement. He had a legal right to throw us out, I suppose, but that would have appeared illiberal.

Instead, he began to pick arguments. Many evenings when I got back to the house from studying at Baker Library, I would meet the professor, lying in wait at the base of the stairs that led to my apartment. His reading glasses halfway down his nose, he would be going through the day's edition of *The New York Times* or browsing through a book on Latin American politics. There would be a single lamp, dimly lit, by which he could read. The rest of the room was always dark.

One night Rich and I happened to walk back to the house together from an evening of studying. Professor Segal did not often argue with Rich, because Rich was not the arguing type.

This particular evening, though, Segal was definitely in the mood for an argument, and our conversation went something like this.

"Hello Professor," I said, ready for the rhetorical blizzard.

"I ought to make you pay extra rent for all those thumbtacks you put in my walls hanging up all that political propaganda," he grumbled. It was his odd little way of making a joke.

"I did not actually make any new holes," I said. "I used the old ones left by the previous tenant."

"How can you support Reagan?" he asked, "He's against abortion."

This struck me as an odd way for Segal to begin his attack on the president. He could have talked about his economic policies, arms control, or something like that. But then it occurred to me that his hatred of Reagan was not connected to the management of government. Segal was aroused by a fundamental disagreement as to the nature of Man, what he is and where he came from, assuming he wasn't aborted.

"It has always struck me as hypocritical," he went on, "that you people on the Right, who care so little about the plight of the poor in our nation's ghettos, who care so little about those who die in pointless wars, are suddenly so concerned about the fate of fetuses."

"I don't think anyone likes wars," I said.

"How can you show so little compassion for women?"

"I don't think I am," I said.

"How can you force a young girl to have a child she doesn't want?" His face was now only a few inches from mine.

"I'm not," I said. I searched for a way to end the argument as diplomatically as possible. "It seems that your stand on this issue depends on your overall outlook on things." It sounded so relativistic, I thought Segal would like it.

He didn't. "Why is that?" he asked impatiently.

"Well, either life is of no account, meaningless, or it is a God-given gift that should be protected."

Segal shook his head nervously from side to side. "Well, I don't think life is a God-given gift, and I don't think it is of no account," he said mimicking my voice and cadence.

"What is it then?" I asked.

"The question of where we came from is meaningless, since we can never know the answer. A human life can either be of great benefit to society or it can be a great burden."

Segal looked over at Rich who, through the entire discussion, had not uttered a word. He stood there with his books under his arm and listened. It appeared to me that Professor Segal was trying to anger Rich. "God does not fit into a rational analysis," he said.

"Analysis of what?" I asked.

"Belief in God is no more than superstition. Charlatans like Jerry Falwell, for their own personal gain, play on people's ignorance. The Catholic Church, and Christianity in general, have been responsible for so much war and bloodshed: the Crusades, the Inquisition, the Salem witch burnings."

At this point, Rich finally entered in. "Many more people have been killed in wars over secular causes and ideologies than in religious wars, especially Christian wars. Both world wars were disputes over secular matters. The entire point of my faith is to praise life, to praise being, and to praise God as creator of the world. Either Christianity is true, or it isn't. Human mistakes don't change the final truth of it."

Professor Segal looked confused, not by the argument, but by the sensibility. Rich had an outlook on life that was utterly reasonable, but not often found in the modern world. There was no room for argument here. In fact, there was little room for three people in the

104

professor's stairwell. Rich and I said good night and went on up the stairs, as Segal folded and refolded *The New York Times.*

I don't believe I ever missed Sunday Mass while living across the hall from Rich Shoup. He made it seem the right thing to do. Rich always got up early, around six o'clock. One Sunday I decided to get up, too.

"I almost became an anthropology major," Rich said that morning. We were sitting on hard wooden chairs. He was leaning back, his feet up on his desk.

"What interested you about anthropology?" I asked.

"Anthropology is the study of man," Rich said. "I'm very interested in man."

"What made you decide against it?"

"I found that anthropology here has almost nothing to do with the study of man."

"I don't understand."

"I mean, they begin by ruling out something called the unknowable. These things they label unknowable happen to be the most commonly held beliefs of men."

"For example?" I said.

"For example, the vast majority of men in history have been members of some religion or other. But God's existence is unknowable according to the accepted doctrine in the anthropology department, as are questions like: Is man mortal or immortal? Predestined or free? Does man have free will, or is his sense of choice an illusion? Does he have a conscience, and should he listen to it? Are there such things as miracles?"

"We can't know these things for certain," I said. "Wouldn't it be presumptuous for a professor to assert something as true if it can't be proved?" I asked.

Rich was in high spirits. He scratched his head for a moment before answering.

"Sometimes we have to draw conclusions from inference," he said.

105

"How do we do that?"

"Well, I've always believed the opinion of the multitude of ordinary men is of more value than the opinion of a single expert. The vast majority of men through history as well as today have believed in God. There have not been many atheists, not many at all."

"Is it so bad to say, I don't know?" I asked.

"About some things it is. Agnostic is a modern term. It fits the modern anthropologist's position, uncommitted. At some point, we must make a decision."

"But can a university impose a morality on its students?"

"It does every day. The question is, which morality? Our belief, disbelief, or indifference toward God has a tremendous effect on the formulation of the curriculum."

"How so?" I asked. "Can't we study literature, history, and philosophy and analyze their relative merits in an objective way?"

"No, I believe an education has to be rooted in a certain set of values."

"But who's to say what values?"

"I happen to believe in Western values. Our view of the universe is fundamental to our study of literature, history, philosophy, or anything else."

"But maybe your values are wrong."

"Perhaps. But is it possible that the whole history of Western thought is based on error?"

"It could be," I said.

"If you say yes, then that will have a profound effect on your reading of these people."

"How so?"

"Well, either Dante has something worthwhile to say, something we should pay close attention to, or he is merely interesting—a clever man, but wrong. He is only for amusement."

"So either we are dilettantes, or we are trying to get something of real value from reading these people."

"That's right." Rich's face lit up. "Building a cathedral makes

106

sense, or it is completely insane. It depends on how you look at things. If the thing upon which it was built, Christianity, is a mistake..." Rich paused for a moment, turned his head toward the window and looked directly at Aquinas House, which is just up the street, ". . . then it really makes no difference if our entire education is founded on Eastern culture—which is also interesting."

"Have you met Monsignor Nolan?" Rich asked.

"No, I haven't," I said, "but I like his sermons. I want to meet him."

"I think he might be a great man. He built Aquinas House about thirty years ago in the face of tremendous opposition. A pamphlet was widely circulated explaining how Aquinas House would ruin Dartmouth. Then the college decided not to allow the Catholic Student Center to use the Dartmouth name. The Monsignor was permitted to say only that Aquinas House was the Catholic Student Center *at* Dartmouth. It had to be clear that Aquinas House was not part of the college."

"Aquinas House seems to be the most active organization on campus today," I said.

"From the start, Monsignor Nolan made everyone welcome—Protestants, Jews, atheists, agnostics—whoever wanted to come. You see a lot of non-Catholics at Mass. Nolan gets between fifteen and thirty converts a year. Two or three Aquinas House students every year enter the priesthood. Did you know there's a higher attendance rate at Mass among Catholics here than at any Catholic university in the country?" Rich said.

I was amazed.

"I don't know if Nolan's name will be remembered a hundred years from now. But I think he has accomplished great things, while offending as few people as possible."

"What's the Catholic situation like at Harvard and Yale?"

"Leonard Feeney, a great man in the estimation of many people, was chased off the Harvard campus in the Fifties. The official reason was that he had a doctrinal disagreement with the Pope about the definition of the Church. The real reason, though, was that he was converting the children of too many rich Protestants. Temple Morgan was one of his prominent converts."

"What happened at Yale?"

"John Courtney Murray, who was considered one of the important theologians of this century, taught at Yale. He was denied tenure."

"What was the problem?"

"He was too noticeable."

"What has happened on the campuses since?"

"Today there is virtually no Catholic presence at Harvard, Yale, or any other secular college, except Dartmouth. Where the flamboyant personalities and important thinkers failed, Nolan succeeded."

"It's almost eleven o'clock," I said. "We better get to Mass."

"I'm playing the organ today," said Rich. "I'd better run."

It was a gorgeous Sunday morning. The sun was bright, the sky clear, the breeze cool. The grass was still wet from the dew. Cars were lined up along the side of the road, as there were not enough spaces in the parking lot. Students were strolling down Webster Avenue, past the fraternities' lawns littered with plastic beer cups, a reminder of the parties the night before. Most of the students going to Mass were dressed in their Sunday clothes. Some wore blue jeans, but it didn't matter. The point was, they were going. Out of the four thousand students enrolled at Dartmouth, about eight hundred went to Mass at Aquinas House.

Rich played "Hail Holy Queen Enthroned Above" for the entrance hymn. People were still filing into the packed building when Monsignor Nolan walked down the aisle with two student servers. He took his place at the front of the congregation. He said the opening prayer, welcomed everyone to Aquinas House, sat down, and waited for a student to finish the Old Testament readings. He then ascended the wooden stairs to the pulpit, his robes streaming behind him. He read from the Gospel, then delivered his sermon—a sermon that one out of five students on campus would hear.

"The entire meaning of Christianity is contained in the phrase in the Creed, 'He descended from Heaven.'"

Nolan's deep voice boomed out across the room. At sixty-two, he had, in some ways, grown more powerful with age. His mind had become sharper and his thoughts more poignant. For many of the more serious students, he was a true father figure, the source of moral and spiritual guidance.

"God is the most obvious fact of human experience," said Father Nolan. "You can see His presence in people's faces. You can see it in the stars when you look up at night. You see it in nature. But if God is so easy to find, why do so many people say they have not found Him? It is as if these people are in a dark room. They say, I can't find the light, when all they have to do is raise the blinds . . ."

"One common charge against Christianity is that it is too simple, too childlike. It is true that we can explain Christianity simply. Essentially, it is a love story between God and Man. It is simple if you want to stop there. But if you want to ask what really happened, be prepared for a difficult answer, no, an incomprehensible answer. . . .

"It is a most natural tendency to try and explain life simply. Isaac Newton, for example, thought he had discovered the law of gravity. Everyone accepted his law as truth. But then Einstein came along and told us that, in fact, there is no such thing as gravity—there is something called relativity, a theory which says that something called matter has a strange effect on something called space and something called time, which are somehow connected. Thus we have new laws of science, and the old ones are thrown out. These laws will also be thrown out when we find that reality does not fit this theory either. Existence is not what it seems. It is not simple. It is odd, unexpected. It is a surprise, but I think it is a pleasant surprise. . . .

"Reality is not something one would have guessed. That is one reason I am a Christian. Christianity is not something one would have guessed, either. If it was, and it offered me just the kind of world I expected, I would have thought it made up. It is not the sort of thing anyone would have thought of. It has that strange unexpected quality that real things have. . . ."

Monsignor Nolan's sermon seemed to speak directly to me. I myself had thought Christianity was too simple to be true. I once thought of it as some kind of wonderful fairytale. To many, Nolan's thoughts would not have been new. These ideas had been expressed by some of Christianity's great popularizers, like G. K. Chesterton, C. S. Lewis, and Fulton Sheen. But these ideas were new to me. Nolan's power, though, came not so much from what he said, but the way he said it and the kind of man he was. He never got caught up in the latest fads and never brought politics into his sermons, or private conversations. He gave the students what they wanted, straight Christian doctrine. He told us that our first responsibility was to look at our own lives before trying to change the lives of others.

During this period, I began to think very differently about Jesus. I began to understand Rich Shoup's conviction that our particular religious belief is crucial to our understanding of Western culture, to our comprehension of the staggering collision between Athens and Jerusalem. I had gone to Mass before out of habit, or because my parents went. Now, on a single Sunday morning, Rich Shoup and Monsignor Nolan had come close to convincing me of the truth of Christianity.

THE ESTABLISHMENT RELIGION

AS I have said, there was a time, under the presidencies of William Jewett Tucker and Ernest Martin Hopkins, when Dartmouth students were required to attend daily chapel. No one took attendance, but most students wanted to listen to the president of their college say a few thoughtful words at the start of the day. William Jewett Tucker, president around the turn of the century, was originally a Protestant minister. And President Hopkins, Jewett Tucker's successor, stressed every day that belief in God was crucial to the moral, spiritual, and intellectual development of the student.

Hopkins and Tucker would usually begin by making some points about the Christian faith and then tell the students about the duty they had to their country, their community, their family, and their college. Their daily talks would give the students a sense of the basic philosophical position of the college. What students took with them from chapel was a set of agreed-upon beliefs that provided the moral foundation upon which a coherent education could be built.

I have spent a good deal of time reading the diary my grandfather kept as an undergraduate. What left the deepest impression on him, the thing he wrote about most, was daily chapel. "I will never forget Dartmouth because of President Hopkins's talks to us each day at daily chapel," he wrote in the year 1919. "Even though I have only talked briefly with him in person on one occasion, I feel that he is like a father to me. I arrived at Dartmouth an agnostic. Now I am a believing Christian and hardly can understand how I could have been anything else. I never think of President Hopkins as being too authoritarian because what he says always makes sense to me, and it makes sense to most of my classmates."

In the Thirties the college shifted to a new policy. Administrators decided that to require daily chapel was no longer possible. Maybe, in a way, it wasn't. This does not mean that religion was no longer practiced at Dartmouth. It just was not officially blessed by Dartmouth officialdom.

Aquinas House, indeed, began to flourish under the leadership of Monsignor Nolan. By the Fifties, Catholics were turning out for Mass in record numbers. The Protestant churches were also very active, and there began to develop a strong Jewish presence on the campus. Monsignor Nolan, though, had by far the greatest influence on the student body of any figure at Dartmouth, either religious or secular, far more than the president of the college, far more than any professor.

During the late Sixties, cultural relativism settled in as the orthodoxy at Dartmouth. "Value judgments" were evil. We were to be "nonjudgmental." What they really meant to say was that the core values of the West were now defunct. They eschewed the word "enemies." Communism, for example, was not a bad thing, it was merely an "alternative political system." That Stalin killed 30 million of his own people was "unfortunate." Thus, relativism, by discrediting the idea that someone could actually preach to the students, as President Hopkins had done, gave way to the new liberalism of the Seventies, which began to make value judgments of its own. Suddenly, the conflict in Central America became *our* fault, and the nuclear arms race was a result of *our* failure to reach an agreement with the Soviet Union (never mind all the arms agreements the Kremlin had broken). The presidency of John Kemeny was a product of this *new* liberalism.

So was Dartmouth's Tucker Foundation. Its purpose, as explained in its charter, was to "foster morality among the students." This was a multimillion-dollar, college-funded organization, and the morality of which it spoke had nothing to do with the morality of Ernest Martin Hopkins or William Jewett Tucker, for whom it was named. As a substitute for presidents Hopkins and Tucker, moral guidance at Kemeny's Dartmouth came in the form of two ministers named Warner Traynam and Richard Hyde, who were hired to be the college chaplains.

Traynam was a distinguished-looking black, with an impressive handlebar mustache. He had the nervous habit of batting his eyelashes very rapidly while he talked. His politics were moderate Left. No one knew what he thought about God.

Richard Hyde, an ordained minister, was a former Catholic, and appeared very bitter toward the Catholic Church. Politically, he was extreme Left. I never saw Mr. Hyde smile, and he seemed incapable of containing his extreme hostility toward anyone who held a political opinion contrary to his own. I am not being hyperbolic about this or exaggerating to make a point. I am simply describing a man who had been given responsibility for the moral guidance of Dartmouth students.

Both Traynam and Hyde made it clear that they did not believe in the moral relativism championed by an older liberalism. In an essay that was mailed to every student, Traynam wrote: "The Tucker Foundation seeks to reinforce the institution's commitment to moral and spiritual values. We are empowering the students. We ought to say something implicitly and explicitly about the use of that power. We cannot guarantee the outcome, but we owe it to society, to ourselves, and most of all to the students, to provide some guidance."

The Tucker Foundation, headed by chaplains Traynam and Hyde, in pursuing its program to give the students a definite moral code, sponsored antinuclear demonstrations; draft evasion panels;

prolesbian films and workshops; lectures against United States involvement in Nicaragua, El Salvador, Guatemala, or anywhere else; marches against the college's investment in corporations that do business with South Africa; and abortion information centers.

The Tucker Foundation's half-million-dollar annual budget comes mainly from the college endowment. It funded things like student internships in the ghetto and such organizations as Planned Parenthood, rape crisis centers, the Headrest Program, and resource centers for "nonviolent protest" against nuclear power.

It is important to note that this new morality, this official *ethos* that was being vigorously and extravagantly promoted by the Dartmouth administration, was not generally held by the students. A very small percentage of students ever entered the Tucker Foundation offices, which took up about half of an administration building. Hardly anyone consulted a member of the enormous staff, or went on the amply funded Tucker Foundation internships. There were not that many people who saw a compelling need to work for Planned Parenthood. In fact, the peculiar philosophy promoted by the Tucker Foundation was a kind of campus joke. The propaganda that students received in their mailboxes was generally ridiculed and promptly discarded.

It did not take any degree of political acumen to see that Traynam's newsletters to the students reflected a sharply liberal-to-left bias. In one campus mailing he described President Carter's draft registration program as "unnecessary, and in a significant way subversive to the values of society . . ." Note that he used the word *society* rather than *America*. It's all part of the *ethos*. In conjunction with Traynam's letter, the Tucker Foundation sponsored a panel at which counselors described methods of evading draft registration.

Please put yourself in the place of an ordinary freshman going to his or her mailbox. You expect to get the usual junk mail from the dean's office, advertisements for new courses being offered, and maybe a letter from someone back home. You find a letter from the

114

college chaplain. His name is Warner Traynam. You are not familiar with his name because you are only a freshman. You expect some thoughtful advice with regard to religion, morality, ethics—something like that. You begin to read:

> The sexual patterns by which Western humanity at least has related are being challenged just as the social patterns have been. Feminism and the gay movement address the problem of roles. The need for procreation is lessened, indeed procreation is fast becoming a limited value. . . .
>
> It is little wonder that the emphasis has shifted from the production of people to the development of love and the nurturing of the life that exists. Once men and women have the real option of whether to procreate or not, it is little wonder that those whom society has shunted aside, in part because they did not reproduce their kind, should claim our attention. . . .
>
> The Apostle Paul, at one place, observes that "all things are lawful, but not all things are helpful." (I Cor.6:12) I have a friend who once commented that he felt desire toward a male friend of his, which was reciprocated. They talked about it and decided that it was real and deepened their relationship. Neither could handle it. As an exclusive pattern homosexuality precludes many of the goods society and individuals value. It is not for everyone any more than celibacy is. So persons for whom it is a possibility should consider it, if they are prepared for the natural and social problems of such an existence and, if not, explore the possibility of change. Not because it is evil but because for the present, at least, it is a difficult mode of life. But for those who know they are Gay and accept it, no apologies are necessary. For them the expectation that society should recognize this reality and the value of it, is a legitimate expectation, and they should embrace it as God has given it to them, confident that it is not only for their own good but for the good of society.

A defense of the active homosexual life was not enough, how-

115

ever, as the other chaplain, Hyde, sent out a newsletter assailing the United States for its participation in the arms race against the Soviet Union. Hyde's mailing included the claim that 70 percent of the nation's budget was spent on the military—it was only 23 percent at the time, according to the Bureau of Statistics, but factual accuracy must never become an impediment to ideology.

The other chaplains brought in by the Tucker Foundation seemed to share a similar zeal for the peculiar. The Reverend Isabel Carter Hayward, one of the first women priests to be ordained by the Episcopal Church, denied the omnipotence of God in a sermon in Rollins Chapel, the home base of Traynam's and Hyde's "ecumenical" activities. Her talk, a Tucker Foundation feature titled "Redefining Power," explained what she referred to as the "nature of real power," which she said "is relational power, shared and exchanged mutually between persons. . . . Power cannot be possessed by a single entity." This woman seemed unfamiliar with the nature of both God and electric chairs.

Mr. Traynam's and Mr. Hyde's program of what they called "facilitating debate," was typical of their idea of "free and open exchange of differing viewpoints on vital issues." When these two used words like "free and open" to describe a Tucker Foundation-initiated "discussion," one knew immediately that it would be nothing of the kind. For example, they sponsored a series of lectures on the "issues of nuclear power," entitled, "The Atomic Legacy: From Hiroshima to Haig." This was to coincide with a protest march from Washington, Vermont, to Moscow, Vermont. (As you may recall, 159 out of a possible 189 Vermont towns, including a town called Orwell, voted for a complete freeze on anything nuclear.) The Tucker Foundation also sponsored a large and expensive seminar on the subject of disarmament. Their brochure promised that "a variety of viewpoints and expertise will be offered." It would have been interesting to listen to a debate on the issue. When I arrived I found that all the debaters agreed on all the major points. They all agreed the arms race was out of hand and that America was primarily responsible and had to begin disarming immediately. There was only slight disagreement as to how far the United States should go in disarming. Two of the participants thought America should do away with the military completely and devote all the extra revenue to the funding of government-run social projects.

November 11, 1981, VETERANS DAY: The Tucker Foundation decided to sponsor a "consciousness-raising" seminar on "The Threat of Nuclear Power." Its agenda included what purported to be a *discussion* of "nuclear issues and the arms race." There was a lecture by someone whom no one had ever heard of on "the need to disarm immediately," and a peace march that featured professors, administrators, counter-culture residents from the area, and a few students. The protesters were dressed up as mutants, apparently victims of radioactive poisoning. Most observers thought they were observing the subject of a psychology experiment gone awry. There were children dressed up as mutants, Grandparents for Reducing the Arms Race, mutants on stilts, and a huge model of a missile.

This extravaganza appeared suddenly on the Green. The procession began with a single trumpeter calling the participants to order. The march around the Green was led by a mutant Madonna and Child, followed by others dressed mostly in black. One mutant girl, dressed like a skeleton, approached me and tried to sell me an unattractive button. When I said "No, thank you," she called me a "fascist war-mongering motherfucker."

When the procession ended, the mutants huddled together at the center of the Green, and two generals fought symbolically. Soon it came time for the bomb to explode. One could have predicted it. Someone hit a giant gong . . . Boom! The protesters died in a kind of mock Hiroshima. Two dogs were seen fornicating in the carnage.

"It's Veteran's Day," I thought to myself, and remembered that I was supposed to attend a holiday celebration in the room of Michael Keenan Jones. His was the one with the huge American flag waving out the third-story window. This would be quite a contrast to the Tucker Foundation's protest march. Drinks would be served, with marching music by John Philip Sousa playing in the background. We would listen to a recording of John F. Kennedy's inaugural address on the hi-fi. We all agreed that this was one of the great political addresses and that it was especially appropriate for Veteran's Day. "Put out more flags!" Jones would yell out the window, alluding to his favorite Evelyn Waugh novel, before filling his glass with more brandy.

The Tucker Foundation also invented something called "Women's Weekend." The agenda included "Non-Violence Training for the Women's Pentagon Action." There was a massage workshop, where female students "came to grips" with lesbianism. During this Women's Weekend, capital W, there was an "all-male discussion on the merits of feminism," followed by a lesbian dance. It must have been difficult for the few males present to cut in. At other Women's Weekend seminars, speakers included an abortionist, a self-defense expert (the bouncer for the lesbian dance?), and an editor of *Ms.* magazine. All events were held in the Common Ground and sponsored by Traynam, Hyde, and their crew from Tucker.

The peculiar little issues that Traynam and Hyde found so important were a source of great amusement to the ordinary student. But the duo made one really foul play in what became known as "The Great Oxfam Deception." Oxfam is an old British charity, which at one time had a very noble purpose, to feed, clothe, and provide shelter to the poor. It was also, at one time, apolitical. The fund drive for the Oxfam America charity was organized on the Dartmouth campus by the Tucker Foundation for the ostensible purpose of getting food to the Cambodian citizens who were starving under the insane and genocidal regime of Pol Pot and the Khymer Rouge. It seemed to most people a very worthwhile cause. In an effort to promote the charity, the Tucker Foundation put up a huge sign on the Green with the statement: "7,000 PEOPLE IN A REFUGEE CAMP IN THAILAND LIVE IN AN AREA SMALLER THAN THE GREEN."

The program set up by Tucker was this: students were asked to give up at least one meal at the college dining hall. For every meal given up, the dining hall would contribute $1.25 to Oxfam.

Where did the money go? . . . Not to the "7,000 PEOPLE IN A REFUGEE CAMP," as advertised on the poster. That program had been terminated many months before the Oxfam drive began on the Dartmouth campus, according to J. H. Miller at Oxfam America's main office.

The odd feature about the Tucker program was that not only were students expected to contribute at least one dining hall meal, but they were also supposed not to eat elsewhere. The idea was to *fast* for one meal and thereby gain a greater "awareness and understanding" of the starving Cambodian's situation. Wouldn't a homeless and destitute refugee be happy to know that a group of rich Ivy League preppies, ten pounds too fat for their summer swimsuits, had decided to miss a meal on their account so that they could better *relate* to their hopeless plight? It was certainly more practical for Dartmouth to get their money this way than to persuade daddies to donate their yachts.

"It's so wonderful, what these students have done in the Oxfam effort!" cried Elise Boulding, professor of sociology, tears of joy welling up in her eyes.

Many students, including myself, did not understand that approximately 60 percent of the money donated by giving up a dining hall meal did not go to Oxfam. The average cost of a meal at Dartmouth was $3.50. The dining hall was contributing $1.25 of that to Oxfam and keeping the remaining $2.25.

You might ask: if the money that actually went to Oxfam did not go to feed the 7,000 destitute refugees on the poster, where did it go?

Well, 19 percent went to Oxfam fundraising that year. The cost of general administration, salaries, bonuses, et cetera, accounted for another 19 percent.

If at one time Oxfam did, in fact, dedicate itself to feeding the hungry, that was no longer its chief pursuit. Oxfam had instituted a rapidly expanding program called "Development Education," the objectives of which were purely political. For example, a study

119

tour, sponsored by Oxfam's "Development Education" division, traveled to Cuba. According to the Oxfam newsletter, available at the Tucker Foundation, "The participants had detailed briefings and learned about *popular power.*" Cuba's "ongoing experiments" with economic development, its relations with the United States and Central America, and "popular participation," were themes throughout the week, according to the newsletter.

Oxfam also provided funding for a program called "Partnership Nicaragua," intended to "raise the consciousness of Americans" about the "history, needs, and aspirations of the Nicaraguan people." And, if they could not raise people's consciousness, they could at least raise money. This program began *after* the Sandinista guerrillas seized control of the country. One of the newsletters explained that "Oxfam continues its strong support for the *new* Nicaragua." Oxfam has also funded projects in Bolivia, "in a concentrated effort to upgrade the social and economic status of women in the district."

What were Oxfam's positions on the politics in other countries of strategic importance to the United States? Well, another one of their brochures labeled the El Salvador Land Reform Program a "cruel hoax. No reform or development is possible under existing conditions." Oxfam distributed literature on El Salvador that sympathized with the guerrillas. One could order such pamphlets as the *Response of the Farabundo Marti National Liberation Front-Democratic Revolutionary Front to the Charges of the North American Government*—good light reading for summer vacation. One could also order movies like *El Salvador: Another Vietnam* and a slide show that promoted the Revolutionary Front as the solution to El Salvador's problems. With a little luck, maybe last year's Cambodian genocide will raise enough money to fund apologetics for next year's Latin American genocide.

Oxfam published on the op-ed pages of *The New York Times* an advertisement opposing U.S. involvement in El Salvador, and pleading for a "humanitarian solution." The "humanitarian solution" for Oxfam would be a government run by the Cuban-armed guerrillas, the same people who were shooting at the Salvadorian citizens who were trying to vote. But the far Left has never put a premium on elections.

None of this information was contained in the Tucker Foundation's huge promotional campaign for Oxfam on the Dartmouth campus. Most students thought their money might help put food into a few hungry bellies. Most students thought this was a legitimate attempt to relieve suffering in Cambodia. I, too, in my previous innocence, gave up a day of meals.

GOD AND MAN . . .

DESPITE the Tucker Foundation and Dartmouth officialdom, much of the knowledge I acquired on the campus itself was of great value. There were times when I would escape the squabbles of college life and look on my bookshelves for one of the books I had always wanted to read. I made reading a sanctuary, where I thought about the words that had built our civilization and shaped the minds of Western man.

I took a course with Kevin Brownlee, in which we read Dante for ten weeks. So many other writers seemed either chained to the world and a worldly conception of grandeur, or completely separated from both, as were a number of medieval poets. But Dante's glimpse of a nine-year-old girl walking down the street in Florence could lead him to the beatific vision and an understanding of God's love for the world. At the hub of religious and social upheaval, Dante understood the meaning of the Incarnation. At a time when philosophers were saying the world was evil, Dante showed them that the mind and soul, liberated but not separated from the problems of daily life, could capture the beauty of the world and state the ineffable.

There was a certain amount of spiritual fulfillment in the beauty of the Dartmouth campus itself, but I found a deeper fulfillment in the office of Monsignor Nolan. On his bookshelves could be found the intelletual and spiritual history of Western man: Saint Thomas Aquinas, the Church fathers, Saint Augustine, Nietzsche, Kant, Karl Barth, Saint Teresa of Avila, Saint John of the Cross, Hume, Camus. But the Monsignor's office also held crucifixes, relics, a statue of the Virgin Mary—and so was alien to most of the religion department. For the most part, the academics over there considered Christianity to be of anthropological interest only. But for me, walking into the Monsignor's office turned out to be one of the pivotal experiences of my college life, because, when he spoke, it was with the whole depth of history behind him. The bonfires, the football games, the fraternity parties, the towering pines, the lawns, the office of the president himself, seemed small in comparison to Nolan.

He helped crystallize all my foggy notions about life. "It's important to understand that romance and religion are connected," he once told me. "You really can't have one without the other." He saw in me what he thought was a healthy suspicion of bureaucracies and illuminated the folly of what he called "the trendies": Hans Küng, William Sloan Coffin, and the "Studies" departments at Dartmouth. But Monsignor Nolan also advised me not to be bitter in my criticisms.

One evening, early in spring terms, I went to the Monsignor's office because I had some questions about my religion. Leaning back in his leather desk chair, hands clasped behind his head, the desk lamp throwing light onto his white hair, he smiled at me as I sat across the room on a stuffed sofa.

"How do we know Christ wasn't a liar?" I asked. "How do we know Christianity is not some gigantic mistake?"

"I suppose it might be a mistake or a lie," said Nolan. His deep voice, black suit, and Roman collar gave him a measure of authority. "If it is a lie, though, it would be an incredible lie indeed. In fact, the lie would be as great a miracle as the truth."

"I'm not sure I follow you," I said.

"Think for a moment. Is it really possible that people would follow this carpenter's son, this teller of stories, this man who claimed to be God, who rode into Jerusalem on the back of a donkey, this almost preposterous sight, unless they thought he was telling the truth? Is it possible that this incredible liar, who died for his lie, was so talented that he could make people believe that he had risen from the dead? This would be a truly amazing accomplishment. Is it possible that these lies could convert an entire Roman Empire? Is it possible that while this six hundred-year-old empire fell, the lie lived on to build another civilization, another completely different culture called Europe, a civilization totally dependent on belief in the lie?"

"It does seem incredible."

"Think about the revolution that was brought about by this single man's lie, a man who never wrote a word, a liar without a manifesto. The classical world with all its great writers and thinkers, Homer, Aristotle, Plato, Virgil, came crashing down. But the lie survived. It lived through the Dark Ages. Then medieval Europe was built around the great monastic movements started by Benedict, Francis, and Dominic. It appealed to the sensibility of a troubadour like Saint Francis of Assisi, and the mind of a logician like Saint Thomas Aquinas. If this was a lie, it was not like one that had been told before."

"It seems it would take a greater leap of faith to believe that Christianity is a lie than to believe it is the truth," I said.

"Exactly," said Nolan.

His optimism lifted my spirits. It gave me hope that my years at Dartmouth, as long as I did not do something very foolish, would lead me toward ancient villages, enduring ideas, and some understanding of the great tale of Athens and Jerusalem—the intellectual and spiritual force that built the West.

Although I am not an especially religious person, I could understand Rich Shoup's and Monsignor Nolan's outlook much more easily than I could understand Warner Traynam's, Richard Hyde's, and Professor Bernard Segal's. Like Rich and the Monsignor, I was basically optimistic about the ultimate fate of things. Optimism, though, might be the wrong word to describe my acceptance of existence, with all its flaws. I knew there were famines, wars, nuclear missiles, evil regimes, and incurable diseases. These facts seemed to me at the root of the Left's opposition to anything overtly religious or even pro-American. "If there is a God, why did he make this obviously flawed world?" "If America is so great, why do we still have people who can't get health care?" One might just as easily ask, how the cosmos of the atheist or agnostic would be improved? Or, if the Soviet Union is so great, why do they need a gulag? Why are so many Cubans, Red Chinese, Vietnamese, and Cambodians fleeing for their lives from the workers' paradise? It seemed to me the Left's arguments against religion and America played on emotion, and not reason. So my acceptance of the world was not really optimistic, but rather patriotic, as is my acceptance of America. It was a matter of loyalty to existence itself, better than nonexistence, and loyalty to the nation of which I am a citizen, a nation with flaws, but I think better than most.

One simply has to look at the alternatives to understand how I arrived at these conclusions. Compare America, or any west European nation, with any communist or third-world country. Compare the Judeo-Christian God with the God of Islam or the Marxist utopia, which is really a substitute for religion. Warner Traynam once accused me of being "Eurocentric." If he meant I favored an advanced culture, a free market economy, democratic government, and the Western tradition of morality over their opposites, then he was 100 percent correct.

There is a certain kind of person, one found generally on the faculty or in the administration of American universities, and Dartmouth was no exception, called a universal skeptic. He is a kind of cosmic critic, not at all interested in improving what he criticizes. For him, criticism is an end in itself. There is, on the other hand, constructive criticism by those fundamentally loyal to what they want improved. But many critics, and one can usually identify them by their method of attack, are, in fact, for the enemy.

Rarely in the university does one hear any serious criticism of communist regimes. But we do hear unmitigated attacks on American anticommunists, usually labeled "superpatriots," a derisive term in the minds of these critics. We hear excuses for the Soviet Union all the time, even for the butchery in Afghanistan. Pol Pot exterminated one-fourth of Cambodia's population. Stalin murdered at least 30 million of his own people, Mao 60 million. Half the world is ruled by communism, which is aggressively expanding. But for some reason, it is Senator Jesse Helms who is the "warmonger" for pointing out that it is the Soviet Union, not the United States, that routinely violates SALT.

I have suggested that, in my view, in order to be an orthodox Christian, one must feel an allegiance to existence and in fact be a cosmic patriot. What strikes me wrong about the universal skeptic is that he is actually a cosmic antipatriot, one who is sour on everything, in some respects won over by the enemy.

This view became fundamental to my attitude toward religion, politics, and academia. It is a view based primarily on loyalty to that of which I am a part: loyalty to my universe, my world, my civilization, my country, my college, and, finally, my family. This view was squarely at odds with the most vocal segments of the Dartmouth establishment.

It was near the end of spring term. I remember walking back to my apartment late one night after studying long hours for my finals. There was a cool breeze, and the rushing wind caused my eyes to fill with water. There were some lighted windows scattered around campus, and I could hear the faraway sound of a typewriter. It was a clear night, and I was struck by the enormous distance of the stars, which made me think of other things that were now distant. I remembered my high school days, the friends I had there and the girls I had known, who seemed to dance past me with their frosty seductive laughter. I thought about Melissa, and about my first day in South Fayerweather dormitory when I met Jeff Kemp. It seemed only yesterday that Jeff and I had roomed together. I thought about the racial protests and the Shaun Teevens "Indian skater incident," and about my first hours at Dartmouth and how alone in the world I felt then. I began to worry for a moment about the passage of time. It suddenly dawned on me that I was almost finished with my junior year. Before long, my days as an undergraduate would be over. As I passed by Baker Library and looked up at its magnificent spire, a pleasant shiver went up my spine. A lot had happened to me at Dartmouth.

TRASHING DEMOCRACY

THE one thing my father tried hardest to teach me was the value of fair play. Whether in sports, in school work, or in politics, he said, if you had to cheat, you haven't accomplished anything except to prove your own inferiority. He placed particular importance on the vote and once said, "If you can't convince the majority of people that your views are correct, there is a good chance that they are not."

At Dartmouth I witnessed what must have been one of the most peculiar elections to take place anywhere (outside Chicago). The tale begins in the fall of 1979 at a party in the living room of Beta after the homecoming football game against Princeton, when I met John Steel, a surgeon from La Jolla, California. He had striking good looks. His hair was silver, short, and parted cleanly on the side. Three of his four children attended Dartmouth. The oldest, John, Jr., was perhaps the best tennis player the college had ever had. Dr. Steel had graduated with the class of 1956 and was active in his alumni club in San Diego. He loved Dartmouth and had bought a second home in Hanover. He could be found on the campus for many big weekends, for which he flew across the continent. He didn't mind the rock music or the stale smell of beer

129

that seemed to permeate the woodwork at Beta. (Actually, Beta put on a pretty elegant party for the alumni on homecoming weekend. The brothers wore jackets, ties without soup stains, and behaved in a respectable way. Cocktails were served instead of grain alcohol, and there were plenty of attractive hostesses. This was not the usual Beta "horror show.")

Dr. Steel was eager to talk with students, but the student he talked most about, and seemed to like the best, was Shaun Teevens. For Dr. Steel, Shaun embodied a Dartmouth seen more in the Fifties than the Eighties, a part that was rowdy, high-spirited, and a lot of fun. One more thing about Dr. Steel—he liked to wear an enormous button on his lapel with a picture of an Indian on it.

In my conversation with Dr. Steel I found that he sensed problems at Dartmouth, and because of this he was running for trustee. Normally, a committee set up by the board of trustees nominates someone who they think is qualified to fill a vacant seat on the fourteen-member board. Under the rules, however, it is possible to run against the committee's nominee if there is sufficient support among the alumni for an alternative candidate. Support must be indicated by signed petitions. Dr. Steel was the alternative candidate. He had been encouraged to run by a number of dissatisfied alumni, among them George Champion, former chairman of the Chase Manhattan Bank, and Ave Raube, a crusty old fellow who graduated with the class of 1934. It was originally Ave Raube's idea that Steel should launch a campaign against Dartmouth officialdom. I was eager to hear Dr. Steel's views on what direction Dartmouth should take in the Eighties. I asked him why he felt it necessary to challenge the committee's trustee nomination.

"For the last ten years, under the leadership of President Kemeny, there has been a de-emphasis of the traditional liberal arts curriculum," he said, "and too much catering to special interest groups. We are doing a real disservice to the minority student by telling him to specialize in black studies. It's too narrow. The education of the student should be as broad as possible."

"Do you know that President Kemeny had the Hovey Grill murals covered over?" I asked.

130

The murals were located in a faculty dining room and portrayed Dartmouth's first president, Eleazar Wheelock drinking rum with Dartmouth's first students, to celebrate the founding of the college. These murals of Wheelock and the student Indians were described by President Kemeny as "racist, and offensive to native Americans on the campus." They weren't too kind to white drunks either.

"Art should not be censored," Dr. Steel maintained, "even if a particular painting does not happen to suit someone's special taste."

These seemed a normal set of beliefs, and I doubted if most Dartmouth alumni or, in fact, the average citizen would find fault with his opinions. Steel's platform statement outlined exactly what he told me that night at Beta. He submitted it to the secretary of the election process, J. Michael McGean. His statement, along with the *official* candidate's, would be mailed to the alumni voters. Dr. Steel assumed this would be a routine election and the winner would be seated. It was part of the procedure to include statements by the two candidates with the ballots. He did not understand the *ethos*.

Steel knew that he differed with John Kemeny about the direction of the college. He did not like the Tucker Foundation, college-funded gay groups, racially segregated living accommodations, and college-funded disarmament rallies. He did not like the editorials in *The Dartmouth* calling him *bigoted, reactionary, stupid,* and *dishonest*. He did not like these things, but he thought they could be discussed . . . "worked out," to use his words. He did not understand that the *ethos* was simply right, and he was wrong.

J. Michael McGean, secretary of the college, ran the trustee election from an office on the top floor of Blunt Alumni Center, near the middle of the campus. He was a nervous man with a stiff neck and a pair of spectacles with pink plastic frames.

McGean assured Dr. Steel that his unedited statement would appear with the ballot. But on receiving Steel's platform statement, McGean raised numerous objections, saying that the material was "very different" from the *official* candidate's (the candidate whom McGean publicly supported and, admittedly, with his job at stake, the candidate whom he had no choice but to support). McGean

131

complained that Steel's platform injected "the flavor of a political campaign."

McGean was correct. Steel's statement was a piece of campaign literature, because he considered himself a *candidate* in an *election*. His statement called for a revision of college policy. McGean decided, or someone decided, that this was unacceptable. McGean demanded that changes be made. Steel refused to make any.

McGean referred the matter to a man named John French, the chairman of the committee that appointed another committee that selected the official candidate. To no one's surprise, French agreed with the committee's choice for trustee. He demanded that the Steel statement be reorganized in style and format to conform with the committee candidate's and that Steel's biographical statement be shortened. It was difficult to see how Steel's biography could have been made shorter, since it was merely a list of his accomplishments and the organizations to which he belonged.

Steel decided to insist upon adherence to the original agreement that there would be no editorial control by the balloting committee. French then asked for time to consult with McGean on the matter. Several hours later, French announced his decision that the "mailing piece will, of course, be mailed as you wrote it."

Nevertheless, McGean several times delayed sending Steel and Ave Raube, Steel's campaign representative, a final copy of the ballot statement that was to be mailed out. When a final copy did arrive, even McGean agreed that Steel's statement had been significantly altered, "emasculated," as Dr. Steel put it. Whole paragraphs had been moved. Headlines had been deleted or changed.

Further, when Ave Raube phoned McGean to ask that the statement be returned to its original condition, he was told that "there just isn't time to reset the type or rearrange the text." The statement, McGean told Raube, would have to be released in what Steel called, "a form which had distorted and completely changed, in some instances, the meaning of what I had to say."

Despite pleas from Dr. Steel over the next three weeks, McGean refused to make the requested changes. McGean defended the alterations saying, "I just didn't realize that style was part of the agreement."

At various times, McGean responded differently to questions concerning the number of times Raube, Steel's representative, had contacted him to ask that the statement be returned to its original form.

"I think I recall making all the changes the first time," McGean said. But express mail receipts produced by Raube indicated that there were many exchanges with regard to alterations of Steel's ballot statement. McGean later admitted to at least two exchanges, saying, "I haven't got all the dates written down."

Steel's trouble was not over. He cites three conversations in which McGean agreed to open ballots only after Steel representatives were present to participate in the counting. McGean told Steel that he would "not consider opening any envelopes until your representatives are here in my office to help count them."

On the first day ballots arrived, however, McGean told Steel's representatives that they could count only the number of envelopes containing the ballots, not the votes themselves—a procedure, he said, that protected the results of the voting. On May 23 all the ballots would be opened at one time. Steel agreed that this was fair.

But Steel soon learned that McGean had already opened and counted the first four thousand ballots to arrive in his office. This was out of a total of twelve thousand. Steel protested, but McGean said that he was compelled to count the votes and would continue to do so under "my own constitution." Steel representatives continued to protest, but McGean continued to exclude them from the counting.

Finally, Steel decided that he must fly from La Jolla, California, to Hanover in order to save the election. He hired a lawyer to attempt to secure an injunction to prevent McGean from opening more ballots. Cary Clark, the college attorney, was called in to negotiate with Steel. They decided to place the four thousand opened ballots in Cary Clark's safe, and McGean was forced to leave the remaining ballots sealed. Well, they weren't exactly "sealed," since anyone could see who voted for whom, right through the envelopes, which were made of very thin paper.

Despite the antics of McGean, Dr. Steel won a considerable victory over the official candidate, getting sixty percent of the alumni vote. Undoubtedly, the administration knew that Steel was going to win, and win big, because McGean had already tallied a third of the vote. This fact created a panic-filled atmosphere in the administrative ranks, including the office of college secretary J. Michael McGean.

President Kemeny denies ever holding a position on the Steel candidacy, and Alex Fanelli, an assistant to the president, said he never discussed the Steel election with Kemeny. But a college employee, who must remain unnamed for the protection of this person's job, told me that President Kemeny and Alexander Fanelli spent hours discussing Steel and the implications of his victory. According to Steel, Kemeny actually threatened to resign his post as president if the trustees approved Steel's seating.

Would John Steel, an exceptionally qualified man who obviously loved Dartmouth, who won a landslide election victory, be seated on the board? A casual observer might conclude that there would be no question, that the trustees would simply approve the decision of sixty percent of the alumni. Alumni donations account for more than fifty percent of the college's income. In fact, in 1981, Dartmouth alumni raised $9,027,586, more than any other alumni body in the country. And there is sixty-six percent alumni participation, far greater than any other college or university in the nation. How important is ideology to these people? Would President Kemeny bend a little and allow one dissenting voice on the board to keep happy alumni dollars pouring in? After all, it was Kemeny who, with trustee approval, got to spend the money. And, so far, the trustees had been more than accommodating to Kemeny's suggestions. Steel was a sticky problem, but Kemeny could have solved it by simply ignoring him. Instead, Kemeny made the seating of Steel a moral issue. The *ethos* struck back.

Charges began to emerge from the corridors of Parkhurst Hall that John Steel was a racist and a sexist. No evidence supporting these charges was forthcoming. There was no acknowledgment of the fact that many blacks, Indians, Hispanics, and women were among Steel's most ardent supporters. Most notably, Reggie Williams, the great linebacker for the Cincinnati Bengals and a hero in the black community when a student at Dartmouth, endorsed Steel's candidacy. Most people did not take the charge of racism seriously. The charge of sexist was odd, because Steel had a daughter attending Dartmouth, and he publicly supported coeducation.

Steel was invited to the June 6 trustee meeting. He was told to wait in another room. After a delay of several hours, he was told that he would not be installed at that meeting. The reason given was that John French, the president of the Alumni Association, had informed the trustees that there were "irregularities" and "misrepresentations" in Steel's ballot statement. The trustees said the charges were confidential and refused to explain them to Steel.

Later, Steel found out that the administration claimed that two of the twenty-four people he had listed as supporters had not intended to endorse him. The names of the two men were Bill McCurine and Ron Campion. McCurine sent a letter to the trustees saying that he did not want to support Steel publicly, but that he could understand how Steel had misunderstood him and put his name on the list of public endorsements. McCurine wrote to Steel: "I believe that you have certainly acted in good faith and that this is an unfortunate mistake that happened as a matter of chance."

That Ron Campion "misunderstanding," however, was of a very strange nature. He charged that he was listed as a supporter without permission. But, on March 9, Ave Raube, Steel's representative, had written to Campion "up to now your name is included along with the enthusiastic affirmation of John Steel. But if for some reason you prefer that I eliminate your name *please let me know.*"

Raube received no reply. Many people might have considered this implicit permission to go ahead and leave Campion's name on the list of endorsements, since he had already indicated his support verbally. But, wanting to make sure that Campion still approved,

Raube sent Campion a copy of Steel's platform statement listing Campion as a supporter. Raube again received no reply. Raube did not accept Campion's silence as implicit permission to keep his name on the list of public endorsements. Raube telephoned him again, reminding Campion that his name would appear on the platform statement as a Steel supporter. Raube also referred Campion to his earlier communications. "Promptly and without question," Raube reported, "Campion said yes."

Following the election, Campion told French that he was "surprised and upset" that his name had appeared on the ballot. When asked about the letters and the phone call from Raube, he said, "I thought that I was merely giving permission to put my name on a mailing list."

I had the following conversation with attorney William Clauson, while sitting in his office several months after the election.

"The issue is this," he explained, his feet up on his desk. "The McCurine misunderstanding occurred long before the Campion problem. Steel, however, did not know that McCurine had taken back his support. Only French knew. In fact, French knew a full month before Steel found out. My question is, why didn't French ever phone Steel to ask him for an explanation?"

"I don't know," I said. "It seems that a lot of confusion could have been cleared up if he had."

Clauson looked at me from behind his wire-rimmed spectacles and brown mustache, as if to say, this kid really does not understand how these people operate; he does not understand the *ethos*. It was the same look he must have given Steel, when Steel expressed his shock and disappointment at the way he had been treated.

"The answer," said Clauson, "is that French apparently did not want an explanation."

"When he got McCurine's letter, French must have known that it was an honest misunderstanding on Steel's part," I said.

"Of course, he did," said Clauson. "That's why he had to find more errors in Steel's statement. So French, who had an obvious bias against Steel, phoned Campion to see if it was true that

Campion meant to support Steel. Now, it is important to understand that Campion did not phone French. French phoned Campion."

"What's the significance?" I asked.

"Well, unless you're calling a friend, usually you don't phone someone unless you want something. French wanted to prevent Steel's seating by showing that Steel had 'misrepresented' himself," said Clauson.

"Ron Campion was the obvious target," I said. "He was the most vulnerable of the Steel endorsements."

"Of course he was," said Clauson. "Campion lives in Hanover, and Campion owns a store on college property."

"Do you think French explicitly told Campion to renounce his support for Steel?" I asked.

"No," said Clauson. "He didn't have to. If Campion gets a phone call from John French, out of the blue, asking if he actually meant to support the opposition—the enemy of approved views—the candidate who has made the Dartmouth administration hysterical with fear and loathing—someone whom they will go to any lengths to defeat—you can bet that Ron Campion will decide that he has made a mistake. He has no interest in making life difficult for himself. He will say, without hesitation, 'Of course, I don't support Steel.'"

William Clauson had no real interest in the college's dispute with John Steel over policy. He had no real interest in Dartmouth whatsoever. He had gone to Bowdin and saw Dartmouth as too pretentious for his tastes. His interest in the Steel case was in examining the psychology behind the administration's hostility toward *outsiders*. Mr. Clauson saw the Ivy League somewhat sardonically. Steel, even though he was an alumnus, was an *outsider*. He was not nominated by the college committee. He did not believe in their *ethos*. Clauson was a populist. This showed in the way he dressed, which was downright poorly. He liked wearing dark trousers, dark shoes, and white socks. He sported button-down-collared shirts that were wrinkled. Instead of a briefcase, he carried a brown leather bag. He hated Richard Nixon, but he liked Ronald Reagan. Reagan reminded him of FDR. Clauson's office was austere. He sat on a wooden chair behind a wooden desk. Almost nothing hung on the walls. He did not look like a Wall Street lawyer, but he was the best courtroom lawyer I have ever seen. He could have charged whatever fees he wanted. He could have been a counsel for Exxon. Instead, he was very inexpensive, because he was bent on helping the little guy, or the *outsider*. He had an intuitive sense of the arrogance of those in power, their secret "understandings," and, often, their sheer dishonesty.

"It's the little guy who is usually cheated," he said. "That's why I was interested in this trustee election. It was a typical case of the individual versus the egotism of those at the controls."

"It's funny how those in power are usually so suspicious of the vote," I said.

"They wouldn't have to be if what they stood for made any sense to ordinary people," said Clauson.

"Why," I asked, "is the administration so horrified by Steel? He's only one of fourteen trustees."

"You don't seem to understand the issue," said Clauson. "What Dartmouth does not want is the perception that there is dissent among the alumni. That would be poisonous to the fund drive. The situation is comparable to many parents' relationship to their children. Mothers and fathers will often go to great lengths to hide problems from their kids. The father might be losing his job, the mother might be on the verge of a nervous breakdown, the marriage might be about to break up. But they will never let their children find out until the explosion finally occurs. This is a common problem, and it's the problem at Dartmouth. The administration will stop at nothing to keep its alumni in the dark, ignorant of anything of substance happening on campus. Parkhurst Hall does not trust its own alumni, and elections have a tendency to bring things out into the open. That is the problem with the Steel victory. The defeat of the official candidate underscores the relationship between John Kemeny and the vast majority of Dartmouth graduates."

138

There are a few more items of interest in the alumni election fiasco.

Back in early April, French phoned Steel's representative, Ave Raube. French explained that he and his committee were responsible for the balloting procedure, and he wanted to make sure that all claims made in the Steel copy were true. In particular, French was interested in the statement that a number of administrators supported the Steel candidacy. He wanted their names. At first, Raube refused French's request because he felt that administrators who supported the opposition, Steel, ran the risk of losing their jobs; which is why, in the first place, Steel did not name them individually on his list of endorsements. French, however, persisted. He said that he wanted the names only for his own "personal background information." He went on to promise Raube that he would never release the names to anyone under any circumstances. "I had complete faith in French's word," Raube said, admitting to a momentary state of stupidity. "I decided to give French three names of administrators who supported Steel, provided he would once again state his promise of confidentiality." French repeated the promise, and Raube gave him the names.

After the meeting on June 7, at which the trustees voted not to seat Steel, Steel met with the chairman of the board, David McLaughlin. McLaughlin said that all the trustees knew the names of the administrators who Steel said supported his candidacy. It became clear at this point that French had broken his promise to Raube and Steel about the complete confidentiality of the names of administrators. French told the board that he had confronted the administrators with their alleged support for Steel. French said that they denied support for the opposition, as one might expect they would if they had any career hopes at the college. Raube told French that he was "shattered by the broken promise."

In a letter to John Steel, French wrote:

> . . . I did not feel that I was violating any confidence when I disclosed these names to David McLaughlin (chairman of the board of trustees). For it seemed to me that the basic assumption on

139

which it was given—that these administrators were your supporters—proved erroneous.

In my opinion, French was saying he lied because he thought
Steel had lied. It is not surprising that, again, French never
bothered to contact Steel to get an explanation.

It stands to reason that out of the hundreds of people working in
the Dartmouth administration, at least some would have supported
Steel. Indeed, this turned out to be the case. The entire caper
appeared to be an organized effort to smear Steel's campaign with
charges that would provide an excuse to prevent him from being
seated on the board. (Joe McCarthy, call your office.)

At the time, no one really understood the meaning of this elabo-
rate effort to destroy the reputation of Dr. John Steel—no one, that
is, except William Clauson. Neither Steel nor Raube really understood what was happening. They did know, however, that whatever it was, it worked very well. Steel wrote to John French:

The inconsiderate and pre-emptory way in which the post-election
decisions and actions were made and handled besmirched Ave
Raube's and my reputations in all areas of the United States where
the accusations of irregularities and implied dishonesty and chi-
canery were disseminated and published. As grave as the uncons-
cionable damage is to us, the harm to Dartmouth College is
greater. Was there not someone involved in these decisions and
actions who recognized this?

The need for prompt action is crucial. Admittedly, such
promptness will do little, if anything, for Ave Raube's reputation
and mine. But it can help Dartmouth.

Sincerely,

John F. Steel

Many alumni, however, were not persuaded by the massive

publicity launched against John Steel's character, disseminated through the *Alumni Magazine*, college press releases, bulletins, other official publications, and at the grassroots level through alumni clubs. Al Louer, head agent for the class of '26, wrote to Dr. Steel:

> I am amazed to learn that the trustees are attempting to delay, if not prevent, your taking the seat you won on the board. They could not have invented a way to further divide the alumni. They must think that the only fair election is the one that comes out the way they want it. . . .
>
> I am already advising my various college and class colleagues that, if you should be denied your seat on the board, at that moment I quit as Head Class Agent, Class Campaign Coordinator, cancel my bequest already included in the Campaign for Dartmouth, and stop all further financial support of the College until we have a board that I can respect.
>
> By all means, John, try not to let all this get you down. I feel sure that the board's tactics are for this purpose. They hope that you will reach a point and quit, rightfully concluding, "Why should I take all this abuse for a job I didn't seek?"
>
> Best wishes and keep in there.
>
> Most admiringly,
>
> Al Louer '26

Eventually John Steel, the outsider, was seated on the board of trustees.

Other strange things began to occur.

At first there was widespread talk inside Parkhurst Hall of not having another trustee election, prohibiting them altogether. The more politically astute, however, knew that this would be going too far and convinced the ideological purists that strict guidelines

141

would be preferable, making it extremely difficult, if not impossible, for an opposition candidate to defeat the approved choice in an election again. These were the new guidelines:

> RULE ONE: All signatures must be on OFFICIAL forms, which cannot be obtained sooner than two months before the deadline for them to be returned to the office of the College Secretary, J. Michael McGean.

This rule makes it very difficult even to get on the ballot. A potential candidate must convince at least two hundred alumni to request a petition form from McGean's office. Assuming that McGean does not delay, all two hundred official forms must be completed and in his office within two months, a very difficult task considering that alumni are scattered all over the country.

> RULE TWO: Ballot statements will be limited to four hundred words.
> RULE THREE: Active, organized, or funded campaigning, either by a candidate for trustee, or on his behalf, will be prohibited.
> RULE FOUR: The College will have complete editorial control over the statements themselves, and all biographical material will be written by a college official.

All these rules were designed to allow the college to limit, or play with, the information on the candidates, if it so chose. It was clear to most observers that the new rule changes were made by someone unhappy with the election of John Steel. J. Michael McGean, though, denied this, and said that the new rules were made in the interest of "depoliticization" of the election process.

President Kemeny correctly interpreted the election of John Steel as a rejection of programs and policies central to his philosophy, a philosophy that had almost nothing to do with liberal arts education, in the traditional sense. Cary Clark, the college attorney, called such elections "divisive." He would later call the emergence of *The Dartmouth Review,* a generally conservative student publication, "divisive." That was the party line at Dartmouth, a liberal arts college supposedly devoted to free expression and open debate.

It struck me as odd that the local administrators had such a low opinion of the intelligence of alumni who are, after all, products of a Dartmouth education. The view generally held in Parkhurst Hall was that the alumni were too out of touch to absorb information on two candidates and choose between them. So the administration had two choices: either have only one candidate, or allow two candidates but control the information made available on the issues. They chose the latter.

So we find that devotion to open debate and democratic procedure in our liberal arts colleges is not as firm as it may appear. A speech by President Kemeny, delivered at MIT and later reprinted in *Technology Review,* raises questions about his own commitment to the vote. "Jeffersonian democracy," he says, cannot work in the complicated world of the 1980s:

> ... My last point, and the most important one, is for our nation to recognize that the present system does not work. It was designed for a much earlier and simpler age. Even two hundred years ago, the founding fathers made choices. They opted for democracy, but they did not opt for Athenian democracy. It would have been totally impractical to use an antiquated model that called citizens into the market place to vote on every issue as it occurred. And yet today we have essentially the same system, now itself outmoded, that we had two hundred years ago. It is time to rethink the issue, because I believe that Jeffersonian democracy cannot work in the year 1980—the world has become too complex.

The desire manifested through Kemeny's speech is for a government by "experts." Only expert opinion counts. It seems clear that at Dartmouth the opinion of nonexperts, in this case the alumni, is an official embarrassment. President Kemeny himself once asked the students: "... please don't write letters to the *Alumni Magazine*

143

that say something is wrong and somebody here ought to do something about it, because this college depends very deeply on its alumni. . . ."

It was hard to keep a straight face when on another occasion he gave students the following advice: "I . . . am going to recommend to you a very old fashioned virtue: *honesty.*" And, in an address to the graduating seniors, he said, "If there is a single thought I would like you to carry away with you, I hope it would be respect for the truth."

Until recently, the alumni have not had much reason for concern over accepted official decisions. For the first time in Dartmouth's history an important election was held. Steel won and the *ethos* lost.

Moral of the story: Elections at Dartmouth are disturbing and give rise to all sorts of hell. The guardians of the *ethos* would prefer that nobody, especially alumni, knew what went on behind those closed doors upstairs in Parkhurst Hall.

ALL THE TRUTH THAT'S FIT TO PRINT

ONE late spring afternoon in 1980, following the Steel election fiasco, Jones and I were waiting for Rich Shoup upstairs in the Segal house. Out of politeness, Jones had left his shark, Chesterton, downstairs in Segal's kitchen just to let Segal know that Jones was in the house. He had placed his feet on Rich's desk and was leaning back so that the chair balanced on two legs.

"Did you hear what happened to Greg Fossedal?" Jones asked.

Greg Fossedal was editor of *The Dartmouth*. We never understood how he got to be editor, because he was known to be conservative, while the rest of his staff ranged from moderate to extreme left. As a result, he was having a terrible time at the paper; his proposals and ideas were usually ridiculed and voted down by other staff members. He wanted to make *The Dartmouth* a first-rate paper, but his staff wouldn't even let him write editorials. Greg had been editor for six months and by now must have been a miserable young man.

"He was just fired as editor of the paper," said Jones.

I was surprised.

"Remember that column he wrote in support of John Steel's

candidacy? Well, no one over there liked it," said Jones, "least of all the administrators who sit on the paper's board."

"That's outrageous," I said.

"No big campus outrage," said Jones. "If he'd been fired for being a Trotskyite, we'd never hear the end of it. You know, I was thinking that this campus needs another student publication, and in a bad way."

"If we had a paper, we could print your columns," I said.

"Can you imagine? The newspaper would feature columns by me." Jones laughed. "We could make an all-out assault on the *ethos*."

"We could combine news, culture, and opinion," I said. "People would have to read us."

"We need money," Jones said pragmatically. "We can raise it from the alumni, the same people who voted for John Steel. That would give us about seven thousand subscriptions to start with."

"We can also sell advertising to local merchants."

"Let's do it!" yelled Jones.

"What's going on up there!" an irritated voice yelled from downstairs.

"Michael Jones is up here!" I yelled down to Professor Segal.

"I know," said Segal, "I have his shark. Do you want to keep the noise down?"

"Sorry," I said, and whispered, "I'll bet Greg Fossedal would be interested in our publication."

"He can be the editor," Jones said. "We'll need money for the first issue."

"We'll worry about that later," I said. "First let's get our staff together."

"The most important thing is to be completely independent from college authorities. It's the only way to maintain credibility," said Jones.

"Absolutely."

"What are we going to call it?" Jones asked.

"We'll have to give that some thought."

"Let's get Fossedal in on this thing right away," said Jones.

"I'll call him," I said.

"I'll get some champagne."

"Where is it?"

"In my room," Jones said.

"How are you going to get there?" I asked.

"I'll call a cab," said Jones, grinning. He used Rich's phone to call the Dartmouth Cab Company before running down the stairs and out the door past Professor Segal who was still busy reading the gospel according to *The New York Times*.

I called South Massachusetts dormitory. The phone rang maybe fifteen times before Greg finally answered. Like an owl, Greg was a nocturnal animal.

"What is it?" he asked in a groggy and slightly irritated tone.

"Greg," I said, "this is Ben Hart calling. Can you meet me and Keeney Jones in five minutes in the Segal house? I think you'll be interested in what we're doing."

"What is it?" he asked again.

"We're starting a newspaper. You're going to be the editor."

"What newspaper?"

"It doesn't have a name yet. The first issue will come out in two weeks. It'll be the graduation issue."

After I explained the idea to him, Greg got excited.

"I've been waiting for something like this for a long time," he said. "I've always wanted to start my own paper."

"Here's your chance. You can now write your columns endorsing unapproved candidates. Jones can write unapproved ideas. This will be a completely *unofficial* publication."

"I'll be right over," said Greg and hung up.

I heard Jones's voice outside and looked out the window to see him paying the cab driver. He came into the house and met the professor sitting in his chair at the bottom of the stairs.

"Hello, Professor Segal," I heard him say.

"Hello," said Segal.

"We're starting a new newspaper," said Jones, "It's going to be edited by Greg Fossedal."

"Fossedal?" said Segal. "Isn't he the fellow who got fired from the 'D'?"

"Yup," said Jones. "They didn't like his views much over there."

"We don't like his views over here," said Segal, rapidly becoming a prisoner in his own home.

"But we like his views up there." Jones must have pointed upstairs. "Have you seen Ben's posters?" Jones asked.

"Yes, I've seen them," said Segal.

"Some great shots of Reagan," Jones said. "Come on up and have some champagne with us to celebrate the founding of our new campus publication."

"I think I'll stay here," said Segal. "I'll watch for it."

"Oh, you won't have to look hard," said Jones in the most cheerful voice. "You won't be able to miss it. It'll shock the socks off this place."

"What's it called?" asked Segal.

"Uhhhh..." There was a silence. *"The Dartmouth Review!"* he exclaimed suddenly.

"What?" asked Segal.

"The Dartmouth Review. That's what we'll call it, after, you know ... *National Review."*

"Great," Segal said, his voice a strange mixture of sarcasm and dejection.

Jones ran up the stairs. When he got to the top, he shot the cork, which ricocheted off the ceiling. Champagne bubbled out of the bottle onto the floor. "Have a glass," said Jones.

Within minutes we heard Greg Fossedal enter the house, slamming the door behind him.

"My name is Greg Fossedal." He had met the professor.

"Christ, not another one," Segal groaned, as Greg stomped up the stairs, rattling the professor and most of the house in the process.

148

Fossedal's skills as a reporter were unmatched by any other undergraduate, and his expertise in the mechanics of putting together a publication was invaluable to us. After he was fired at *The Dartmouth*, there was an immediate drop in subscriptions, advertising revenue, and the quality of news coverage, as the "D" declined from being a poor newspaper to one that was almost painful to read.

"How's it going, boys?" asked Greg as he stepped into the room.

"Sit down," said Jones, "and have some champagne."

"Let's think of a name," said Greg.

"I've already thought of one," said Jones. *"The Dartmouth Review."*

"Sounds fine to me," said Greg.

"Who can we get to work with us?" I asked.

"I think we can get cartoonist Steve Kelley," answered Greg.

Kelley was a junior. For two years running, he received an award as the top college cartoonist in the country. *The Dartmouth*'s editorial editor, however, often canceled Kelley's daily cartoon slot if he judged the material "insensitive," or offensive to special interest groups on campus. In disgust, Steve stopped submitting his stuff. Kelley was a conservative, and his cartoons often showed an irreverence toward the local pieties. During my years at Dartmouth I discovered that, generally, guardians of the *ethos* do not like cartoonists, satirists, or jokers of any kind. Its true believers tended to be grim. These people saw nothing funny in Steve Kelley. And to their lasting chagrin, he found lots that was funny about them.

"I'm sure we can get Dinesh D'Souza to work for us," Fossedal went on.

"What does he do?" I asked.

"He's a dark-skinned fellow from Bombay. Dinesh D'Souza, or Distort D'Newsa, as he is called by his critics. He's only a freshman, but he's already won awards for reporting. He also quit working for the 'D' recently. He's now sending his stuff to outside publications."

Poisoned Ivy

During Dinesh's four years as an undergraduate I'm sure he published more material than any student his age in the country. He was a regular reporter for the *Manchester Union Leader* and the *National Catholic Register*. His stuff has been in *National Review, Policy Review, Reader's Digest, Conservative Digest,* and countless others. He later became editor-in-chief of the *Review*. By age twenty-two, he had written two books. "Even though I happen to be from India," he liked to tell newsmen, "I take great delight in slaughtering the sacred cows around this place." While at Dartmouth he maintained a 3.8 grade point average and was admitted to Harvard Business School.

"I'd like to meet this guy," I said.

"I'll get him on the phone right now," said Greg.

"See if you can get Kelley over here too," said Jones, "and what about that girl friend of yours?"

"Rachel?" asked Greg.

"Let's get her selling advertising," said Jones.

"I'll try," said Greg. "I'll also see if I can convince Gordon Haff to jump on board. He's invaluable to *The Dartmouth*. I don't think he likes it over there, and he's an expert photographer and layout man."

Greg phoned everyone, and within a matter of minutes Steve Kelley, Dinesh D'Souza, Rachel Kenzie, and Gordon Haff were marching past the harried Professor Segal, who was still parked in the kitchen with his *New York Times*.

"Hello, Professor Segal," each would shout.

Icy silence. But then Rich Shoup walked through the door, lugging a small mountain of religious texts, and the professor stirred himself.

"Can you find out what the hell is going on upstairs in *my* house?" he barked.

"Why, haven't you heard?" asked Rich.

Another moment of glum silence.

"I guess I have," said Segal, staring at his thumb.

150

"Put on some music!" Jones yelled from upstairs. "Have some champagne!"

For Professor Segal, it would be a long night.

The Dartmouth Review was launched. It was a tabloid newspaper, only twelve pages, with a mix of humorous and serious content. In its portrayal of the antics of Dartmouth's administration, the *Review* has been described as the *National Lampoon* of the Right. It was, in a way, but there were also think pieces by such people as Milton Friedman, Thomas Sowell, Walter Williams, George Will, the student editors, and others.

The first issue featured a cover cartoon by Steve Kelley; an interview with Dr. John Steel; some items on the Steel election; a column by William F. Buckley, Jr.; and Aleksandr Solzhenitsyn's address at Harvard's commencement ceremony.

Greg Fossedal funded our first issue by cashing his student loan check, with which we paid the printer. In addition, Greg wrote most of the copy, during the week before finals. Not only was Greg able to put out a top-quality newspaper during final exam week, on almost no advance notice, he also got straight A's in his courses and scored 796 out of a possible 800 on his Law School Aptitude Test. He would later turn down admission to Harvard, Yale, and Stanford law schools to go into journalism full time. At age twenty-four, he would take a job on the *Wall Street Journal* as the youngest editorial writer in their history. It is no overstatement to say there would have been no *Dartmouth Review* without the talents of Greg Fossedal.

Newsreel. SCENE ONE: "Men and women of Dartmouth. In the trying times we live in, I ask you to avoid the sin of apathy. I ask you to get involved in the great issues of our time. When the call to public service came, I responded as well." *(Heroic music sounds. The image of a college president inhaling the smoke from his cigarette, causing him to choke, cough, and wheeze, fades from the screen.)*

SCENE TWO: *(A close-up) In the spring of 1980, a group of Dartmouth students decide not to be apathetic. They begin publishing a campus newspaper called The Dartmouth Review.* It is to be an independent, freewheeling, and, on the whole, conservative voice on campus. *(Ta Da!)*

What follows is a documentary description of this student newspaper's adventures with the Kemeny administration.

On June 2, there suddenly descended upon the strawberry blonde head of the publisher, Miss Rachel Kenzie, a junior and a girl friend of Greg Fossedal, the following welcome from Dean John Bryant:

> As I understand it, *The Dartmouth Review* will be incorporated in New Hampshire as a not-for-profit entity. . . . Given the fact that *The Dartmouth Review* is a corporate entity distinct from the college, the college cannot recognize it as a student organization. Student organizations are formed within the college and exist at the pleasure of the college . . . your separate corporate status also excludes you from access to the Hinman mailboxes, the assignment of office space, and other services such as telephone, etc.

Two days later, college attorney Cary Clark joined the welcoming committee.

> John Bryant of the dean's office has informed me that you and others are in the process of starting a new publication, which you intend to call *The Dartmouth Review*. . . . I must inform you, and through you, your associates in your new venture, that Dartmouth College objects to your intended use of the name *The Dartmouth Review* in connection with your proposed publication and demands that you and your associates refrain from publishing, distributing, and selling any publication which is entitled *The Dartmouth Review* or which in any way includes the name of the college.

After absorbing this harrumph, and taking some laundry in a DARTMOUTH cab to the COLLEGE Cleaner, stopping at the DARTMOUTH Bookstore to buy some books, and going to the DARTMOUTH Travel Agency to check some bus schedules, the students went ahead and published a graduation issue. They also retained the services of lawyer William Clauson.

In official publications the college maintained that its principal objection, indeed its sole objection, to the *Review* concerned the use of the name "Dartmouth." So when the *Review* asked presidents of alumni clubs if they knew of some members who might be interested in reading the newspaper free of charge, the welcome mat came out again. On July 22, Mr. David Orr, associate secretary of the college under J. Michael McGean, directed the following communication to all alumni club presidents:

> We understand that you recently received a communication from the Business Manager of *The Dartmouth Review* concerning the use of the club mailing list. The Club Officers Association has long ruled that club mailing lists should be used only for publications by college-recognized organizations for college-related business. ... Therefore, it would be quite contrary to the rules that have been applied over the years to authorize the use of club mailing lists in this case.

The college had thus protected itself from contamination by this scurrilous publication. It was still presumably threatened by the dry cleaners, the cab company, the bookstore, the travel agency ...

Nothing much happened during the summer. The *Review* did not plan another edition until the fall. On August 5, 1980, during Dartmouth's summer term, the official student newspaper, *The Dartmouth,* printed an editorial comparing the election of trustee John Steel to Watergate. The editorial was imaginatively entitled "Steelgate." The official student newspaper had already printed an editorial claiming that voting for Ronald Reagan was like voting for Adolf Hitler, presumably because neither of them subscribed to the *ethos.*

153

AND
CONSEQUENCES

"**I**N court you people won't have a chance," the chief attorney for Dartmouth College said to us as we sat submerged in deep leather chairs in the dean's office.

From where I sat I could see, through a large picture window, the center of campus. The mid-morning sunlight was hard and dry. Students and faculty strolled across the Green. On this Saturday morning the scene was more crowded than usual. It was a football Saturday, crisp and clear. In a few hours the team would play their first Ivy League game of the season against the University of Pennsylvania. And even though the windows were closed, the brassy sound of trumpets and tubas and the deep booming sound of base drums could be heard as the band marched toward the center of town. On the street outside, a group of students rode by on an ancient fire engine, all brick red and brass, bells clanging, and the sound of laughter rose through the thin air of autumn.

"We're not going to let you do it," thundered Cary Clark, the college lawyer, an owlish and overweight man in his late forties. "No way."

The dean of Dartmouth College looked at him, saying nothing. He popped a purple candy into his mouth.

155

Poisoned Ivy

"I just don't see what you're so upset about," said trustee John Steel. He looked at the dean and the lawyer, and then at the half-dozen other people in the room. Bitterness was in the faces of the college officials, particularly lawyer Clark.

This was the first time in my three years as a student at Dartmouth that I had seen the office of Dean Ralph Manuel. On fraternity row, he was known as Mean Danuel, the "Ralph" of Dartmouth. As far as students were concerned, he embodied college bureaucracy. He had a round face and neatly trimmed brown hair. He smiled often and told everyone what they wanted to hear—within certain limits. He never departed from college policy as set by Kemeny. Manuel was a bureaucrat's bureaucrat. He represented what most people referred to as the "new" Dartmouth. Manuel enjoyed being dean; everyone assumed he would remain dean for a long time.

Manuel had replaced the legendary Carol Brewster, who was affectionately known on fraternity row as Brew Deanster, the "Carol" of the college. President Kemeny thought Brewster got along all too well with fraternity types, and too often seemed to be having a good time in the fraternity basements, drinking beers with the brothers. Brewster had also been a fervent supporter of the Dartmouth Indian. It seemed appropriate, he said, since Dartmouth was founded for the purpose of educating Indians. John Kemeny did not like Brewster's argument. In fact, he did not seem to like Brewster, so he replaced him with Ralph Manuel.

Manuel popped another hard candy into his mouth.

Fossedal, John Steel, William Clauson, and I had set up a meeting with Dean Manuel in his office in Parkhurst, in hopes of working out some sort of *modus vivendi* with the Dartmouth administration. Representatives of the college included Dean Manuel; vice-president in charge of finance and administration, Paul Paganucci; and college attorney, Cary Clark.

Cary Clark had a mannerism of sweeping his right hand across the top of his white skull and through his thinning hair. His job was to explain to Greg Fossedal, John Steel, William Clauson, and

156

myself, why the *Review* should not be permitted to use the Dartmouth name in the title of the publication. The conversation took place primarily between the two attorneys, Clauson and Clark, with the others only occasionally adding a comment or two. Dean Manuel never said a word. I would have had trouble believing it, had I not been present.

Clauson, gazing at Clark through wire-rimmed spectacles, began the conversation by asking: "So what exactly is it then that Dartmouth objects to?"

"We object to the use of the Dartmouth name in connection with this publication," said Clark.

College vice-president Paul Paganucci put a large cigar between his lips, inhaled deeply, then exhaled a cloud of greenish smoke into the room. Smoke was about all that came out of his mouth during the entire conversation.

"Why do you object?" asked Clauson. He took off his spectacles and looked icily at Clark.

"The college has property rights to the Dartmouth name."

"These students have First Amendment rights," answered Clauson.

"We are willing to enforce our property rights in court," said Clark.

"You would take Dartmouth students to court?"

"If we have to," grumbled the college lawyer, who was on retainer.

"Well," said Clauson, "if Dartmouth ever had sole rights to the Dartmouth name, which I doubt very much, it gave those rights up long ago when it made allowances for the Dartmouth Cab Company, the Dartmouth Bookstore, the Dartmouth Travel Agency— not to mention the fact that there is a Dartmouth, Massachusetts, a Dartmouth, England, and an eighteenth century Earl of Dartmouth. Why the selective enforcement of your alleged property rights in regard to this particular student paper?"

"The Dartmouth name is valuable," said Clark, "and we will not permit this publication to use it. We intend to protect ourselves." (There was no telling what trouble could be made by two towns of people and a deceased earl.)

"I think," interjected John Steel, "that this confusion can be cleared up if Dartmouth would simply grant these students a license to use the name. That way Dartmouth's property rights would be protected, and everyone would understand that they are using the name with the permission of the college. After all, these are Dartmouth students writing about Dartmouth."

Clark stared at Steel through his gray eyes, narrowed to slits. Of all the administrators under John Kemeny, Cary Clark, in my judgment, disliked Steel the most. "We will have to think about that," he answered.

"Sounds like a good idea to me," Clauson added.

"I don't think so," said Clark. "We are worried that this might develop into a potential 'Princeton Situation.'"

"What is a 'Princeton Situation'?" asked Clauson.

"At Princeton," said Clark, "there is a group of alumni who have raised millions of dollars. They are holding this money in escrow until the Princeton administration changes some of its policies." (I found out later from a friend at Princeton that there was, in fact, no "Princeton Situation." There did exist a group of Princeton alumni who began publishing an alternative alumni magazine called *Prospect*. To use the words of their publisher, Steve Manacek, "The alumni magazine that comes out of the Princeton administration is a joke and presents a very distorted picture of what is going on at Princeton." So, there was no escrow fund and, therefore, no "Princeton Situation," as Clark described it. And no one with *The Dartmouth Review* had expressed any interest in starting an escrow fund at Dartmouth.)

The conversation continued.

"Well," said Clauson, "I've never heard of this 'Princeton Situation.' Princeton alumni, of course, would be well within their rights to withhold their own money for the purpose of influencing policy there. I know that's not at all what these students have in mind. All they want to do is publish a weekly newspaper, written and edited entirely by students, funded by advertising revenue and alumni contributions. . . ."

"But, that's exactly what we object to," interrupted Clark.

"What?" asked Clauson.

"We don't want a publication going out to Dartmouth alumni under the title of *The Dartmouth Review*."

"Why?" asked Clauson.

"Because alumni might confuse *The Dartmouth Review* with other official publications like the *Dartmouth Alumni Magazine*."

"Ha, ha, ha, ha," broke in Fossedal, no candidate for the diplomatic corps. "That seems very unlikely. But if it will make a difference, we can print 'Not Published by Dartmouth College' on page one, right under the title."

"We can't accept that," answered Clark, shaking his head and shifting his bulk so that he would not have to look at Greg who was sitting next to him.

"Why not?" asked Clauson. "That sounds like a reasonable proposal."

"Because we object to the fact that this publication is going to Dartmouth alumni," he said, engaged in rhetorical break-dancing.

"Why do you object to that?" asked Clauson, putting his spectacles back on and trying hard to look serious about Clark's seemingly endless objections.

"Because we don't think that it's a good idea for alumni to receive two opinions about what is happening on the campus."

"Why not?" asked Clauson.

"Because two opinions can be very . . . *divisive*," answered Clark.

"What on earth does that mean?" asked Fossedal.

I looked at Steel, who was sitting next to me with his legs crossed and his hands folded in his lap, the very picture of a proper trustee. While absorbing Clark's remarks, Steel had been running his fingers through his silver hair. He looked as though he wanted to say something, but seemed to stop himself, and wrinkled his eyebrows as if to say "It's really no use trying to reason with this man—is it?"

"I think," said Clauson, "that Mr. Clark is saying that Dartmouth alumni are not intelligent enough to judge the relative merits of more than one view."

"That's not it at all," Clark cut in. "We think it would be fine if there were many different views about life on campus going out to the alumni. But we think it very destructive and *divisive* to the Dartmouth community as a whole to have only two opinions to choose from."

"One opinion, then, seems much worse," Fossedal interjected.

"No. One opinion is better than two," Clark answered, "because two opinions tend to *divide* the community. Many opinions, on the other hand, would not have this polarizing effect."

"This is a lunatic conversation!" said Fossedal, turning a light shade of red. "Are you saying that if we began publishing many different newspapers, all expressing different points of view, and mailed them out to alumni, everything would be all right?"

"Of course not," answered Clark. "That would be an unreasonable request.

"Look here," Clark blurted. "Dartmouth has property interest in protecting its name. We intend to do so, if necessary, in a court of law."

"I think," said Clauson, "that if any sober-minded judge listened to you for five minutes you would be laughed out of court. I don't think this conversation is getting us anywhere. Let's adjourn."

"We'll be in communication with your office," said Clark.

Greg and I were the first to leave Dean Ralph Manuel's office. The others followed close behind. It became clear that the objections of the administration really had little to do with the use of the Dartmouth name. They had everything to do with the kind of information the alumni might get.

I paused for a moment on the steps outside Parkhurst and looked across the campus. People were wearing hats and brightly colored sweaters. Some blew horns and yelled "Wah-Hoo-Wah." The sound of the band playing "As the Backs Go Tearing By" could be heard in the distance, and mobs of people walked toward Memorial

Stadium with their friends or dates. All, of course, were oblivious to the distressing conversation I had just heard.

I thought of Jeff Kemp, who would lead the team against the University of Pennsylvania. I wondered what must be going through his mind at that moment. I knew that hundreds of alumni would be leaving their tailgate parties about now, heading toward the game that was about to start.

On the other side of the Green, leaving the Hanover Inn bar and gradually making their way toward the stadium, were Anthony Desiré and Keeney Jones, the latter pulling his blue foam-rubber shark close behind. I watched them for a moment, as they waved and said hello to people. In a moment they vanished from sight, swallowed up by the mob.

The sun was bright and warm, but as I looked across the campus to the distant hills and admired the brilliant shades of red, yellow, and green that characterized this northeast corner of New England in autumn, I felt a cold gust of air whistle through my hair and shivered slightly. Winter was not far off.

On September 23, 1980, *The Dartmouth* published a front page feature length story: "The College May Take Suit Against Publication."

At about the same time, a supporter of the *Review*, a woman from Beverly Hills, California, and a widow of a wealthy alumnus, wrote a $10,000 check to support the paper. The check was deposited in a college account, as the *Review* did not yet have tax-exempt status. The college blocked the woman's money from reaching the *Review* on the grounds that the publication was an outside organization and had not yet received its tax-exempt status, which was pending, and that her own intentions were unclear. Well, she made her intentions crystal clear by phoning Parkhurst Hall, hinting that she might cut Dartmouth out of her will if her $10,000 was not in *The Dartmouth Review*'s bank account by the end of the week. We received the check in the mail the following day. She also indicated that it would be in Dartmouth's best interest to allow the students to use the college name.

161

Eventually, college attorney Cary Clark, with additional prodding from *Review* attorney William Clauson, agreed, at least in principle, that the college would grant the paper such a license. The first draft of a proposal, submitted by Clark to Clauson, had nineteen points, some of which were very complex, a few of which Clark himself could not explain. Various lengthy drafts went back and forth, along with some amusing correspondence. On October 17, Cary Clark wrote as follows to William Clauson:

> It would be difficult to measure my disappointment upon receiving your letter of October 16, 1980, in which you enclose a proposed form of license agreement. I would have expected something like this on or about October 1, but it is inconceivable that you would choose to place on the table a document such as this at this point in the negotiations.

Clauson replied in a letter dated October 21:

> It would be difficult to measure my great dissatisfaction in dealing with your office.
>
> Simultaneously, I have received instructions from Attorney Daschbach that you did not want me talking to you or anyone in your office and that I should deal exclusively with Mr. Daschbach, while I have received telephone calls and letters from you requesting me to deal directly with your office. Simultaneously, I have received instructions from Attorney Daschbach that you did not want me meeting with any members of the Dartmouth Administration while receiving invitations from your office to meet with members of the Dartmouth Administration . . .
>
> You provided us with what you call the "controlling" case law in the issue. Case law which established that young ladies in pornographic films who parade half naked should not call themselves the Dallas Cowgirls because it would offend the Dallas Cowboy organization. In light of your "controlling" cases, our position was unchanged and we responded by sending you cases which respect our first amendment rights.

162

We then received from you a proposed agreement with one silly section after another:

> *The Dartmouth Review* shall not directly or indirectly affiliate with any organization or any person.

You could not explain what this meant or what it was for. I pointed out that I assumed *The Dartmouth Review* had "affiliation" with its advertisers, with its writers, with its subscribers, with almost anyone it came in contact with.

You proposed to require that *The Dartmouth Review* be "of first quality and in good taste."

Again, you couldn't explain what this meant, but *The Dartmouth Review* was expected to agree nonetheless. As I pointed out, the main objection of *The Dartmouth Review* was that your proposed agreement required *The Dartmouth Review* to waive all its rights without any similar concessions on the part of the College.

On October 14, you asked me to prepare a draft which would be acceptable to *The Dartmouth Review*. I told you that I was extremely busy this week, but you nevertheless asked that I give it my prompt attention. I prepared a draft which eliminated the language of "affiliation," the arbitration paragraph, which made no sense, but provided the essential protection (indeed at some points better protection than you had requested) as to the issue which you had attempted to articulate. You find our proposed draft "disappointing" without explanation. Indeed, I have been told by an attorney in your office that our proposed licensing agreement is "illegal." This is obvious nonsense and, obviously, the attorney refused to explain or attempt to justify this rather strange opinion.

It seemed to us that the point of all this harassment on the part of the college was to intimidate us into not putting the paper out at all.

It was no longer the leftish students who had the energy, the wit, and new ideas necessary to launch a successful assault on a stuffy, Philistine conservative Establishment. The Sixties were gone. Today, it is conservative students who are writing the satire, ridicu-

163

ling the pompous and comfortable members of the liberal Establishment, many of whom had not heard, or had, a new idea in over a decade.

Dinesh D'Souza, for example, wrote the following article, titled "Feelings," that drew shrieks of outrage from many of the faculty:

"Feelings" is the in-game for the Fall of 1980, and it's both amusing and illuminating. It teaches you how to conduct a liberal conversation or write a liberal political speech—in the unlikely event that you would want to do either.

The idea is that you pick one word from each of the three columns below, any three words, and string them together in a phrase. What you get is perfect liberal music. Try it!

Thus you can have a "profound dialectical relationship," or a "meaningful communal oneness." You can have "genuine contextual linkage." Or "sophisticated humane consensus." Or "genuine humane dialogue."

COLUMN X	COLUMN Y	COLUMN Z
Profound	Interpersonal	Awareness
Diverse	Emotional	Oneness
Genuine	Dialectical	Relationship
Subjective	Harmonious	Network
Complex	Communal	Correspondence
Objective	Contextual	Linkage
Sophisticated	Humane	Consensus
Realistic	Interactive	Communication
Meaningful	Collective	Dialogue
Mutual	Societal	Forum

In case you are filling out an application for a grant from the Ford Foundation, a graduate application to Harvard, or running for office in California, the "feelings" machine will come in handy.

What's truly liberal about this game is that you can play it all by yourself.

164

And Consequences

The following is an example of a Keeney Jones column, this one comparing President Jimmy Carter with President John Kemeny, titled "Presidents of a Feather":

Both men have rather odd accents. Both have dominating wives. Both have been challenged by the forces of the right. And both are on the way out.

The similarities don't stop there. Indeed, they beg documentation.

Jimmy Carter was an outsider to government in Washington... Jimmy Carter has an excellent educational background—valedictorian of his class, nuclear engineer. His weaknesses notwithstanding, many people think Carter to be a sincere and virtuous man.

John Kemeny has the credentials too: research assistant to Einstein (note the nuclear link), math innovator, Ivy League president.

Both the credentials of Mr. Carter and Mr. Kemeny look terrific on paper. Carter is President of the United States. Kemeny holds down the same job here. Both positions are something to be proud of.

Yet both failed. Jimmy Carter has led this country into an economic and strategic cesspool. Kemeny has simultaneously made Dartmouth the Ivy League pit . . .

Kemeny is great at making plans. He instituted his own plan for year-round education—a plan in which everybody seems to be beginning and ending but never doing. He scored a big victory for the First Amendment when he came down violently on the traditional Indian symbol.

Kemeny's idea of a major is Policy Studies. It is Policy Studies majors who are responsible for the affirmative action and busing programs in this nation—programs which on paper epitomized sincerity and fair play—but programs which in practice are a ghoulish nightmare.

The Kemeny administration is a bureaucratic blunder full of yes-men, growing exponentially every day. The faculty consists

165

mostly of underpaid nontenured junior members (this way the college saves money by first hiring young faculty and then five years later by denying them tenure). And the staff . . . well the Dartmouth staff consists of many people like the receptionist in housing. You know—she's the one with the robin's nest hair-do and the personality of an electric chair.

Hey, all of this doesn't matter. You can make a few mistakes. John G. Jimmy did. Inflation. Unemployment. Iran. Afghanistan. UN botches. Energy plans. Running for re-election.

But despite the dismal performance in the office, many of us think John Kemeny to be a sincere and honorable man. Right? Well . . .

Last June—for the first time in Dartmouth's history—a man, independent of the college strings, sought and won a position on the Board of Trustees. But to John Kemeny this man was anathema. . . .

Just two weeks ago our own Jimmy Carter, the man who "loves each and every American" and who teaches Sunday school, chose to call Ronald Reagan a racist and warmonger.

Even Carter's decision not to participate in the debates can be seen as Kemenyesque. Rather than defend the last ten years of Dartmouth against Steel's criticisms, Kemeny lashed out at Steel's character—much the way Carter did to Reagan while side-stepping the issues.

In short, if John Kemeny is an indication, Mr. Reagan has nothing to fear from Carter's vicious campaign. Reagan, like John Steel, will be seated. And it's probably not coincidental, but rather divine plan, that around the time Ronald Reagan mounts the Capitol steps to take the oath of office as fortieth President of the United States, Dartmouth College will have a fourteenth president.

Some editors of the *Review*, as a joke on college funding for the Gay Students Alliance, tried to persuade Dartmouth to pay for the

166

social activities of "The Dartmouth Bestiality Association." *Review* contributor Scott Lamb (his real name) was the group's first president. He pleaded eloquently in front of the College Committee on Student Organizations on "the need to raise people's consciousnesses about alternative sexual orientations." "According to surveys, .05 percent of the world's human population prefer animals to people," explained Lamb. "But a lot of animalphiles are afraid of what society might think, so they remain silent, and are thus sexually and emotionally inhibited."

The college denied funding to Bestiality Alliance, stating that this was not a legitimate group. "To the contrary!" exclaimed Lamb. "This is a very serious subject, and your denying us funding demonstrates that the college is making value judgments on the lifestyles of students."

All this was reported in the *Review*.

The paper also made an effort to promote Dinesh D'Souza, a *Bombay* Indian, as the new symbol for Dartmouth, since the American Indian was no longer acceptable to liberals.

The *Review* uncovered scandal in the administration; exposed shenanigans in the trustee election; ridiculed college policies; printed uninhibited evaluations of professors and their courses; published irreverent articles poking fun at such favorite liberal icons as Affirmative Action, Women's Studies, college-sponsored disarmament rallies, college financial support for organized lesbian activity, and so on. The liberals were ill-equipped to deal with this new kind of protester. Every Friday they braced themselves for that week's outrage to be published in the *Review*. College bureaucrats and faculty would scan the pages nervously and then breathe a sigh of relief if they found that their names weren't mentioned. Paranoia began to grip the Dartmouth Establishment. In short, for a change, it was no longer comfortable to be a *liberal* on the campus.

The administration did not know how to handle what they considered to be a major problem, a student protest with broad-based alumni support. It became routine for the editor of the

Review to receive in the mail this kind of pompous, humorless harrumph from Ralph Manuel, dean of Dartmouth College:

> ... You should not in the future expect the College's administration to accept at face value your assurances that higher standards of responsibility will be forthcoming from your editorial policies. You should also not expect the College to cooperate with you in the preparation and distribution of your publication. Your organization thus far has not shown the interest you professed in assuming a responsible role at the College. We in turn have no wish to be a party to your total disregard of the College's legitimate rights to its name in the publications field or your continuing unwarranted personal abuse of members of the Dartmouth community.
>
> Sincerely yours,
>
> Ralph M. Manuel

And, in the June 1981 issue of the *Alumni Magazine*, the official news from Parkhurst, which goes out to all Dartmouth graduates, there appeared this article entitled "Straight Talk," written by Donald Rosenthal:

> ... despite its mudslinging and fantasies its writers have managed to pass off as objective reporting, *The Review* has managed to convince some alumni that it is the victim of college harassment intended to prevent the terrible secrets from reaching alumni ears. For instance, the disagreement over the use of the name "Dartmouth" in the title of the paper was a commonplace dispute over the legal right to use of the name. What it wasn't was an attempt to squelch dissenting views. There's a considerable logical gap between the two. If anything, the College has leaned over backwards to let *The Review* say what it will—whether out of respect for freedom of speech or the wallets of some wealthy benefactors I cannot say.

168

And Consequences

> *The Review*, it seems to be, has destroyed any credibility it might
> have earned with its never-ending half-truths and vitriol, with its
> incessant attacks on President Kemeny, the Board of Trustees,
> liberals in general . . . communists, John French '30, Senator
> Kennedy, Jimmy Carter, critics of the Indian symbol, homosexu-
> als, Latin American rebels, anti-apartheid protesters, the College
> administration, the Undergraduate Council, feminists, the organ-
> ized black community, the staff of *The Dartmouth*, Maryssa
> Navarro, supporters of minority studies, and so on down the line.
> *The Review*, in short, deals in hate. And, as we all have cause to
> know, hate justifies everything.

All this, of course, made great material for the paper, and we
reported it immediately. Subscriptions began to pour in by the
hundreds, not only from alumni, but also from people outside the
Dartmouth community, who wanted to see what all the fuss was
about.

For the most part, people in the outside world saw *The Dartmouth Review* in a different light from local bureaucrats and
academics at Dartmouth.

William F. Buckley, Jr., wrote:

> *The Dartmouth Review* is a vibrant, joyful, provocative challenge
> to the regnant but brittle liberalism for which American colleges
> are renowned. It is serious, in the best sense of the word; it is lively,
> it has spirit, and it has a considerable capacity to meditate on its
> own weaknesses. I would hope that the Dartmouth administration
> would welcome this paper, especially as its rhetoric pays so much
> attention to the vigorous exchange of ideas.

William Simon, former Secretary of the Treasury, wrote:

> A new breeze is blowing in the land; a breath of fresh air for a
> country choking on the bureaucratic exhaust fumes of the last fifty
> years. One sign of this freshness is the bright and thoughtful

Dartmouth Review. Lucidly written and impressively organized, *The Review* proves that the tedious old cliches which have dominated academic life for so long are now defunct. *The Review* conclusively demonstrates that alert and active young minds are very much alive on our campuses.

Columnist George F. Will wrote:

. . . a significant development. I have followed with interest the trend of *The Dartmouth Review.*

George Champion, class of 1926, and former chairman of The Chase Manhattan Bank, wrote:

These young students are performing a great service to Dartmouth College. To me, it's perfectly remarkable evidence of ability and dedication which needs nurturing in our world today.

Newsweek magazine, in a feature story on the publication, wrote:

They call for a renewed emphasis on Western Civilization in the curriculum and demand a return to Dartmouth's traditional Indian symbol, which was banished a decade ago as offensive to Native Americans (American Indians). Given the times, it would not be surprising if their limited success inspired campus conservatives, with similar funding to mount offensives at other colleges.

Since the emergence of *The Dartmouth Review,* students at Harvard, Yale, and Princeton have produced similar publications. In the fall of 1982, one hundred newspapers modeled after the *Review* had begun publishing. These papers, too, were free of administrative control. William Simon decided to use his influence with foundations across the country to help get these papers started. In the end, however, every paper would have to be a

170

self-sustaining enterprise, financed completely by the alumni, advertising, subscriptions, and assorted promotions.

The administration obviously did not see eye-to-eye with our supporters—people like William Simon—but one would not expect them to. The *Alumni Magazine* ran three pages of letters against the publication, asking alumni not to support it. Consider this typically thoughtful, carefully crafted letter printed in the front section of the house organ:

> Throw those *Review* bums out before I take my lily-white fist and burn a big black hole in their pointy little heads! How embarrassing!
>
> Free speech? I suppose that's how Hitler got his start. Well, it ain't going to work in my house, because I learned long ago to exterminate rats whenever and wherever I find them.
>
> Filth and vermin breed more of the same. Dartmouth, for God's sake, clean up your act.
>
> Steve Pennypacker '63

Clearly, educational standards began slipping earlier than we suspected.

In its first year of operation, the *Review* raised $106,000, mostly in contributions from alumni, and gained nearly two thousand subscribers. In its second year, subscriptions doubled to about four thousand. That number continues to grow.

For an idea of the panic that gripped Parkhurst Hall, take a look at a few lines from a letter circulated by a prominent college official, Ed Sheu, among the alumni of Casque and Gauntlet, a senior honors society. The letter is a four-page diatribe against the paper. Here are a few of the highlights. The *Review*, writes Sheu, is an example of "just the worst kind of hate mongering." He goes on to say "even the editor doesn't believe in what he is doing, but obviously cash flow is more important than the truth." (I might interject that the *Review* is run completely by volunteers, and no salaries are paid except to a part-time secretary.)

Poisoned Ivy

Sheu rages on:

> They would have you believe their successful promotion of Dr.
> John Steel in last year's election is an indication of massive support
> emanating from the alumni body. In my judgment, persuasive
> rhetoric (Indian symbol, fraternities, etc.) and personal alumni
> endorsements (two of which were not authorized) were sufficient to
> defeat . . . superb candidate Raymond Rassenburger '48. This was
> an election in which less than one-third of the alumni voted and in
> which Ray was given no outside support as per the unwritten rules
> of the election.
>
> *The Dartmouth Review* started last year ostensibly as a "conser-
> vative" student newspaper—a weekly alternative to *The Dart-
> mouth.* But it became quickly clear *The Review* had no intention
> of being your typical student newspaper. *The Review* was out for
> bigger game—to discredit John Kemeny, gain several seats on
> Dartmouth's small Board of Trustees, and ultimately to exercise
> considerable influence over the policies of your college.

The fact is, *The Dartmouth Review* did not exist during John
Steel's candidacy, so it would have been difficult to promote his
election.

Sheu concludes: "The goal of *The Dartmouth Review* is to
control all seven alumni trustee seats by 1984."

He asks in his letter: "Will Dartmouth survive this contrived
onslaught of unfavorable comment from the right?"

Following Sheu's letter, a series of events transpired that I would
hesitate to print, since they seem so unlikely, if verification of the
facts could not be found in *The New York Times* and other major
newspapers across the country.

INCIDENT: On Saturday, October 3, 1981, around eleven A.M.,
an employee of The Hanover Inn (owned by the college) was
observed depositing several hundred copies of *The Dartmouth
Review* in a garbage bin behind the inn. These had been left on a
table in the lobby, alongside other newspapers, to be picked up, free

of charge, by anyone who was interested. Asked what he was doing, the employee said they were "old copies." In fact, they were current. Later that same day, Robert Merrow, a supervisor of the inn and a friend of many students on the paper, phoned *The Dartmouth Review*. He explained that he had that morning received a call from Parkhurst. He was told not to allow the *Review* to be put on the table in the inn lobby.

INCIDENT: The *Review* was formally informed in a letter from the sports information office that police would be used if necessary to prevent the newspaper from being distributed at football games. When the college talked to the police about "the *Review* problem," one of the town officers explained that there was nothing he could do. "The students have a right to distribute the paper," he explained.

INCIDENT: *The Dartmouth Review* applied for a grant from the John Olin Foundation and received $10,000. Former Secretary of the Treasury William Simon sits on the board of the foundation. An alumnus of Lafayette College, he received a call from the president of Lafayette, trying to block the grant to the *Review*. Parkhurst Hall had been at work again. Instead of blocking the grant, Simon moved to make $100,000 available to applicants from other colleges to start similar newspapers.

INCIDENT: A prominent businessman, Richard J. Press, of J. Press Clothing, contributed $500 to *The Dartmouth Review*. This was deposited in a Hanover Bank account. A few days later, Press received a call from one of his class officers. "Why did you contribute $500 to this newspaper?" he was asked. Enraged, Press contributed a lot more. No one knows how the class officer got information about Mr. Press's contribution.

INCIDENT: All administrative departments at Dartmouth were informed of a new "official policy," via a memo by college attorney Cary Clark. No interviews were to be granted to *The Dartmouth Review*. Now, interviews with college administrators do not make for lively copy, but this struck us as a bit odd.

INCIDENT: Two senior administration officials told the *Re-*

173

view that they were threatened with the loss of their jobs if they cooperated with, or provided information to, *The Dartmouth Review*.

INCIDENT: A freshman reporter for *The Dartmouth Review* approached Mrs. Dolores Johnson, secretary of the Council on Student Organizations, and asked for information about student groups. Mrs. Johnson said she would have to check with the office of the college president. She did, and said she had been instructed not to say anything to the paper. She would not even provide the reporter with information "as a student," since "students are entitled to information about the [student] groups, but not students affiliated with *The Dartmouth Review*."

INCIDENT: A Dartmouth senior, while distributing copies of *The Dartmouth Review*, was bitten by an upper-level black college administrator.

INCIDENT: Three days after that assault, the Dartmouth faculty voted 113-5 to censure, no, not the punching, kicking, and biting college administrator, but the newspaper the Dartmouth senior had been distributing, *The Dartmouth Review*.

Yes, something important has happened at Dartmouth, and it has national implications. The importance of the *Review* has been measured by almost every major newspaper, radio station, and television news show across the country. Keeney Jones and I appeared on the *David Susskind Show* in New York. Keeney went on *Phil Donahue* and other talk shows in New York, Chicago, and Boston. For the most part, the coverage has been superficial, ... it was the old "Dartmouth administrator bites student!" story. People were used to protestors with long hair, posters of Che Guevara, placards, pot, and the rest of it. It had all become somewhat boring. But *this* was news. Here were conservative dissidents, honor students, women as well as men, black, white, and brown, Catholics, Jews, and Protestants, with heavy support from contributions, advertising, and foundations ... tax deductibility, tax exemption, nonprofit. It all looked very different from the routine hairy-

174

protestor stuff. But the significance of this whole movement goes deeper than that.

The Dartmouth Review, along with the hundred other papers springing up everywhere in imitation, represents the Eighties at war with the academic holdouts from the Sixties.

The academy has, of course, always been the ideal place for rebellion. Students, with lots of time on their hands, have always had a good time making trouble for their elders. In the middle of the eighteenth century, John Wesley's Methodist movement came roaring out of Oxford to change the face of Protestantism in England and America. Later, John Henry Newman's inspired movement toward orthodoxy within English Protestantism led to a Catholic revival. There was, of course, the rebellion of the Sixties, which for most people was not primarily a protest against the Vietnam War but a reaction against another kind of entrenched, stuffy, Establishment *ethos*. The students of the Sixties were protesting against a form of Babbitry. The campus has always been a lively place.

I have some sympathy for administrative fixtures in any establishment, those whose fundamental wish is for business as usual. In my view, however, there is a counter-revolution brewing on campuses, and it is going to roll back much of what we are left with from the Sixties. The weapons employed by the new revolutionaries will not be pot, placards, riots, and a sloppy physical appearance, but ideas, wit, and creativity.

THE GAY STUDENT ALLIANCE. During the spring of 1981, the paper printed a short piece by future editor in chief Dinesh D'Souza criticizing the GSA, an organization that enjoyed college office space and financial support. The piece was sober and objective, and printed the names of the GSA's president, vice-president, treasurer, and social chairman. Implicitly, but not explicitly, the article raised the question of whether college funding ought to go to an organization based on sexual preferences—an interesting question. There was campus outrage over the article, even a demonstration involving not only gays, but militant women and various minority groups, along with the usual host of faculty members, administrators, and assorted friends of the *ethos*. It all seemed a visual metaphor for the radical coalition of the Sixties. The *Review* staff threw even more coal onto the fire, demonstrating irreverence by holding a croquet match near the protest rally and having drinks and sandwiches catered by The Hanover Inn.

CURRICULUM: The *Review* has been severely critical of the "special interest" courses that emerged from the ferment of the Sixties: Women's Studies, Black Studies, Native American Studies, Policy Studies, Urban Studies, and so on. Some students dismissed them, perhaps too easily, as "bozo" courses, dilutions of a legitimate curriculum. In one college course, for instance, the movement of European settlers to the New World was presented as "The European Invasion of America." This was hardly a legitimate history course. It was that new academic discipline, Native American Studies. It's not surprising that at the same time that this program was instituted, the Indian symbol was banned as offensive, not only to Indians but to racial minorities in general and even to women. We were told that the symbol represented the entire spectrum of American *racism, sexism,* and *oppression. The Dartmouth Review* was skeptical of the charge of a wider American racism, which at bottom was what the whole argument was about. The *Alumni Magazine* published letters by militant women professors complaining about the "emotional damage" caused by *Review* criticisms. I am happy to report that students on the *Review* have not suffered emotional trauma, despite repeated characterization as racists, bigots, chauvinists, fascists, hate-mongers, and you name it.

BLACK MILITANTS: Even though the *Review* has black students on staff (both in the writing and business departments), who do not seem disturbed by its editorial policies, the paper has been the constant target for charges of racism. The paper has always opposed discrimination, including reverse discrimination (also known as Affirmative Action). It is also impatient with the fact that, while for years liberals have campaigned for busing and forced integration, there are two black segregated social organizations on campus, the Afro-American Society and the fraternity Alpha Phi Alpha.

It is a fact that blacks on campus have made great gains in recent years. That many of them may feel particularly sensitive to criticism of Black Studies, reverse discrimination, and segregated black social institutions is understandable. But all this has to be assessed from the point of view of the good of the institution and the individual student. It is my own feeling that reverse discriminatory policies have failed because they have put almost unbearable pressure on the qualified black students, for example, forcing them to be "super students." Many blacks feel they have to take the toughest classes and more than the usual load. Segregated social institutions have been denounced by everyone from Andrew Young to John Hope Franklin, an Afro-American historian, as a narrowing and restrictive force at an important stage of a student's development. My own feeling is that many of the "gains" for blacks during the Seventies were not really gains at all.

The entire conflict can be understood simply by observing the argument over the college symbol. We can see, for example, that the Left often embraces contradictions: (a) that the "Indian symbol" was trivial, and thus beneath serious discussion; but (b) that it also had cosmic moral importance. In a way it did.

As was mentioned earlier, an official college bulletin called *The Dartmouth Review* "blasphemous." The word is significant because the entire debate on college policy and curriculum was, in a certain sense, a "religious" quarrel. It seems to me there is an important distinction between politics that actually attempts to solve problems, and *feel-good* politics. Campus politics tends to be of the latter sort.

The game played on campus is to take political positions of great symbolic importance (to those taking them), but of little or no practical consequence. For example, removing college investments from South Africa would in no way penalize South Africa but would chiefly hurt students whose tuition bills would rise as a result of divestment. Similarly ineffective are positions on expunging the Indian symbol, disarmament, reverse discrimination, minority studies programs. Nobody believes any of these programs and policies really do anyone any good. This grimly frivolous politics lies behind the labeling of John Steel and the student editors of a conservative journal as *racists, sexists,* and *fascists.* No objective observer would think such charges are really true, but it *feels good* to make them.

QUESTIONS REGARDING FEEL-GOOD POLITICS: Was it really necessary for classes to be cancelled over Nixon's invasion of Cambodia? Did President Kemeny really have to defend widespread student riots at the time as "not unreasonable"? Did undergraduates really have to receive academic credit for agitating against the war? Did McGovernite actress Shirley MacLaine really deserve an honorary degree, while Nobel Prize-winning economist Milton Friedman, who lived just ten miles up the road, was ignored? Did the Dartmouth faculty really have to denounce Ronald Reagan formally, immediately after his election? Why were so many speakers who were brought to the Dartmouth campus outright leftists?

The answer is simple: "It felt good."

I ran across a somewhat startling study, by Seymour Martin Lipset, on the political views of faculty in universities across the country. Some two-thirds supported George McGovern in 1972. More than half regard the United States as an evil force in the world. More than half regard right-wing dictatorships friendly to America as more of a threat than communism. Socialism commands wide support, and so on down the line. Perhaps most startling, Leftism grows as the prestige of the college or university goes up.

Race, feminism, pacifism, homosexuality, the Third World, U.S. oppression, reverse discrimination—the whole McGovern menu at the 1972 Democratic convention: *The Dartmouth Review* has offended every official and unofficial aspect of it. "It's like shooting snakes in a barrel," said Dinesh D'Souza. "It's Dunkirk for Liberalism," wrote Keeney Jones.

178

And Consequences

"Abortion, Amnesty, Appeasement," went the polemical anti-McGovern chant of 1972. Defeated elsewhere, the corpses have come marching back onto the campus, in mummified form. McGovern himself, the "prairie populist," as *Time* called him, who attacked the three-martini lunch, has now put his $600,000-house up for sale. For the nation as a whole, the show is closing, but it's closing slowly. The Left is still deeply entrenched in the academic Establishment.

It's apparently a legitimate educational endeavor for a college administrator to bite a dissenting student. Perhaps ordinary American citizens should demand that campus officials wear muzzles. We at the *Review* think our articles were in good taste, but we didn't want to be literally eaten. And, while the Dartmouth faculty condones violence against those who do not conform to the *ethos*, we eschew it (excuse the pun). As U.S. Senator Gordon Humphrey said, "It's a good thing the student had the biting college official in a headlock rather than a scissors hold."

I suppose the editors of the *Review* should have been aware that bad taste is the sole prerogative of liberals, for whom bigotry, *ad hominem* attacks, exaggerated charges, and physical violence against demon conservatives, like me, Shaun Teevens, and John Steel—who are probably nazis under it all—becomes respectable. College news service director Bob Graham called the *Review* "a baneful influence on campus."

Will biting students and cheating in elections, once popularized, also become "a baneful influence" at this institution for higher learning?

Food for thought.

179

THE REAL RACISM

I first met April Cooper, by way of a mutual friend, at Peter Christian's tavern on Main Street in Hanover. She did not like our dissident publication, because she sensed it was a disruptive force on campus. I suspect she half-believed the charge, disseminated primarily through Dartmouth officialdom, that beneath our calm opposition to Affirmative Action and our desire to reinstate the Indian symbol, we were probably antiblack, anti-Indian, and generally opposed to people who do not look and think exactly as we do.

I had noticed April before, as had everyone at Dartmouth, and I think it's safe to say she was one of the most strikingly beautiful women on campus. She had large brown eyes, dark wavy hair about shoulder length, stood 5-feet 8-inches tall, and could cause an unsettling feeling in any male who saw her walk down the street. She had long legs that gave her something of the appearance of a gazelle, smooth and sleek. She also had a warm smile, that revealed a perfect set of teeth, white as ivory, which were especially striking because her skin was the color of mahogany. Her personal reason for disliking the *Review*, I think, stemmed from our steadfast opposition to segregated social and living arrangements. April was a member of a predominently black sorority, spent a lot of time at the Afro-American Society, and lived for a time in Cutter Hall, an all-black dormitory. It was natural for her to do this, because many of her friends belonged to these organizations. But April interpreted the *Review*'s criticisms of all-black institutions as an attack on black culture. In fact, she had circulated a petition earlier that year denouncing the editorial positions of my publication.

I wanted to meet April because I found her very appealing to look at, but also because I thought it was important for her to understand that different views on matters of public policy did not automatically reflect a fundamental difference in moral composition. It was possible, in other words, to oppose Affirmative Action and not be a racist. It has always surprised me how many people disagree with that simple premise. But because a thing like Affirmative Action has been placed in a category called "civil rights," its critics, almost by definition, fell into the role of defendant.

As I mentioned earlier, the mutual friend who arranged my first meeting with April was named Eva Simmons. Eva was also very pretty and was part American Indian and part black. Her father would become Undersecretary of the Interior in the Reagan Administration, and she would often meet me for lunch. Neither April nor Eva appeared to be victims of society, and neither looked as if she needed special treatment on account of discrimination. In fact, a professor once remarked that these two were such a stunning pair that when they walked into class together a few minutes late, it was a disruptive event. Eva once informed me, however, that April could not understand how she could be such good friends with me, or anyone associated with *The Dartmouth Review*. So I asked Eva to invite April and a number of her friends to dinner at Peter Christian's tavern.

I arrived and was greeted by Eva and her friend Doug Graham. April and her friend Paul appeared a few minutes later. For the first twenty minutes of the meal, April monitored my every movement, listened intently to whatever I said, and did not talk, beyond the formalities of our initial introduction. I mentioned something about *The Dartmouth Review* employing the belly laugh as a weapon against the pompous, self-righteous, and morally indignant. This must have caught her off-guard, because she began to chuckle, and then joined the conversation.

"I don't dislike everything your paper prints," April said. "In fact, a lot of it is very funny and, listening to you speak, you sound like a reasonable person."

"I'm glad to hear that," I said. We had ordered a carafe of white wine and a couple of cheese and meat platters.

"What are you majoring in?" I asked, deliberately steering the discussion away from politics to the kind of small talk that might take place on any campus between two people at their first meeting.

"I've got a double major in English and biology," she said. "I hope to go to medical school. But I also enjoy literature."

"A double major is tough," I said.

"It's difficult, because I often have to take four courses instead of the usual three."

"What year are you?" I asked.

"Technically, I'm a junior," she said. "But I already have enough credits to graduate, if I want."

"When do you think you'll graduate?" I asked.

"Probably with my class, although if I keep going at this pace, by the time I leave here, I'll have forty-four credits, instead of the required thirty-three."

"It's hard enough for me to carry the normal course load," I said. "How do you do it?"

"I just sleep a little less," she said. Her eyes twinkled in the soft light. She put her elbow on the table, and stared at me for a moment. I felt a distinct ease in the initial tension between us, and I was quite happy the focus of our conversation was not *The Dartmouth Review*. Political discussions have a tendency to ruin what otherwise might be a perfectly fine evening. Her expression indicated that she no longer thought I was such a bad fellow.

"Where do you usually study?" April asked me.

"The eighth floor of Baker Library," I said. "Come visit me, if you get the chance."

"It looks as if you two are hitting it off," Eva cut in, obviously teasing April, as she nudged her under the table.

"Appearances can be deceiving," April said. But she smiled.

The following afternoon, a girl snuck up behind me as I was studying, put her hands over my eyes, and said, "Guess who."

"I give up," I said.

"Not very observant for a journalist, are you?" she said. "You can't recognize my voice?"

"April!" I said.

She removed her hands from my eyes. "I was in the area," she said. "Would you like to go downtown for an ice cream cone?"

"Sure," I said. "I'll treat."

I really liked this girl. I found her to be more than good to look at. She had a gifted mind as well. She wasn't especially interested in politics; her subjects were science, in particular, biology, about which I knew nothing. But she could also talk about literature, and at one point tied her understanding of my subject, English, to what disturbed her most about my publication.

"I haven't made up my mind yet about Mencken," she said. "His iconoclasm works when he's making fun of the stuffy Establishment types, but falls flat when ridiculing those who are down on their luck. He was the perfect writer for the Twenties, but, I think, because of the very irreverence that made him famous, he became unpopular during the depression."

"Humor is risky," I said. "There is a fine line between satire and something blatantly offensive. The *National Lampoon* treads that line."

"*The Dartmouth Review* crosses that line on occasion," she said.

"The problem with humor is one is always trying to top the previous joke." I said. "One function of the iconoclastic style is to expand the boundaries of what can be said. I do believe that a joke, even a poor one, is a blow in favor of freedom. Anyone in Russia today who is caught joking about the authorities will soon find himself working on the Siberian pipeline. I think *The Dartmouth Review* is "unstuffing" Dartmouth. Maybe in another year, it will be impossible for the administration to call anyone to task for dressing up as an Indian."

I very much enjoyed talking with April, perhaps, in part, because she could disagree with me in a civilized way. I think, though, we were in basic agreement on many points. I was so taken with her that on the way back from the ice cream shop, I decided to do something really nutty.

"Would you like to go to Beta's formal with me?" I asked.

The question threw her off guard, and suddenly I felt awkward having asked it. She appeared visibly shaken at the thought.

"I don't know," she said.

A moment or two went by when neither of us said anything. I had felt so comfortable with her that the question rolled off my tongue naturally.

"Yes," she answered.

"You'll go with me?" A surge of energy went through my body. At that same moment, she looked as though she were having second thoughts about it. I wanted confirmation that she would come with me. "It's two weeks from today," I said.

"There must be some blonde-haired preppy you would prefer to go with," she said.

"Obviously not," I said.

"I'd be glad to go with you to the formal," she said.

Her answer filled me with a sense of romantic speculation. I did not realize at first how difficult it was for April to say yes, not just for a date, but for a date with a controversial campus figure to go to a predominently white fraternity formal. I was naive enough to think that, in this modern age, differences in skin color were no longer a social barrier. I don't think she would have had such a problem dating me, either, had it not been for some of her friends at the Afro-American Society.

She almost canceled out on the formal on several occasions

185

because she had quickly become anathema to the militant black community, and some members of her sorority thought she should resign—all because she had been spotted having dinner and going to films with me. There were, of course, plenty of black students who found nothing wrong with April dating a white male, or even someone associated with *The Dartmouth Review*. In fact, many people told us we made a very attractive couple. Nevertheless, the controversy put quite a strain on our beginning any kind of relationship. It was especially cruel to April, because she was basically apolitical and placed great value on being liked by people. She started missing classes because of the hostile stares she would encounter from former friends on entering the classroom.

April felt not only emotional effects from the controversy, but physical effects as well. She began to feel ill, with headaches and an upset stomach. Often, when she came under stress, she would get a bloody nose. She canceled our first three dates due to bloody nose problems, and it looked for a while as though the formal might be in jeopardy. Repeatedly I would arrive at her door and find the following message scribbled on her note board: "Ben, I can't make it tonight. Bloody nose again. Sorry."

In a few days, however, she pulled herself together and got a defiant look about her.

"I don't care what they think," she said to me. We were sitting in the Hopkins Center snack bar. "I'm going to see whomever I want."

One day she had a rose delivered to me. Attached was a card that said, "Happy Twelfth-Day Anniversary. Love, April." I began to send her flowers as well, and notes that said something like, "Hope you have a nice day." I knew my attraction to her was not some sort of momentary exotic infatuation, but assuring her of that was another matter. One day, while sitting outside on the lawn just beneath the window of President Kemeny's office, April said, "So, what is it exactly that you like about me?"

"Besides the fact that you're intelligent, fun to be with, and one of the most beautiful women on campus, I can't think of anything," I said.

186

April laughed. "I mean really," she said. "Sometimes I wonder if you're just using me to prove that you have nothing against black people."

"That's a judgment you're going to have to make for yourself," I said. I was thrown by her statement, because I knew that's what people over at the Afro-Am thought. There was no easy way to prove how thoroughly I had fallen for her.

"I'm sorry," she said. "That was an unfair question." She then leaned over and gave me a kiss, which startled some lower-level deans who were staring out the windows of Parkhurst Hall.

I didn't see April again until the formal, which was the following evening. She went into a twenty-four-hour hibernation. I talked to her once on the phone, and she said she was thinking of quitting her sorority, and she was worried sick about Beta. She didn't know the brothers but thought I might be treated by them as she had been by a segment of the black community. She asked me several times if I wanted to go through with it.

"Of course I do," I said. "You still want to go, don't you."

"I think so," she said. "I don't know. Couldn't we just go out to dinner or something?"

"I tell you what," I said. "Get ready to go to the formal. We'll go out to dinner, and if you decide you don't want to go to Beta afterward, we won't go. We can go to a film, or go dancing, or something else."

"Okay," she said.

I took April to the Parker House, which was the best restaurant in the region. She was gorgeous in her white evening dress, pearl necklace and earrings, and a red ribbon in her hair. I had on a black tuxedo and white, pleated shirt.

"I feel better now," she said, as the waiter brought her lobster. "I'm so happy you asked me out."

"I don't think you would have said that earlier today," I told her.

"I wouldn't have before now," she said, the candlelight reflecting in her eyes.

"I'm glad you agreed to come."

We spent most of the dinner chatting about campus life, our

backgrounds, April's parents who still lived in Chicago, and where she thought she might like to practice medicine. Mostly, though, we just looked at each other and smiled a lot. I was somewhat disappointed when she said she planned to go back to Chicago after graduation, because I didn't think my career would take me there. But, then I thought it was awfully dumb to think she would change her plans after dating me for two weeks.

The formal went very well. Everyone had on evening dress, and Beta looked especially good. But, if I may boast a bit, no one's date compared to April. My friends were immediately drawn to her. There was almost a scene at one point, when one of the brothers abandoned his date momentarily to talk to mine, and the young lady he was with stormed into the women's room, her face red with rage.

The dancing went into the early hours of the morning, but April and I left around midnight. We walked around Occum Pond. The night air was clear and fresh. As the sounds of laughter and music faded into the distance, she clasped her hands around my arm and kissed me on the cheek.

"I wonder what your friends think of us," said April.

"My guess is, they were too jealous to think," I said.

PLAYING FAIR

THERE were people in my class who never went to a football game, who spent their afternoons in the library stacks studying their economics texts so that they could get into business school. Some of these people may discover later in life the spectacle that occurs every autumn just down the street from the library. They may discover what is beautiful, remarkable, and fun about football. It is never too late. As for me, I have always loved football, as spectator, amateur statistician, and failed participant. I played briefly in high school but, having always been small for my age, was too light to play the game well. I stopped playing when I sustained a few minor injuries and realized that I did not have the raw physical attributes needed to become an outstanding halfback. My enthusiasm for the sport remains, however, and is probably the foundation of my friendship with Jeff Kemp.

When Jeff and I first became roommates, I knew that he had been recruited for football, but I had no idea how good he was, nor did anyone else for that matter. In write-ups by the sports information office, he had been mentioned as someone with a lot of athletic ability and potential, but he was as yet untested. Back at his high school in Bethesda, Maryland, he had not faced stiff competition.

189

During his first week at Dartmouth he sustained a minor shoulder injury and began his career as the fourth-string quarterback on the freshman team. For a month he never got one chance to run the offense, not even in practice, although his shoulder had long since healed. He just stood out there, breathing into his hands to keep them warm, waiting for a chance to prove his ability, while his friend and classmate Joe McLaughlin ran the team. The coach completely ignored Jeff. Jeff got pretty depressed.

"They still have you on fourth string?" I asked one day.

"Yes, I'm the last string quarterback. Can you believe that?"

"You can throw the ball twice as far as anyone out there, and the coach puts you last?"

"He doesn't even seem interested in looking at me."

The season was two-thirds over when freshman coach Robert Weiss put Jeff in for a few plays, completely without warning. Jeff had no chance to warm up his passing arm and no chance to go over the play-calling strategy. He simply had to go in and run the team. Things could not have gone worse. On the first play from scrimmage, Jeff fumbled the snap from center. He recovered the ball himself. On the next play he dropped back to pass, slipped, and fell down. No one touched him, he just fell down. On third down and twenty, he was hit hard as he tried to throw the ball. It was intercepted by a defensive back who almost ran it back for a touchdown. Jeff made the saving tackle.

The atmosphere back in the room that evening was very gloomy. "Why do I play this game?" he asked, holding an ice pack over his right eye. "It's so pointless."

"What did Coach Weiss say?" I asked.

"Nothing. That's what hurts most. I know I did a terrible job out there today, but he wouldn't say anything. Most coaches would tell me that I stink, or ask why I didn't dump the ball off to a back when I saw the right side linebacker blitzing, but Weiss just ignored me. I can't wait for the season to end."

Jeff's sophomore year went considerably better. He never got into a varsity game, but got a lot of junior varsity experience. As the season went along he moved up to second string, behind the legendary Buddy Teevens.

Teevens had the highest pass completion percentage of anyone to play for Dartmouth, a season average of 62 percent. He led a team picked by most sportswriters to finish last in the league, to an Ivy championship. He was only 5-feet 8-inches tall and weighed 170 pounds, but could bench press 360. Teevens will probably be remembered as the greatest quarterback ever to play for Dartmouth because of his performance against a heavily favored Brown team. Of his first sixteen passes that game, he completed fourteen, for a total of something like two hundred yards. He rolled up thirty-one points, and the contest decided the Ivy championship. Teevens was picked for first team All-Ivy and first team All-East.

Teevens was a legend, partly because of his exploits in athletics, but also because of what he represented off the playing field. He could always be found in the Beta basement playing *William Tell* with a plastic cup and a keg of beer, or wrestling on the floor with his younger brother, Shaun. In fact, it was Buddy who put Shaun up to the "Indian skater incident." Buddy Teevens represented the old Dartmouth, Dartmouth before John Kemeny. He was what everyone thought the Dartmouth quarterback should be. It was with Teevens that Jeff Kemp would always be compared. Teevens set the standard to which Kemp would have to measure up.

In his junior year, Jeff won the starting quarterback job from senior Larry Margerum and classmate Joe McLaughlin. It was something Jeff had sweated for all summer, lifting weights, running, and throwing hundreds of footballs. He was 6-feet tall, weighed two hundred pounds, and could run forty yards in 4.6 seconds. In fact, he was one of the two or three fastest men on the team. Jeff hated training, especially running. But he was out there every day in the heat, cold, or rain, getting himself into the kind of condition that I would have given ten years of my life to be in. He would have given anything to lead Dartmouth to an Ivy League title.

One Thursday night I was walking back to my room from the

library when I met Jeff, who was standing at the center of the Green looking at the stars. It was midnight.

"What are you doing here?" I asked. "You should be in bed. The Princeton game is only two days away."

"I know," he said apprehensively.

"You're not nervous, are you?"

"I'm scared to death. I've never played in front of so many people before. I'm used to the J.V. games. No one goes to those, so no one sees you mess up."

"No one sees you when you play well, either," I said.

"I guess I'm a little worried, too, because my dad's going to be there with the rest of the family. The Ivy League's a little different from the pros, you know."

"I think he knows that," I said. "Remember, he went to Occidental—not exactly a football powerhouse."

"Yeah, that's true. He's just happy I'm playing. But I want so badly to do well against Princeton. I have a feeling if we win this one we could go all the way to a championship."

"Don't worry," I said. "You'll do just fine out there on Saturday."

"Let's go take a look at the football stadium."

The place looked eerie in the moonlight. A cool wind blew through our hair as we looked around silently.

"Have you ever thought of what a legend you can become?" I said.

"Right now I only want to beat Princeton."

Jeff was a superior college athlete, but up until this time he lacked the complete confidence needed for greatness. I think he always looked up to Joe McLaughlin, the starter on the freshman team, as the legitimate quarterback. Many people, including most sportswriters, said that Kemp had the edge over McLaughlin, merely because of his name. After all, his father had been All-Pro while playing for the Buffalo Bills. This charge hurt Jeff. I think that deep down he thought they might be right, maybe he was starting against Princeton because of some inherited right. And somewhere in the back of his mind there lurked the myth of Buddy Teevens, which could never be recreated.

The following evening, I did not see Jeff at all. I was told that he had skipped his classes and locked himself in his room all day. He wanted to study his plays for Saturday.

It was homecoming weekend. At seven P.M. the band began to play faintly in the distance, the songs rising to concert volume as the musicians marched up Massachusetts Row, with a mob of people following behind, singing "As the Backs Go Tearing By." By eight o'clock, a 60-foot structure that had been built by the freshmen was ablaze at the center of the Green. Tongues of flame rose to heights of two hundred feet, and the orange glow could be seen from miles away. The entire town turned out to watch the spectacle. Even though this scene had occurred in exactly the same way for as long as anyone could remember and would occur again for as long as anyone could foresee, it was dazzling. On this night, all the campus characters lost their significance, all detail was gone. The Georgian walls rose up majestically, but even they were finally consumed by the brilliance of the towering flame. Everything seemed to melt like colors in a sunset.

On the day of the game, the roads were packed with people and cars that came to an inexplicable halt, while a policeman tried in vain to untangle the confusion. A high-school-age kid was standing on a street corner yelling, "Programs! Programs! Get your programs! Read about this historic rivalry!" Farther down the road there was an old man yelling, "Pennants! Dolls! Pins! Footballs! Balloons! Anything you want, I have. Hey, you there, get your date a pennant."

It didn't matter at all that the stuff was junk. Everyone was swept up in the excitement and bought souvenirs, hot dogs, popcorn, Cokes, even though no one really wanted a balloon, and no one was really hungry or thirsty. I wished April had been on campus that term. I'm sure she would have wanted a pennant.

People filed by the ticket window, looking at their watches. Many of the older alums had trouble finding the stadium because they had had an especially good time at the tailgate parties and class tents. In another five minutes, the streets outside were empty. I felt the sweat dripping off my own brow and wondered what must be going through Jeff's mind.

The stadium was like a dream, unreal, with its mobs of undergraduates, alumni, players, and all the meaningless, but somehow essential, hoopla of a spectacular show.

Ivy League football wasn't exactly the big time, but there was something more important in the Dartmouth-Princeton rivalry, which had been going on for almost a century, than, say, the Oklahoma-Nebraska contest. Other games, although higher-caliber ball, somehow lacked the emotional intensity of Ivy League contests, probably because a place like Oklahoma is more a farm team for the pros. A student who plays for Dartmouth knows that, after his senior year, he will almost certainly never play again. That consciousness tends to bring out the best in an athlete.

On Dartmouth's 1970 Lambert Trophy team, for example, a team that was ranked thirteenth in the nation, there was a young man named Murray Bowden. He played middle linebacker and weighed only 175 pounds. He made All-American because he was the best at his position in the country. Calvin Hill, the great running back for the Dallas Cowboys, was once hit so hard by Kansas City's 250-pound linebacker Willie Lanier that his helmet was knocked twenty feet in the air and Hill, unconscious, had to be carried off the field. Later he was asked by a television commentator whether that was the hardest he had ever been hit. "No," he replied. "When playing for Yale, I was hit harder by a little guy from Dartmouth by the name of Murray Bowden."

Murray Bowden gave everything he had to play football for Dartmouth. He will feel pain in his knees for the rest of his life. In the fraternity basements, late at night, over a few beers, the legend of Murray Bowden's accomplishments on the gridiron can still be heard. Whatever those people from the Midwest may think of Ivy football, there is nothing more important to the players than the Dartmouth-Princeton game.

The men, dressed in green-and-white uniforms, ran out onto the field in the midst of a mob of freshmen who were there to greet them. They were like figures from another world, strange, romantic, blurred by the throbbing of band music and cheers. I finally picked out Jeff—number 14. Thinking of the responsibility resting on his throwing arm, I could almost feel his pain. He was completely alone now, as were all the players—alone with a strange combination of fate and skill. Sitting two rows in front of us was the whole Kemp family, who had flown up from Maryland. I had never seen parents prouder than the Kemps were when Jeff jogged out onto the field to take control of the offense on the twenty-six-yard line after the kickoff return.

The first three plays were magnificent, as the ground attack ripped off two first downs; in one, Kemp kept the ball himself as he ran for ten yards around the right end. Pandemonium broke loose, and the nervous energy that had dominated the crowd a moment before turned into a kind of blind confidence that we would roll up the score against Princeton. In the pregame picks, Dartmouth was favored by fourteen points; and after the first three running plays, it looked as if it could be fifty to nothing, the way our runners seemed to be able to walk through the Princeton defensive line.

But after Dartmouth had moved to the Princeton thirty-five, Princeton's defense stiffened. Kemp tried three hair-raising forward passes to Dave Shula—who was double and triple teamed—none of which he completed and two of which were almost intercepted. The offensive line seemed totally incapable of keeping Princeton's pass rushers off Jeff. The Princeton linemen charged like wounded buffalo, and Jeff was hammered to the turf by two or three of them after every pass attempt. Chris Sawch came into the game to try a fifty-yard field goal. The kick fell embarrassingly short of the mark and to the left.

From that point on, the game was a total disaster. Princeton rolled up first down after first down, as they ground up the Dartmouth defense behind the running and pass catching of their explosive halfback. Chris Crissy, scoring sixteen points to Dartmouth's zero. Dartmouth got only three more first downs and never got inside Princeton's forty-yard line after that first series of plays. Gloom descended over the Kemp family, and for three quarters the stadium's capacity crowd was completely silent. This was the Princeton game when anything could happen; and something *had* happened.

We lost. No, we didn't just lose. We were humiliated in our own stadium. The melancholy was deep, and the whole responsibility for the disaster fell down on Jeff like so many tons of brick. He had thrown twenty-five passes, completing only six, for a mere eighty-four yards.

I heard a drunken alumnus say, "Why don't they put someone out there who can throw a football? That Kemp kid's a bum."

I wanted to turn around and tell him off. But I knew that he had only said what everyone else was thinking—at least, everyone who didn't know how hard Jeff had worked for this chance and how much it would have meant to him to have turned in a good performance that day.

People would disappear into their postgame parties. Alumni would renew acquaintance with old classmates, and the topic of conversation would be how awful the team looked; and self-proclaimed football pundits would explain why Coach Yukica should have played McLaughlin instead of Kemp.

Beta was having a party, too. Jack Kemp, Mrs. Kemp, their two daughters and youngest son were there. People wanted to talk with the congressman, but not about football; so, generally, the conversation went in the direction of politics. People wanted to hear about the Kemp-Roth tax-cut plan that Reagan would later push through Congress, after years of lobbying by Jeff's dad.

After the postgame cocktail party had been going on for some time, with Jack Kemp as the center of attention, a bruised and battered Jeff Kemp appeared. With him was a recently acquired girl friend named Muffin. He didn't speak much, except to say "hello," and was unable to get off a convincing smile.

It didn't matter any more, the game was over. Still, Jeff listened intently to his father.

196

Most of the players, including Jeff, spent the evening away from the center of the party. After his brief appearance with his father at cocktails, I didn't see him again. But for those who had not played in the game, the party at Beta raged on into the early hours of morning.

The following week, Jeff played against the University of New Hampshire. Usually this is a walkover game for Dartmouth, but this time we managed only a 9-9 tie, and Jeff had his jaw broken. He would not be able to play the following week against Holy Cross.

Coach Yukica decided to go with Joe McLaughlin. He was much lighter than Jeff, only 170 pounds, and did not stand up well under the pressure from Holy Cross's raging front four. He was sacked repeatedly and was able to throw for only ninety-six yards. Dartmouth lost 10-0.

Jeff got the starting nod against Harvard. Dartmouth had not beaten Harvard for five consecutive seasons. There was something ancient in Harvard's stadium that clouded the mind and caused the opposition to make freakish mistakes. Even in the year of the great Buddy Teevens, Dartmouth lost in a heartbreaker, a final-second fluke. This season Dartmouth had yet to win a game.

With Jeff's first play in Harvard Stadium, pandemoniom broke loose and continued until the end of the game. Dartmouth's offensive line rose to the occasion and kept Harvard's linemen off Jeff, who had a spectacular day throwing the ball. Early in the opening drive, Jeff hit Dave Shula repeatedly with sideline passes. Then he began rifling the ball to Dave across the middle of the field. A roar went up from the Dartmouth side when Jeff threw a scoring strike between two Harvard defenders, and Shula made a spectacular, diving, over-the-shoulder catch. Later in the half, there was some confusion immediately behind me. Pushing and loud voices—a man had gotten sick or fainted; I never found out which. Then my view of the field was blocked for a moment by rising bodies. Kemp had just completed another twenty-five yard pass to Shula, and Dartmouth had the ball first and goal on the Harvard five-yard line. Suddenly everything went crazy. The substitutes were jumping around on the sidelines. Kemp had kept the ball himself and, bloodstained, dragged three Harvard defenders into the end zone. The air was full of hats and cushions. A deafening roar went up again, as Chris Sawch kicked the extra point, and the band played "As the Backs Go Tearing By."

However, the game was not over. The Harvard quarterback, Burke St. John, began to engineer what would have amounted to an amazing comeback. With three minutes to go, St. John launched a ninety-yard march down the field. It culminated in a scoring pass to Harvard and Rich Horner. St. John went for two points and hit Horner again over the middle for the score.

Harvard got possession of the ball again. With under a minute to play, St. John began moving the ball. Again and again the public address man would yell to the crowd "ST. JOHN'S PASS . . . COMPLETE!" A roar would go up from the Harvard side, and Kemp could do nothing but stand on the sidelines with a water bottle in his mouth, watch the clock, and hope that the defense would hold out for a few more seconds.

St. John had moved his team to the Dartmouth five-yard line. The clock was counting down, seven-six-five-four-three-two . . . St. John threw up his final pass. A Harvard receiver was open in the end zone, but only momentarily. A Dartmouth defender was able to race in front of the goal post and bat the ball harmlessly to the ground. "ST. JOHN'S PASS . . . FAILED!" said the public address man.

Dartmouth had won. It was a great game—what was described by sportswriters as "an historic game."

I walked down onto the field. Jeff signed autographs until the stadium was almost empty, lingering until the last possible moment. He had come a long way since the Princeton game and had an ecstatic glow on his face. He picked up a clump of dirt that was lodged in his cleats, let it drop to the ground, looked at it for a moment, turned and walked into the dressing room.

There was something in this game of football that could unlodge a primitive spirit in a person, something that could not be discovered in a seminar. On the field, one either won or lost. There were no "ifs" or "buts." It seemed a test of manhood itself. That is, of course, an unacceptable notion in this age. Yet, there it was. And there was nothing John Kemeny, Michael McGean, John French, Bernard Segal, Dick Sterling, and the Tucker Foundation could do about it—at least at that moment.

Jeff Kemp arrived at Beta late that evening, after the long trip back from Cambridge. When he walked in, everyone stood up, clapping and cheering until he sank down into a plush leather chair. From all corners of the room, people came up to shake his hand.

Quite a switch from the usual "Kemp's a bum," or "We could have beaten Princeton if McLaughlin had played instead," or "The only reason Kemp is our quarterback is because of his name." Tonight, suddenly, Jeff had a wealth of new friends. Everyone wanted to be able to say, "Oh sure, I know Kemp. He's a good friend of mine . . . great guy."

Muffin was there. She looked pretty and pleased to be sitting in Kemp's lap, with her long brown hair streaming down her back.

I stepped outside to get some relief from the stale smells and relentless blast of rock music. Webster Avenue that night, as on any Saturday night, differed from everyday Webster Avenue—as a girl in the daytime differs from one at night. Light from the moon and inside the building suggested that things were more mysterious and entrancing than daylight revealed them to be, and the people strolling in and out of the little passageways and alleys shared this quality, as their faces broke the half-darkness. A figure approached. It took me a moment to realize it was Jeff.

"I got a little tired of the noise and hubbub," he said. "It's so crowded in there, I began to feel claustrophobic."

"It's nice out here."

"It sure is," he said, and paused for a moment. "What do you think of Muffin?" he asked.

"She's cute," I said.

"You think so?" he asked.

"Sure."

Poisoned Ivy

"If we beat Cornell next week, we can still win the Ivy title," Jeff said with great enthusiasm.

"I know," I said.

"If we win that one, everyone will forget about the Princeton game," said Jeff.

"Princeton is water over the falls."

We walked back into Beta. Downstairs some people were watching a freshman throw up in a plastic garbage can, while another group watched a kid suck beer directly from the tap. Tap sucking was a popular game, the object being to see who could suck beer from an open spigot the longest. The record that evening was somewhere in the neighborhood of forty-five seconds, which is equivalent to consuming about half a case.

There was something at Beta for everyone. If one wanted to dance and do relatively genteel things, there was the living room. If one wanted to get stinking drunk, one belonged in the basement. Down there, the participants had no inhibitions.

Dartmouth lost a close game to Cornell, but not because of Jeff. He completed passes for more than 200 yards. But Cornell's ground attack chewed up the Dartmouth defense, as some unknown running back by the name of Weidenkopf rushed for 256 yards. Dartmouth won all their remaining games, Kemp having a spectacular day against the favored Brown Bears, throwing to Shula for two second-half touchdowns. Kemp singlehandedly overwhelmed the University of Pennsylvania, throwing for almost 200 yards and running the ball himself for 103 more. Because of our slow start, however, Dartmouth could only manage a third-place tie with Princeton in the race for the Ivy championship.

The mediocre season was over, and Jeff spent the summer throwing balls, working in the dust and heat and sweat, running, lifting weights, and going through the old routine. He was determined to do better the next year.

Jeff Kemp's senior year went up in smoke in a fateful game against Cornell. Dartmouth had a chance to win the Ivy title if they could beat Bob Blackman's team on a miserable day in Ithaca, New

200

York. The temperature was thirty-four degrees. The wind gusted to speeds of fifty miles per hour, and it poured rain. Dartmouth lost to Cornell, 3-0, missing all kinds of opportunities. Shaun Teevens dropped a pass on the one-yard line at the end of the first half. He could have walked in for the score. It was hard to fault him, though, because the waterlogged football weighed about ten pounds. But, even worse, with three seconds to go in the game, Kemp had Teevens again wide open in the end zone. When he threw the ball to him, a huge gust of wind blew the ball off line, just enough so that a defender was able to stick out a hand and knock it to the ground. Dartmouth lost the championship, and the season ended in misery, with Jeff suffering a shoulder separation.

Judging from Dartmouth's won/lost record while Jeff was quarterback, one would not have guessed that he had actually achieved some great things. He broke virtually every worthwhile passing record for Dartmouth—most passes completed in a season, most passes completed in a college career, most passing yards gained. Despite heroic effort, though, Jeff never delivered the championship to Dartmouth. This cold fact was undoubtedly the worst injury he had ever sustained. Not many people could have endured the kind of thrashing he took at the hands of opposing offensive linemen. I never once heard him complain about Dartmouth's horrendous offensive line, which couldn't give him the pass protection he needed. He would always get up off the ground—despite cuts, broken bones, concussions—and stay in the game for yet another series of plays. He had a certain dignity of heart that went deeper than his proud carriage. But most of all, he just loved the game.

The elegiac quality of the Jeff Kemp story is intentional. Anyone who has taken athletics seriously, either as participant or spectator, has experienced intensely the transitory nature of the world. He knows there is a definite end to things: The clock runs out, the nine innings are over, the buzzer sounds, and there is nothing anyone can do about it. An athlete also experiences his own mortality: a running back loses a step, his reflexes are slower, he is injured, he fails to make the team, and is forced into retirement—a kind of early death for many. It is no accident that a tiebreaker is often called "sudden death." Athletics highlights a truth about life that people do not like to face, a truth that is not as readily apparent in the classroom.

Academic intellectuals tend to scoff at athletics. They say sports detracts from the intellectual life, which is the business of the university. President Kemeny, in an earlier convocation speech, spoke about the need for "mental fitness," and suggested that in this country physical fitness is overvalued. He launched a vigorous campaign to "deemphasize athletics," which indeed worked: Dartmouth's men's teams under Kemeny plunged to last place overall in the Ivy League. I've heard professors bemoan the fact that a number of "dumb linemen" were taking their courses.

But an athlete experiences something different from a student in a seminar. Most college football players know their last game will occur on a precise date at the end of fall term senior year. Their athletic careers are *over*. This is not true of a seminar or classroom discussion. There is always more to be said. The conversation can always continue. Even a book can be read again. Judgment is subjective—in the intellectual life. But a won/lost record, the final score, a batting average, a pass-completion percentage is there for all to see in its cold, stark reality. Academics generally don't like this feature, the idea that something can have a definite result, that performance can be measured, unless they are doing the measuring. Academics like the idea of tenure, for example, because if they were measured day in and day out for the quality of work produced, many would not have jobs. Performance, production, results, are not part of the daily experience of most faculty members I met at Dartmouth, and I think this fact is at the root of their hostility toward serious athletic competition. Because it also requires something extra from the participant, in terms of personal discipline, courage, talent, and the desire to pursue excellence (also alien concepts to many academics today), athletics, as Aristotle, Plato, and Homer knew, is vital to a liberal arts education.

Jeff's football career was not over yet. He received a letter from the Los Angeles Rams inviting him to their tryout camp. He performed well, and they let him play in their first preseason game against the New England Patriots. He threw a touchdown pass and continued to do well. He threw for another touchdown against San Diego and connected on a number of long bombs. Jeff made the Ram team as the backup quarterback to Pat Haden, the former star at U.S.C., along with former Alabama star and three-year pro, Jeff Rutledge.

When Jeff arrived on the Dartmouth campus the following summer to visit friends, there was an instant crowd of newly acquired fans who followed him here and there, asking for autographs. Jeff was always friendly but managed to make his way through them in brisk fashion.

I was told that when he and a friend walked into Campions, a local sports and clothing shop, and asked to see their selection of neckties, a salesman said, "You seem to think you're pretty important. Just who do you think you are?"

"His name is Jeff Kemp," said the friend. Jeff looked confident, maybe a little on the cocky side, as his friend added, "What do you think about that?"

"Jeff Kemp from the Los Angeles Rams?!" a chorus of voices exclaimed.

A woman ran up to Jeff and asked him to autograph a football for her twelve-year-old son. The salesman's face lit up, as he forgot his responsibilities to the other customers.

"Mr. Kemp!" he exclaimed. "Right this way please, Sir. Not only will I show you our neckties, I'll show you our Indian paraphernalia. We keep it hidden in our backroom."

NOT
ALL THAT
CONSERVATIVE
A PARTY

IT was November 4, 1980—
National Election Night. *The Dartmouth Review* was throwing
the most elegant party that Dartmouth had seen in recent history,
perhaps since the Twenties. Not all the men wore tuxedos, but
many did, and most women wore long dresses. Instead of rock
music, an elderly woman played a mixture of classical music and
old, seldom-heard, Dartmouth songs on a large gold harp. The
harpist was a Jones touch—a kind of surrealist joke. There were
hors d'oeuvres, cheese, caviar, crackers, vintage wines, sandwiches,
and an open bar.

About two hundred fifty invitations were sent out, and everyone
showed up; they all wanted to meet the staff of *The Dartmouth
Review* and the author of those outrageous, and often downright
irreverent, columns—Keeney Jones. Jones had on a button that
said "DOWN WITH IT." (He kept trying to convice a couple of
administrators to wear a button that said "IT.") On the walls were
large portraits of Ronald Reagan, Richard Nixon, and Dwight D.
Eisenhower.

Even though Beta had planned a competing party that evening,
Jeff Kemp showed up at ours, and so did Shaun Teevens and Mike

Lempress. People knew that this was the place to be, if you wanted to meet the prettiest girls on campus. Some who were not invited stood outside the door and tried to purchase invitations from those enterprising souls who had managed to acquire more than one.

There were three television sets tuned to the three networks. Some listened to election returns; others were only interested in socializing. On one wall was a gigantic map of the United States. As the returns rolled in, Steve Kelley, the cartoonist, would color in the states. If Ronald Reagan won a state, Kelley would color it blue; if Jimmy Carter won, he would color it red. Beside the map was a list of all the Sixties-style liberals who were losing their respective races: McGovern, Church, Magnuson, Bayh, Culver, and so on. The party was by no means limited to conservatives—I think, in fact, there were a good many more liberals there. Invitations had been sent to anyone who was known to be good company. Liberals, as long as they were not bores, windbags, or buffoons, were welcome.

Conversation encompassed the most trivial to the most profound matters, but most of the talk revolved around politics; in particular, the politics of the *Review*. I overheard Anthony Desiré talking with a black campus politician Chris Cannon. A group of people were clustered around them. As I remember, the conversation had become rather heated. It went something like:

"How can you work for this newspaper?" Cannon asked. He was dressed in a fancy blue sportscoat and gray slacks.

"Because it seems obvious to me that the group of students with this publication is the best and the brightest," answered Desiré.

"But do you agree with the underlying philosophy behind the thing?"

"You're asking if I'm a conservative?" Desiré asked.

"Yes," Cannon answered.

"I don't think I'm especially ideological," said Desiré. "I'm interested in what's best for me. If I thought *The Dartmouth* was the best paper on campus, I would work for that."

"The *Review*'s a divisive paper," said Cannon. "It can only hurt Dartmouth."

206

"I disagree," said Desiré. "This paper has put Dartmouth on the map. Everyone is talking about it. It's controversial, and that's why it's read. No one of importance outside Hanover has heard of *The Dartmouth*."

"It's very puzzling to me how a black man can work for an organization like this," said Cannon.

"Why's that?"

"The *Review* is against everything that's intended to help our people," said Cannon.

"Like what?" asked Desiré.

"Like Affirmative Action," said Cannon.

"I don't know about you," said Desiré, "but I don't want to be known as someone who got in here on Affirmative Action. I got in on my merits."

Their debate continued, but I went over to one of the television sets to check the election returns. It was only eight o'clock, and Jimmy Carter had already conceded a Ronald Reagan victory. Cheers went up from some in the crowd; there were sad faces on others. But most people were too busy talking and enjoying the free drinks to be too concerned about what was happening in the election. On the way back to the bar, I was met by a tall, angular gentleman named Nathan Levenson. At the time, he was working as a photographer for *The Dartmouth*. On his blue blazer was a huge button. It said, "I LOVE TED."

"I've always liked the Kennedy family," he told me. Nate was from the Boston area. "I liked Jack's style, and it's out of loyalty to him that I voted for Ted against Jimmy in the primary. I like the *Review*, though, and I want to work for you guys."

"I've heard you're a terrific photographer," I said. "Why do you like the *Review*?"

"I didn't at first; but I read somewhere that the definition of a neoconservative is a liberal who's been mugged. I was mugged by the Tucker Foundation."

"How so?" I asked.

"Well, I went on one of their internships to the ghetto in Jersey City. The idea was that we were supposed to help the poor in some

207

undefined way. When I got there, they put me to work in the welfare office, where I saw the incredible dishonesty—actual theft—that goes on."

"Theft by people who live in the ghetto?" I asked.

"No," said Nate, "by the government social workers. They punch in at 9:30 A.M. and sit around the office, or leave to play golf, and come back at 4:30 P.M. to punch out."

"You must be exaggerating," I said.

"Absolutely not," said Nate. "I knew one guy who had been doing it for many years. He loves the job."

"Do they do any good at all?" I asked.

"They do more harm than good," said Nate. "That welfare office is a racket."

"Did you tell this to the people at the Tucker Foundation?" I asked.

"Sure," answered Nate. "Jan Tarjan, the director of the intern program, spent a good deal of time down there with us. She asked us for our conclusions about the program."

"What did you tell her?" I asked.

"I said that the poverty I saw in Jersey City is not from lack of funds but lack of schooling. Without education, these people have no chance of climbing out of the ghetto. I told her we ought to phase out welfare and food stamps as the most direct incentive for these people to improve their present condition. At the same time, the government should improve the schools. Education is the only solution to poverty."

To me, Nate was convincing. I remembered that George Gilder, author of *Wealth and Poverty,* had an almost identical experience. Gilder was a liberal Republican, until he began working for a government agency. He discovered there that welfare, food stamps, public housing, and so on, actually perpetuate poverty, providing little incentive to improve one's condition. They create a permanent welfare class. Nate's discovery was that success in our system depends more and more on paper credentials. Without a high school diploma, without a degree, without a skill of some kind, the impoverished are doomed to poverty.

"What did Miss Tarjan say to that?" I asked.

"She spent hours telling me why I was wrong. I was unconvinced, so she said I must be unethical. As I grew more dissatisfied with the situation down there, she decided I must be a racist."

"This is Dartmouth's representative you're talking about?" I asked.

"That's right," Nate answered. "Miss Tarjan couldn't understand how I could go on this internship and leave with such *obscene* views. To me, this implied that the entire purpose of the Dartmouth internship was to indoctrinate me with the virtue of government welfare programs. That I didn't see their virtue meant that I didn't understand why I was there. Now, I've always considered myself to be more or less liberal. Most of the students on the Dartmouth program, though, were generally off the American political spectrum. I would come back to the house each night, and they would relentlessly berate me about the evils of capitalism and America. They would say I didn't like the welfare office because the problems of the area were too complicated for me to understand. Day after day they would attack me as racist. They wouldn't argue; all their attacks were *ad hominem*. Sometimes they would just refer to me as 'Nate the asshole.'"

"They would say these things just because you disagreed?"

"That's right, and that's why I want to join the *Review*."

"You're certainly welcome. We need a good photographer."

The more Nate became familiar with how the Dartmouth administration operated, the harder he worked for the *Review*. He became good friends with trustee John Steel, a man whom he had opposed during the election fiasco. He bought the traditional Dartmouth necktie with the Indian logo, a symbol that he had disdained only months before. He replaced his Ted Kennedy button with a Reagan button. The following year, he became president of the paper—all because of Jan Tarjan and the Tucker Foundation's Jersey City internship.

Our harp player, who had probably tired of such revelry during the Coolidge administration, went home at eleven o'clock, but the party went on. Jones decided to play patriotic songs and speeches

209

from Franklin Roosevelt and Spiro Agnew on the hi-fi. Almost everyone agreed that the party was a tremendous success. We learned the next day, however, that the entire evening was an affront to the *ethos*. One of *The Dartmouth*'s editors, Steve Anthony '83, had the following spasm on its editorial page:

> When they started singing "God Bless America" I decided I had to leave.
>
> The Reagan victory party sponsored by Keeney Jones *et al.*, Tuesday night, can only be described as a sordid and decadent affair. What purported to be a gathering to watch the election returns and celebrate an imminent Reagan victory, turned out to be a debutante ball for the ultra-conservative socialites on campus.
>
> Having only received an oral invitation, I arrived at the doorstep of Room 212 at the Hanover Inn in blue jeans and sneakers. Jones himself greeted me, resplendent in his black tuxedo with satin lapels, pleated shirt front, and gold studs. I suppressed a smile.
>
> Fossedal stood at the bar, dressed as if ready for a game of bridge on board a luxury liner, blue blazer, ascot, and matching handkerchief in his breast pocket. He sipped his martini and smiled at me. I gagged . . . Chris Cannon, of the Undergraduate Council and one of very few liberals present, looked more than a little dismayed. I could hardly blame him. The scene resembled a coming-out party at a Wasp country club. . . .
>
> . . . The bar was open and served only name-brand liquors. They even had the Inn's chef sculpt a block of cheese into the figure of an elephant. It was disgusting.
>
> After watching Ronald Reagan become president and cushioning the blow with a couple of gin and tonics, I decided I was awkwardly out of place and had better depart the affair. As I left, I overheard someone remark, "I wonder if Reagan will bring back the Indian symbol."
>
> I think I'm going to cry.

Apparently, this writer saw nothing funny in Jones's harp

player, his buttons, Anthony Desiré's opposition to reverse discrimination, Nate Levenson's switch from *The Dartmouth* to the *Review*, or the election of Ronald Reagan. I can't blame him. After that night, the future for liberals did not look bright.

DR. BUSH, DO YOU HABITUALLY REACH CONCLUSIONS IN THE ABSENCE OF FACTS?

IF you were at a tribunal at which the charges were not specified, at which challenges to the competence and personal biases of the tribunal were voted on by the tribunal itself, at which clear contradictions in testimony of key witnesses were not investigated, at which no offense by the defendant was established, and at which a guilty verdict was handed down after a nine-and-a-half-hour confabulation—where could you be? At a trial in Moscow or Peking? Up on charges before the Ayatollah?

Not necessarily. You might be facing the Dartmouth College judiciary body, the Committee on Standing and Conduct, better known on campus as the C.C.S.C., where your constitutional rights are suspended, where hearsay evidence can be used to suspend a student from school, and where you might be brought up on one charge and found guilty of another.

Greg Fossedal, editor of *The Dartmouth Review*, found himself before this remarkable tribunal. Students were discouraged from bringing a lawyer; they were told that this would work to their disadvantage, angering committee members. Students were advised to keep their hearing secret. Their fates were decided behind closed

213

doors, and by college regulation all evidence was destroyed immediately afterward. Greg, however, brought a lawyer, that same William Clauson who had already jousted with Dartmouth officialdom. He was wise enough to make the hearing public. The press was there to report unusual events, and about a hundred students were present as witnesses.

What follows is a brief documentary of some of the more outrageous features of the Fossedal hearing. You are not reading Kafka. You are not reading Orwell. You are reading recent Dartmouth history.

The Case

For two years, on a weekly basis, Greg Fossedal had been going into the college news service offices to look through the press releases put out by the college. They were hanging on a hook marked "cleared for release."

On this occasion he saw a news release concerning a possible cancer discovery by a faculty member at the Dartmouth Medical School. He photocopied the item, following the same procedure he always had, and wrote up the story for the *Manchester Union Leader*, for which he was a part-time reporter.

Greg's publication of the release angered the researcher, Dr. Leo Zacharski, who had worked with a blood anticoagulant called warfarin, which he claimed could be used to treat lung cancer. Zacharski wanted to publish his research in a prestigious medical journal before releasing it to the major media. Evidently, it is frowned upon in the medical profession for a doctor to print his findings first in nonmedical publications. Each publication of his research, said Zacharski, jeopardized his chance to receive government grants needed to advance his research. No one explained how Greg should have known this.

Zacharski, and two of his supervisors, brought their complaints to the dean's office. They wrote letters charging Greg with "stealing" the information, even though College News Service Director Bob Graham later testified that the information had been hanging on a hook marked "cleared for release" in the offices of the college news service and in the form of a press announcement. In my opinion, the dean's office sensed an opportunity to inflict damage on the editor in chief of *The Dartmouth Review* and thereby intimidate the rest of the staff, and sent the case along to the chairman of the C.C.S.C., Professor Michael Green, also chairman of the Native American Studies department and no fan of Fossedal. The doctors called for Greg's dismissal from school.

The Story

THE DEFENDANT:	Greg Fossedal
THE PROSECUTION:	The C.C.S.C.
THE JUDGE:	The C.C.S.C.
THE CHARGES:	C.C.S.C. Chairman, Michael Green, refused to specify or clarify charges.

The scene had a circus atmosphere. The room was packed with students, reporters, photographers, professors, and administrators. Jones had on his navy blue suit and Sherlock Holmes cap and waved an American flag whenever he thought Michael Green was looking at him. For most people, it was an entertainment, like going to the Friday night fights. It was novel because almost all C.C.S.C. hearings in the past had been closed. What went on behind closed doors had always been subject to hearsay and rumor. People wanted to see if all the horror stories they had heard about this judiciary committee had any basis in fact.

Before testimony began, Greg's attorney, Clauson, challenged the impartiality of six committee members, one of whom was Green. The following is a tape-recorded exchange between Clauson and Green:

CLAUSON: The challenge would be to Professor Green.

GREEN: Excuse me, the chairman will sit in his chair.

CLAUSON: I start off being amazed that Mr. Green has not already disqualified himself. The relationship between *The Dart-*

215

mouth Review and Professor Green has been probably the worst of any members of the committee, which is to say something, because it has not been good with the committee in general. . . . I had the privilege to read a long article in last week's *Dartmouth Review*, which in essence explained how badly the committee had been run under the chairmanship of Professor Green, and went through any number of specific cases and stated exactly what the committee had done which is offensive to most of our notions of fair play. Certainly, if anything in the article in *The Dartmouth Review* is anywhere close to being true on any occasion, then my notions of fair play—everything I have ever learned about due process—is offended.

HIGGINS (*C.C.S.C. member*): Do you wish to disqualify yourself? (*He looked at Green.*)

GREEN: I believe I can sit. (*Riotous laughter from the audience.*)

Earlier in the day, Greg and I had had something to eat at one of the local restaurants. We spent some time talking about the case. Greg told me he was distressed that Green was allowed to remain chairman of the C.C.S.C., despite all the problems the committee had experienced under his leadership. He was particularly worried that Green would use his position against Greg. At the time, Greg still had no idea why he was being brought before the committee. After hearing about his relationship with Green, I was convinced that Greg had good reason to be worried. Greg and Professor Green had had their first dispute two years earlier, when Shaun Teevens, dressed as an Indian, skated into Dartmouth history. Greg, at that time, was sports editor for *The Dartmouth*.

"I was laying out my page and helping out with the news editing," Greg remembered. "Then, in came one of our photographers who said he had a great picture of the "Indian skaters." I convinced the layout editor to run the photo and story on the front page. The editor was skeptical, but agreed that news is news and that the story ought to run. It didn't seem to be an ideological question."

The Native American Studies department thought otherwise, Greg explained. In came an emotionally charged letter denouncing the paper's editorial judgment for printing the story and picture. Evidently, the event should have been kept a secret, even though it had occurred in a sold-out hockey arena. The letter was signed by Michael Green. Greg pulled the letter out of his sportscoat and handed it to me. I began to read: "That Dartmouth students chose to present themselves as racist caricatures is unfortunate; that the college newspaper chose to publicize this example of *class* insensitivity without critical judgment is appalling. Either *The Dartmouth* should make a public explanation and apology for selecting this picture for the front page, or cease to pretend that it is a publication for all segments of the population."

"It would be bad to be thrown out of school at this stage," Greg said. "It's only a few more months until I graduate." His palms were sweaty, and he was visibly nervous.

I remembered Green heating things up quite a bit in the spring after the skating incident. In conjunction with the president of Dartmouth's Native American society, Lennie Pickard, an American Indian, he denounced the pardon of Teevens. Pickard called the pardon a "heinous and racist act."

Greg had incurred the wrath of native Americans, and their most vocal representative, Michael Green, when he put together the annual freshman issue of *The Dartmouth*.

"I was told our selection of photographs was abominable, clearly racist," Greg explained. "The lack of minority photos was seen as deliberate. Actually, it was the kind of thing I would never think of. Who has time to count up the pictures for ethnic content?"

The emergence of *The Dartmouth Review* in the fall of 1980 sparked a good deal of acrimony. In its opening issue, the *Review* ran a collage of fifty years of Dartmouth football program covers; the dominant motif on the programs was the Indian. Professor Green and others complained bitterly to Dean Ralph Manuel and other college officials.

Later that fall, Greg had written an editorial calling for an end to the college's reverse discrimination policies and to racially segregated living and social arrangements. He also proposed the elimination of special interest departments, questioning their academic and intellectual merit. Green was chairman of the Native American Studies department, and his job depended on its existence. Green had not been pleased by the editorial. Now, he was not pleased by Fossedal, generally.

Greg leaned back in his chair and loosened his necktie. On it were Indian heads.

"Isn't it a little risky to wear that into the hearing?" I asked.

"I suppose, but I remember a story that Green was once late to a C.C.S.C. hearing. When asked why he was late, he said that he had been busy tearing down Indian posters that were popping up around the campus. I want to see what he does with my necktie."

I remembered that Greg and Dinesh had done a long investigative story on Green's C.C.S.C., the same story that Clauson referred to in an effort to demonstrate Green's bias. From this article, which contained several pages of interviews with students, one gathers that student paranoia about the C.C.S.C. was at an all-time high under Green's leadership. Two student members of the C.C.S.C. grew so disgusted with Green's performance that they spoke to D'Souza, although they asked not to be identified, fearing what Green and company might do to them if it was learned that they had spoken to the *Review*. Their names, for the purposes of the article, were given as Ellsberg and Deep Throat.

Ellsberg was of a liberal bent and no fan of Greg, Keeney, or the *Review*. In fact, he had frequently written letters to the editor criticizing the paper for this and that. But he was even less of a fan of Michael Green.

Deep Throat was conservative and had done some work for the *Review*. Deep Throat said that Green would go to any lengths to prosecute students who took a position even remotely in favor of the Indian symbol, or those who had criticized the college's reverse discrimination policies.

Ellsberg said that during the Teevens drinking incident (Teevens

218

went before the committee for some minor infraction involving alcohol consumption), "Green was out to screw Teevens. When someone stood up to defend the kid, I heard Green say, 'That's a crock of shit!'" Ellsberg went on to say that "Green made a deliberate point of bringing up the fact that Teevens was the very same kid who skated out on the ice ages ago."

The C.C.S.C.'s obsession with racism and sexism was exacerbated by Dean Karen Blank's frequent use of the term "emotional violence." "That term has become the catch word for severity," Ellsberg said. "Students, particularly women and minorities, have only to charge that actions were psychologically damaging for the C.C.S.C. to impose harsh penalties on the culprit."

The *Review* contacted Green to get his comments on the issue, but he declined. Green said he had forbidden all C.C.S.C. members to talk to the *Review*.

I once heard a student comment, "The C.C.S.C. operates a little like Russian roulette. Their decisions are completely arbitrary."

The sentiment was understandable but did not seem to be true. In my experience, C.C.S.C. decisions have followed a definite pattern. After the Teevens skating incident, not only the C.C.S.C., but college officialdom as a whole, became so riddled with paranoia at offending ethnic groups that one needed only to utter the word *black* for bizarre and excessively severe penalties to be swiftly administered. Remember the "Take an Indian to Lunch" punishment? And it was not at all unusual for students to be thrown out of Dartmouth on charges of *racism* and *sexism*. Merely *the hurt* that a feminist felt could truncate a student's career at Dartmouth.

On the other hand, if one's ancestry showed traces of minority background, or one's family had a history of misfortune (except for Teevens, whose father died over Christmas break), or one's grand uncle was unjustly hanged in 1864, one had little to fear from the C.C.S.C.

What the C.C.S.C. wanted in a student was a Kafkaesque lust for guilt. Total self-deprecation was essential for getting a light sentence. No attempt to defend oneself was acceptable. "We're all guilty in some sense," said the true believers. Exaggerated humility when speaking, an expression of bovine bliss at this opportunity to reform oneself, and a clear demonstration of how *the trial* experience has given one a sense of *self-renewal*, was what was called for, if one expected to continue one's studies at Dartmouth.

Greg Fossedal, however, knew that in his case self-abnegation would not work.

The hearing was peculiar from the start. Clauson's challenge to the committee's impartiality went unheeded, as Green and five other members voted to retain themselves. Clauson's views of the procedure were to the point. "I can tell you that in no judicial proceeding would judges who have been attacked by the defendant be allowed to vote on whether they themselves should be allowed to judge the defendant." Green defended the procedure on the grounds that the C.C.S.C. "is not a judicial body."

Clauson explained that he had received six letters (from college deans, from doctors, and one from Bob Graham, director of the news service). "Nowhere in the letters are the charges against Mr. Fossedal made clear. What exactly are the charges?" asked Clauson.

"It's going to be necessary for you to interpret the charges for your client," said Green. "We will proceed with the hearing."

"Great," said Clauson, the sarcasm in his voice unmistakable.

"If you feel that your violation or alleged violation is a grievous act of some sort," added committee member Steve Godchaux, "I suggest you address yourself to that."

Laughter erupted from the audience. Jones waved his American flag.

During the hearing, Clauson was able to bring out contradictions in witness testimony. Several of these involved the plaintiff, Leo Zacharski, and college news service director Graham. Graham had sent a letter to the dean's office charging that Greg had "broken into his files" to get the press release. At the hearing, Clauson got Graham to admit that the news item had, in fact, been hanging on a hook on the wall, marked "cleared for release." When Clauson asked Graham why he used the word "files" in his letter, implying some kind of locked cabinet, Graham said that he considered the hooks on the wall to be his "files."

"A very unusual definition of *files*, which you said were broken into," said Clauson. (Laughter from the crowd. Graham went back to his seat.)

Dr. Zacharski took the stand, claiming that the press release, photocopied by Fossedal, was only "a preliminary draft . . . I can't take responsibility for any specific wording that was used in this particular, very preliminary, version."

"Greg's not asking you to," Clauson pointed out.

Later, Graham testified that the press release had attached to it a pink slip on which explained Graham, "was a statement that said 'Cleared by Dr. Zacharski,'" but also said "Hold." Graham said that he understood that Zacharski had approved the release as ready for publication.

"But not publication by me," Greg added later.

The numerous letters arriving at the dean's office from the medical school demanding Greg's dismissal from college seemed to have a mysterious origin. There was the following taped exchange between Clauson, Zacharski, and Zacharski's superior, who also sent a letter complaining about Greg.

> CLAUSON: Did you discuss with them [Zacharski's superiors] the writing of letters?
> ZACHARSKI: No.
> CLAUSON: Did you know that they wrote letters?
> ZACHARSKI: Yes. Afterward, I found out that they did.

Zacharski left the room and his superior, Dr. Bush, entered, sat down, and began fielding Clauson's questions.

> CLAUSON: Did you discuss the sending of your letter with Dr. Zacharski?
> BUSH: Indeed.

CLAUSON: Did you send it because he asked you to?
BUSH: No,
CLAUSON: Tell us about the discussion you had with him about sending the letter.
BUSH: He sent me a copy of what he had sent. I asked him if it would be appropriate if I supported him. He said it would. I, therefore, wrote this letter, and asked him if he thought it was a fair statement, if he could make any suggestions about the changing of phraseology, or if it was inaccurate. Then the letter was sent.
CLAUSON: So you had a chance to review Dr. Zacharski's letter, and then you had a chance to draft yours and discuss the matter with him.
BUSH: Correct.

It was clear at this point that Dr. Zacharski was less than candid when discussing Dr. Bush's letter with Clauson.

Dr. Bush went on to demand, in addition to Fossedal's dismissal, a disclaimer in the *Union Leader* saying that Dr. Zacharski had nothing to do with the publication of the release. Bush said that separation from the college was not too serious a penalty for Fossedal because "when one considers the value of the object stolen, when one considers the responsibility and degree of the person involved, when one considers the use of stolen material— you can take all those three things as a pretty serious grievance."

My father was also one of Greg's advisors in the case. He took up the matter with Bush:

HART: Dr. Bush, you have used the word "stolen." What knowledge have you of the circumstances under which the story passed into the hands of Greg Fossedal?
BUSH: I said, I understood from Dr. Zacharski that it had been stolen, and I understood from the beginning of this proceeding that the specific complaint against Mr. Fossedal involved misappropriation.

HART: You knew nothing of the actual circumstances?
BUSH: I am not a detective, and I told you quite clearly where I got my information and what my understanding was.
HART: Dr. Bush, do you habitually reach conclusions in the absence of facts?

It was clear very early that Greg had done nothing wrong or out of the ordinary. He was caught between a couple of doctors who did not want Greg interfering, however benignly, with the publicity of their work, and proponents of the *ethos* who were bitter about Fossedal and what his newspaper was doing to their campus.

It seemed that this committee would have liked to see Fossedal leave Dartmouth. With Clauson and a hundred witnesses there, however, it would have been impossible after such a hearing to actually throw Greg out of school. But the committee found him guilty of misappropriation (a nice word for theft) and innocent of an honor principle violation. Most people found the distinction laughable. But the committee apparently thought they had to find Greg guilty of something. So they put him on college discipline, which is really only a slap on the wrist. Greg considered suing the college, the individuals on the committee, and the doctors, for damage to his reputation, but decided against it, out of loyalty to Dartmouth. "I don't want to soil my college's reputation," he said.

When asked why students were often convicted, despite a good deal of evidence indicating that they had done nothing wrong, dean of students John Hanson replied, "The C.C.S.C. does not have to prove guilt beyond a reasonable doubt. If evidence of guilt exceeds the evidence of innocence, we have to respect that."

Thom Smith, vice-chairman of the Undergraduate Council, compared the hearing to the Spanish Inquisition. He did not think the tenets of due process had been observed, adding, "I went to the trial with a noose in my hand, wanting to see Fossedal hung. I walked out thinking he had been done an injustice." About the jurors who refused to disqualify themselves, despite their demonstrated biases against the defendant, Smith said, "Michael Green's ego is what kept him from stepping down. The whole procedure had the quality of incest—I didn't like it."

Student sentiment was almost unanimously supportive of Greg. But the deanery, and college officialdom in general, had a different view. Deans Ann Craig and Almon Ives (committee members) and news service director Graham all felt that due process had been observed in the Fossedal hearing. Dean Craig said she thought the charges against Greg were "well defined"; while Ives thought "Michael Green acted with great impartiality." Graham said, "I am somewhat disenchanted with Greg's performance, and I am becoming increasingly disenchanted with the performance of the *Review*." This, from a man who had been enchanted enough to confuse his "files" with a "hook on the wall."

THE GRADUATE

WINTER and spring terms were, for seniors, a time of anxiety. Some students were waiting to hear from law, business, and medical schools, while others were the objects of a process called corporate recruiting. Interviewers from the personnel offices of banks, investment firms, advertising agencies, and manufacturers would descend on the campus and pick the two or three best applicants, offer them large salaries, a promise of advancement, and a secure future. Most students, including me, had no idea what they wanted to do after graduation.

I spent my senior spring finishing an English honors thesis. I was writing about American literature in the Twenties. I had a theory that the industrial revolution at around the turn of the century, and continuing up until the stock market crash of 1929, was responsible for the tremendous artistic revolution of the period: the works of Hemingway, Fitzgerald, Eliot, Pound, Millay, Faulkner, Crane. I tried to demonstrate that capitalism, freedom, and art are related and, in fact, inseparable. I thought that a home-run hit by Babe Ruth was, in some sense, comparable to *The Waste Land*, the revolutionary and explosive poem published in 1922 by T. S. Eliot. The transition from the singles-hitting Ty

Cobb to the explosive power of Ruth seemed analogous, and even connected, to the transition from the nineteenth-century Longfellow to a modern and completely *new* T. S. Eliot. Both Ruth and Eliot revolutionized their respective fields in style and form. Both were products of the *new* energy that was created by an influx of capital. Cash, of course, made possible the revolution in technology, industry, and, I argued, art. I suggested that Marxism is a reactionary ideology, a fearful revolt against man's natural desire for freedom and the almost limitless possibilities presented to he who has money. Fitzgerald suggests this in *The Great Gatsby*. Marxism, I maintained, is a retreat from modernity. It is an effort to regain, in some sense, the "lost community"; to go back to an agrarian past and live as peasants.

I knew that my thesis was risky. After many sleepless nights at the typewriter, drinking iced coffee, Coca Cola, and eating peanut butter sandwiches, I turned in, one day after it was due, the 120-page document of my scholarship. I report, with both relief and pride, that I received two A's and was awarded high academic distinction in the major.

I particularly enjoyed my association with my thesis advisor, Professor Don Pease. He was intellectually honest, one of the outstanding young literary scholars on the campus, had written a number of plays produced off Broadway, and his reputation was beginning to extend beyond Dartmouth's boundaries. He published widely, taught a Yale seminar, and often lectured at Harvard.

I felt a certain degree of regret about senior spring. There was so much work with the honors thesis, my courses, countless hours at the newspaper, that I scarcely had time to visit with friends. I saw Jones quite a bit, and the other staff members of the *Review*, but I had wanted to renew acquaintances and friendships with people outside that small circle, people whom I had met in South Fayerweather during freshman year. I tried often to stop in at Beta and join the parties, but it was no good. Not that term anyway. Instead, I spent hour after hour at the typewriter, pounding out papers and articles. It seemed ironic. For four years I had looked forward to these final few weeks when I would do a hundred things I hadn't had time to do before.

April had one more final exam, physics, before she could leave for Chicago, where she would work in medical research for American Hospital Supplies. She would come back to campus next year to complete her requirements for graduation. I had invited her to go on a picnic in Vermont, where we sat by the Pomponoosic River, named after an old Indian chief, and watched a waterfall cascade over the rocks and collect in a pool that formed a swimming hole. The water reflected the pines that lined the banks.

"You know, it's a funny thing that I forget the really rotten times I've had here," said April. She had on a charcoal gray one-piece swimsuit, a wide-brimmed floppy hat, and sunglasses. "What I mean to say is, I'm sure I'll forget the lousy grades, studying all night for exams, the difficult professors, and the small-minded deans."

"It's a little difficult to think of anything lousy on a day like this," I said. "If I ever get married, and that's a big if, I think I'd like my son to go here."

"After all that stuff you've printed in your paper about how rotten things are here, don't you think that's silly?" April asked.

On reflection, my statement did strike me as a little sentimental, but perhaps it was a time for sentiment.

"It's a tremendous institution with a great tradition," I said, "despite the people who now run it. Besides, Harvard, Yale, and Princeton are all in worse shape."

April stood up, took off her hat and sunglasses, and dived off a rock into the river. It was a brilliant June day, and I followed her in. The water still had a sharp chill, and my body went numb for just a moment, but then was invigorated. In a little clearing downstream, a deer was trying to cross the river, fighting the current. When the white-tailed creature got to the other side, it struggled up the embankment, shook the water off its fur, and paused to stare at us for a moment, before darting off into the trees. It was a spectacular afternoon.

"I'm going to miss you when you're gone," April said, as she swam up and grabbed me around the waist.

"I'll miss you too," I said. "But that doesn't mean we'll stop seeing each other."

"I fully intend to see you as often as possible, but we won't be able to see each other every day any more, at least not for a while," said April. "What do you think the chances are of our relationship developing into something important?"

"Something permanent?" I asked.

"Yes," said April.

"I think our chances are good, as long as we make the effort," I said.

"Have you decided what you're going to do with your life?" asked April.

"No, but I'd like to try journalism," I said.

"Why's that?"

"It seems to me journalism is one of the last real frontiers in America. There's a lot of opportunity for adventure. Have you ever read Ernest Hemingway's account of Normandy? That's journalism the way it was meant to be. I mean the invasion of Normandy must have been a truly amazing sight. That's what I think I'd like to do: go to the scene, whatever the scene, and write about it."

"Sounds crazy to me . . . You know, there are a lot of peculiar things happening on this campus," said April. "I mean the students are relatively normal, but the people who work here, the faculty, some of them are real strange."

"You're just finding that out now?" I asked. "Dartmouth's no exception, you know. There was a Samuel Johnson scholar at Harvard who said 'sir' all the time and carried orange peels in his pocket everywhere he went. He wanted to imitate Johnson. No one knows why Johnson did that though. There was the professor who conducted tutorials while rolled up inside a rug, his lectures coming out in muffled sounds as the baffled students tried desperately to scribble down notes. There was George Kittridge, the Harvard Shakespearean, who refused to take his Ph.D., objecting, 'Who would examine me?'"

"Faculty are a strange bunch," concluded April.

"Just take a look at the way the faculty have voted at their meetings over the years. They voted to get rid of R.O.T.C. on the grounds that it promoted a promilitary viewpoint. They voted to cancel classes so that students could protest Nixon's invasion of Cambodia. They voted to abolish fraternities, on the grounds that they encourage racism and elitism."

"What do you know about that little circle of classicists, religion professors, and drama people?"

"They are always putting on 'late-Roman' comedies."

Most students on campus thought that was a real rip, at least ·those who knew what a late-Roman comedy was like. Some of it was really sicko stuff, I mean the equipment that was used on people. . . .

"It's no wonder there is such a fight going on over the curriculum," said April.

"We do sometimes get interesting speakers though, like last week."

"You mean that atheist, Madelyn Murray O'Hair?" said April in disgust.

O'Hair had visited the campus the week before. The auditorium was packed for her lecture with an audience that behaved raucously—whistles, catcalls, and laughter, all directed toward the 250-pound O'Hair. She was passionate about the prospect that God does not exist. The idea of atheism and sexual freedom seemed indissolubly linked in her mind, and she thought it to her advantage to attack what she perceived to be the staid sensibility of her audience. Sex, sex, sex, she was ranting. "I'M COMPLETELY

LIBERATED!" she screamed. "Sex, sex, sex. Everyone's so hung up about the human body. Everyone's so inhibited, afraid to show off what they've got."

Fossedal had raised his hand to ask a question.

"You, over there," she had said, pointing to Greg.

"If you're so liberated," he called out, "why don't you take off your clothes, right there on the stage?"

Laughter.

We pulled ourselves up on a warm rock to dry off and unpacked the sandwiches and soft drinks.

"What do you think of this feminism thing?" I asked.

"I'm for equal pay for equal work," said April.

"So am I. But what was going on over at the Common Ground last week redefines feminism," I said.

"What do you mean?" she asked.

"It was pretty disgusting, I mean this women's support session they were having—people trying on birth control devices, others massaging each other, examining each other's bodies. They invited me to watch, but I had to leave. Some people actually *stank*," I said.

"*Stank?*"

"It was all in the name of this principle, *the principle of unattractiveness*. They want men, and other women, to accept them *exactly as they are*."

"Sounds like the great unwashed," said April, chuckling.

"It's all somehow connected," I said. "Feminism, atheism, Marxism, liberalism, and unattractiveness."

"I think I'll have a sandwich and a soda to wash down all these principles," said April.

Later we went dancing at Beta. They were putting on a rather grand party. People were dressed up. The band played a lot of Fifties music.

"It's getting late," April said finally. "Let's take a walk in the moonlight."

"I'd like to stroll around Occom Pond," I said.

The Graduate

The moon was only a slim crescent. Away from the party at the Psi U, there was darkness everywhere. With her hand resting lightly on my sleeve, I felt the pressure of stored-up memories. When we arrived at Occom Pond, a good quarter of a mile away from the center of campus, April stopped at the water's edge and stared pensively into the darkness.

"I suppose when we come back here for class reunions and all that," she said, "we'll wonder how time could have gone by so quickly."

I did not answer but thought of all the hours I had spent playing hockey on Occom Pond. I dreaded the loss of this little northern enclave among the trees and hills. All the people I had known would soon be scattered around the globe. But that thought did not move me as much as the knowledge that, in one more week, I would no longer be a part of this place. Saying farewell to Dartmouth itself would be even more difficult than leaving my friends. We began to walk slowly around the perimeter of the water. The grass smelled fresh and damp. There were ghosts nearby. The noise of our walking somehow seemed sacrilegious. But then two more couples came, laughing, into view from out of the trees, and brought me back to reality. I looked at April; her cheeks were aglow. I thought she was a terrific girl.

"Are you cold?" I asked.

"No," she said. "But I think we ought to go."

It was time.

Early Friday morning, I woke to the sound of Rich Shoup packing his things. At 8:00 A.M., the sun had already risen above the tall pines across the road from Professor Segal's house. I had always thought that Dartmouth did not need June to heighten her beauty. But these final few days were the kind you commit to memory, despite yourself.

"Look at all this stuff we've accumulated," said Rich, standing in the midst of piles of books, papers, and half-empty crates.

Dumped on the floor of the room were all my dusty and derelict

231

belongings. A golf bag, tennis rackets, skis, and ice skates were strewn all over our apartment. Mildew had appeared on them.

"Rich, what do you say we get some breakfast?" I yelled into his room. He was clearing out his closet.

"No thanks, I've already eaten. Made myself some scrambled eggs about an hour ago."

"I think Keeney wants to eat. I'll try and get him out of bed. See you later," I said.

I ran downstairs and outside into the clear New England air. It was early and still cool. I strolled past Aquinas House and thought for a moment of inviting the monsignor to breakfast. But chances were he had already eaten because he always got up at six. I went up fraternity row, which was quiet, and walked across a large grassy area to Streeter dormitory, where Keeney lived. I was struck by how many reminders of departure littered the corridors and rooms—suitcases, crates, scattered belongings.

"Sorry t'see ya go," said a janitor to a couple of students who were loaded down with suitcases and bags.

I walked upstairs and knocked on Jones's door.

"Come in," yelled Jones. When I opened the door, Jones was in bed.

"Want to get some breakfast?" I asked.

"Sounds good to me," he said. "No sense in sleeping away the morning."

"It's a good one," I said. "Before we go to breakfast, I'd like to go over to South Fayerweather and look in on my old freshman room."

"All right, but let's make it quick. I've suddenly gotten very hungry."

When we arrived at South Fayerweather, I found that the present occupants were sophomores, who had already left for home. They had been living there for two years.

"On the whole," Jones remarked, looking into the room, "they seem to be rather dull fellows."

The Graduate

Jones was correct. Nothing in the room seemed to recommend its present inhabitants. Their books were dull, as were their pictures. Nothing seemed to be there to satisfy a particular taste. It was as if they had looked at a photograph of the model undergraduate's room in the *Alumni Magazine* and copied it exactly. There were textbooks, mostly economics and engineering. There was a green "Class of 1984" banner over the door, and there were a few scenic posters, which they probably had bought downtown at the bookstore.

"It's still a nice room," said Jones. "A little nondescript, but nice anyway."

I walked over to the window and found the following inscription carved in the wood of the window sill: "Jeff Kemp and Ben Hart— Class of 1981."

"Let's get some breakfast," said Jones.

Most seniors went to dinner with their parents, many of whom had traveled across the country to see their son or daughter graduate. After everyone's families were put to bed, Beta threw a gigantic party for the graduating seniors, which went into the early hours of the morning. Jeff Kemp was there; so was Mike Lempress, and Shaun Teevens, who was dressed in Indian garb and performing drinking feats on the roof. Keeney Jones also made an appearance. A number of brothers took his shark away and hoisted it up a flag pole at the center of campus. Keeney didn't seem to mind though and, during the early morning hours, stood in the middle of the green saluting his foam-rubber companion, which waved at him like a flag fifty feet above the ground. Undoubtedly, disgruntled college officials would have Chesterton removed before parents and wealthy alumni woke for breakfast, and that would be the last anyone would see of him. "It's a fitting end to an illustrious college career," I heard Keeney say to a newly acquired girl friend, pointing to his shark. No one had known before that Keeney was particularly interested in women; but there he was with one who seemed

233

enthralled with his every movement, and a little melancholy that his shark was gone. Perhaps it will make its way to the Smithsonian, she must have thought. Probably not.

At Beta, the evening was sad in a way. Everyone tried to have fun. The brothers made a point of singing all the outlawed Dartmouth songs, repeating each several times. Every few minutes champagne corks flew, and Indian cheers went up. But no one said much that was funny or even memorable. Perhaps everyone was tired from the strain of the term, but more likely they were apprehensive about what lay ahead. "Is there life after Dartmouth?" I heard someone ask. Everyone knew this marked the end of something. It wasn't as if we would never see each other again, but we would only run into each other by chance. Never again would we commiserate and rejoice over common experiences: the difficult professor, the Saturday night party, the impossible final exam, the spectacular date, a lecture by a self-righteous dean, the autumn spectacle of football. A few of us would never leave the academic life. Some would go on to graduate school for an advanced degree and wind up teaching, perhaps returning to Dartmouth. But for the rest, our studies were over, and we were forced into the sudden realization that we would have to grow up and meet the outside world, which in all likelihood would not be as friendly as this little northern enclave.

Late that night, walking alone down Webster Avenue, watching the moon settle above an empty Baker Library, I heard the echo of bells in my mind.

I opened my eyes to sunlight streaming through my window. I lay in bed for a while, trying to decide whether I should get up. I looked at a photograph that had been taken at the party the night before, with one of those instant cameras. The quality of the picture was short of perfection, but I could see the faces: Kemp, Teevens, Lempress, a number of the brothers, and some attractive women. The group looked a good deal older than when I first met them four years ago. Jones was curiously absent. I tucked the photo in my wallet.

At ten o'clock I got ready to march in the big graduation procession. All thousand graduates sat directly in front of the commencement speaker's podium, with several thousand relatives directly behind us. Behind them were people who would not get a seat, interested spectators, and reporters who were there to hear the president of Dartmouth deliver his final speech. That's right, John George Kemeny was stepping down as Dartmouth president. He was being replaced by a businessman from Minneapolis, the former chairman of the Toro lawnmower company and chairman of Dartmouth's Board of Trustees, David McLaughlin of the class of '54.

"I have a special charge to your class: I charge you to go out and tell forty thousand alumni about the Dartmouth you know and love," Kemeny told us. His hands were shaking and he seemed passionate about the message he was delivering. A moment later it became clear what the full message was.

> There are many alumni who have not been back for many, many years and thus they have to rely on rumors, on third-hand reports, or on what is happening at other colleges to form their view of the Dartmouth of today. *Or, they are receiving that view from other publications that have ulterior motives—that will twist the truth to fit their own special purposes.*

Everyone interpreted "other publications" as a reference to *The Dartmouth Review*. "That will twist the truth . . ." I wondered what our ulterior motives might be. The paper, it seemed to me, had always been candid in its positions. It made no effort to hide the fact that it was generally conservative, supported Ronald Reagan, liked the Jack Kemp tax-cut proposal, John Steel, and the Indian symbol. It was outspoken in its criticism of the Dartmouth administration's policies regarding curriculum, reverse discrimination, and racially segregated social and living facilities. It was all up front, explicit and argumentative. Nothing was hidden. But President Kemeny was not through:

235

Poisoned Ivy

During the years to come, many voices will speak to you. . . .
Amongst these voices will be one—a voice heard in many guises
throughout history—which is the most dangerous voice you will
ever hear. It appeals to the basest instincts in all of us—it appeals to
human prejudice. It tries to *divide* us by setting whites against
blacks, by setting Christians against Jews, by setting men against
women. And if it succeeds in dividing us from our fellow human
beings it will impose its evil will upon a fragmented society.

The attack had a certain irony. It was, judging by the reaction of
the students, parents, and alumni, the most *divisive* commencement address ever delivered at Dartmouth. Either one agreed with
reverse discrimination policies and segregated living facilities, or
one was a racist. Either one was for disarmament, or one was a
warmonger. Either one believed in funding lesbian groups, or one
hated women. The speech was, to employ a liberal buzz word,
simplistic.

The liberal mind, I found during my Dartmouth experience, is
Machiavellian and melodramatic. It sees itself as pure and its
opponents as haters. It's not enough to attack the opponent issue by
issue. The liberal must conjure up an enemy and call him a Hitler.

After the graduation ceremony, the campus cleared out, and by
three o'clock in the afternoon, Hanover looked like a ghost town.
Most people, I think, didn't like the prospect of saying goodbye to
their friends. It sounded too final. I always hated it when a student
would say to another, "Well, I guess this is it. Goodbye, and have a
good life." How can anyone respond to that? So most people just
drifted off, and that was the end of it.

At about six o'clock, I took a walk around the campus. The
dorms were empty and the library closed. The huge commencement speakers' podium, which had taken two weeks to assemble,
was already dismantled. A station wagon with a U-Haul trailer,
loaded down with four years of accumulated debris, made its way

through the Hanover streets and finally down the long hill to Ledyard Bridge, leaving nothing behind but a cloud of dust.

An elderly alumnus stopped me on the corner where Main Street intersects Wheelock in front of the Hanover Inn terrace. He didn't introduce himself, but he asked where I was going from there.

"I don't know," I said.

"You'll look back on these days as the best of your life," he said.

"I hope not," I said.

POISONED IVY

I HAD been out of Dartmouth for a couple of years, and word got out to Dartmouth officials that *Poisoned Ivy* would begin appearing on bookshelves in the fall of 1984. I began getting panic-stricken phone calls from alumni fundraisers.

"The title sounds negative," one fundraiser said.

"It's a mix of good and bad," I said.

"A lot has changed since Kemeny went back to the math department," said the fundraiser. "This new president, David McLaughlin, is a conservative, and he's changed things completely. I hope you say that in your book."

The alumni had high hopes for David McLaughlin. He was more mainstream than Kemeny, who was doing some part-time work for Alan Cranston's ill-fated campaign for the 1984 Democratic nomination. Both Kemeny and Cranston, it seemed, were symbolic of a decayed, dying liberalism—barely able to muster more than a sliver of the popular vote. McLaughlin, on the other hand, was virile. He had been a tremendous tight end for Dartmouth in the early Fifties, and, in fact, went on to play pro football for the Philadelphia Eagles. When he arrived on campus, he stood six-feet four inches tall and was in extremely good physical shape for a man his age. He even had a deep suntan. His home was in Minnesota, where he was chairman of the Toro lawnmower company. He had seen the disaster unfold at Dartmouth during the Kemeny years, and alumni viewed him as a man who could restore lost traditions and bring rigor back to the curriculum. Everyone else thought he could, too. He did, however, have one major obstacle: the *ethos.*

An example of the kind of thing that went on under McLaughlin's presidency occurred in the fall of 1982, when a sophomore reporter named Laura Ingraham enraged William Cole, a tenured Dartmouth professor, by publishing a critique of his music history course in *The Dartmouth Review.*

Professor Cole, a kind of guru for militant members of the black community on campus, was so outraged by the sophomore's article that he suspended class for two sessions and demanded that *The Dartmouth Review* apologize. "I will not tolerate any sneaky m*th*rf*ck*r to come into my class to write an article," the professor screamed to his bewildered students, according to a follow-up article, again, published in the *Review.*

Dinesh D'Souza, chairman of the newspaper, said Professor Cole's request for an apology was "humorous, because the article was indisputably accurate."

The morning after the article appeared, a Saturday, Professor Cole showed up at 8:30 A.M. at Laura Ingraham's dorm room and banged on her door for almost twenty minutes, screaming obscenities and waking everyone on her hallway. Ingraham wasn't there, and her roommate was too frightened to open the door. Professor Cole left, but came back again at 10:30 and tried to force the door open. The roommate opened the door slightly, peered through the crack, and asked that she be given a moment to put on her clothes. Professor Cole allowed her to get dressed. I was unable to get a verbatim account of this particular verbal flourish by Cole, but the roommate was reportedly stunned, in fact, in tears, over her experience with a member of the Dartmouth faculty.

Professor Cole's cancellation of class and his performance in a

240

college dormitory were reported to the dean's office. The matter was taken up by Hans Penner, Dean of the Faculty. Penner reprimanded Professor Cole for his behavior and told him that he could not cancel classes. Attempting to explain this Dartmouth professor's actions, Dean Penner told the *Review*, "I don't know what it's like to be a black man. He's obviously under emotional stress."

Some understatement. If Professor Cole had been anything but black, he would not have been told to return to the classroom, he would have been turfed off the campus. Dean Penner's statement implies that, because Professor Cole is black, he should not be measured by the usual standards of conduct, which seems precisely the kind of condescension that promotes racism. In Tuesday's class, according to *The Dartmouth Review* and several students in the class, Professor Cole continued the barrage of obscene language, using words like "bastard," "*ssh*le," "m*th*rf*ck*r," and "c*cks*ck*r."

"I'm the professor," the professor told his class, "I have a Ph.D. You all are ignorant ... You are all responsible for this, because you are [the *Review* reporter's] peers, and some of you know her, or are her accomplices."

Despite Dean Penner's warning, Professor Cole announced that his class would be suspended for two weeks, after which attendance would be optional. All requirements would be dropped, except the final exam, for which he passed out the questions in advance. The professor then appealed to the black students in the class to confront the administration because, "My job's on the line, man." He went on to say that "black people are the only ones who understand freedom and justice." At the end of Professor Cole's speech, a few black students gave him a standing ovation, but most students, black and white, were dumbfounded and remained seated. "I would expect more from a Dartmouth professor," said one student.

Two months later, Professor Cole filed a lawsuit against *The Dartmouth Review*, Laura Ingraham, and the staff for $2.2 million, which is unresolved.

While the Professor Cole story is odd in itself, the really disturb-

241

ing news is that the Dartmouth faculty supported him. In fact, fifteen faculty members including the John Phillips Professor of Religion, the Arthur R. Virgin Professor of Music, the John Sloan Dickey Third Century Professor, the Geisel Professor in the Humanities, among others, sent a letter around appealing for money to support Professor Cole's war against the *Review*. The Geisel Professor in the Humanities, John Appleton, added an especially colorful touch, saying that, if he were Cole, he would have "busted Ingraham's kneecaps." Even the Dartmouth administration must have thought this too harsh a punishment for a sophomore reporter.

There was no comment on the Professor Cole affair by Dartmouth president David McLaughlin.

More peculiar things began to occur under McLaughlin's leadership. The Tucker Foundation, for example, in conjunction with a number of Dartmouth's endowed committees, launched an extensive campaign to lobby for a "nuclear freeze" on American weapons. During the 1982-83 academic year, a total of 60 speakers made their way to the Dartmouth campus, including professional propagandists from Moscow, of which 46 called on the United States to end its production and deployment of nuclear weapons. Only eleven thought a strategy of "peace through strength" was a good idea; the other three speakers were more or less neutral on the issue.

Students, for example, were treated to a presentation by William Sloan Coffin, the protestant minister who hailed the arrival of the Ayatollah in Iran as "progressive." Coffin labeled American soldiers who fought in Vietnam "war criminals" and asserted that Moscow's "proposals have been more reasonable than those of Reagan." In one of his calmer moments, he pronounced America "morally bankrupt," and called on citizens to withhold from the Internal Revenue Service the percentage of their tax bill allocated for our national defense.

From the Catholic side; Robert Drinan, a priest and former U.S. congressman (who was told by the Pope to get out of politics following a vote supporting federal funding for abortion) trundled in from Washington to inform students of Ronald Reagan's "irrational cold war mentality" and scorn the American president's "hostile obsession with communism." Father Drinan went on to define the "peace through strength" idea as "pathological" and dismissed criticism of the nuclear freeze as "a nonsensical onslaught." On a similar note, there was a presentation by Martin Sherwin, a writer for *The Nation*, who advised students to be thankful for "every Reagan administration day we survive."

Beyond its lecture series, however, which was hopelessly lopsided against the idea of deterrence (a strategy that has prevented war for 40 years), the nuclear freeze concept also became an integral part of the Dartmouth curriculum under President McLaughlin. E. P. Thompson, for example, was hired to teach a course on disarmament, and announced to befuddled students that the CIA is sabotaging civil rights movements in the Soviet Union and Eastern Europe. On the question of the Soviet massacre of Afghan women and children, and Moscow's position on Afghan civil rights, Thompson argued that "we need not base our actions on preference for one bloc or another." Right, but what about basing our actions on their actions? (Thompson, incidentally, heads the Campaign for Nuclear Disarmament and has been a major figure in the European Freeze movement.)

There was also a course entitled "The Control of Nuclear Weapons," taught by a visiting professor from Princeton, Harold Feiveson, who writes for the magazine *Dissent*. The titles of the required readings provide the gist of Professor Feiveson's message: *Protest and Survive, Nuclear Nightmares, A Smoking Radiating Ruin at the End of Two Hours, The Bomb, Dread, and Eternity*, and so on.

But Dartmouth went even further than polluting the curriculum to advance disarmament for America. The Tucker Foundation, Dartmouth's psuedoreligious outfit, in conjunction with a left-wing group called "Bridges for Peace," sponsored a visit to the Dartmouth campus by a delegation from the Soviet Peace Committee, which included the following speakers:

Poisoned Ivy

—Yuri Bandura, a Soviet propagandist and deputy editor in chief of the leading government newspaper, *Izveztia.*

—Galina Sidrova, a reporter for *New Times,* another Soviet publication. She spoke to the students about Reagan's "repressive measures" and said his comments on Poland were "red-threat signals."

—Yuri Zamoshkin, head of United States Studies and the United States and Canada Institute of Moscow. His writings, published widely in Soviet government publications, describe America as "an authoritarian bureaucratic structure" that frustrates the aspirations of the American people. "Conservative right-wing extremist groups have been able to redirect feelings of national humiliation and shame and channel support for chauvinism, great-power imperial policy, and militarism," he says.

In addition, there was Ivan Knietz, the head of the biochemistry department at the Latvian Academy of Sciences; Karina Pogosovia, acting secretary general of the United Nations Associations; Vladimir Rudko, vice-rector of the Moscow Institute and member of the Soviet Commission of Physicians for the Prevention of Nuclear War; and Lumilla Tarasevich-Skrylnikova, a history professor at Moscow University and a member of the Soviet Women's Committee. There was even a Soviet clergyman, Alexander Zavgorodny, a bishop in the Russian Orthodox Church, who stressed that there was no religious persecution in the USSR. His church, according to *Twentieth Century Peace,* a Soviet magazine, has been extremely cooperative with the Soviet peace movement. It had also ceased being a church and had become an arm of Moscow's propaganda machinery.

Zamoshkin seemed to impress a number of faculty members when he said the USSR was becoming more democratic and that the Soviet peace movement was picking up steam. The Soviet peace movement consists of denouncing President Reagan as the gravest threat to world peace since Adolf Hitler. It is Ronald Reagan who is the focus of evil in the world, according to these travelers from the Soviet bloc.

244

"Give peace a chance," said one of the Soviet speakers. For me this phrase has a chilling effect. We had given peace a chance in Vietnam, Cambodia, and Laos, and what we got for it was genocide—millions killed by Pol Pot and the Hanoi government, thousands handed over to the Soviet Union to work in slave labor camps, thousands of refugees drowning or dying of disease, while trying to escape on their rafts. The word "peace" has become a kind of boomerang word. It changes course in mid-flight and turns into its opposite. The peace rhetoric coming from the Dartmouth campus was Orwellian.

The peace movement is not actually a peace movement at all. It's a surrender movement. What peace really means to these people is permitting the Soviets to crush all resistance under the threat of nuclear war. The Soviets like to play on people's fears. They try to frighten people into believing the peace rhetoric. They say, give peace a chance, or we'll blow you off the face of the earth.

The Dartmouth Review commented weekly on the "red parade in Hanover," and was mailed out to thousands of alumni, who began phoning President McLaughlin for an explanation of what was going on. He also had the difficulty of confrontations with militant members of the Dartmouth faculty, who would storm into his office on a weekly basis and demand that he close down the *Review*, to which he could only respond, "There's nothing I can do." He could not control these dissident students. In addition, McLaughlin had no academic credentials other than a Dartmouth undergraduate degree and an M.BA., and so carried no weight with the faculty. For David McLaughlin, the problems began to mount.

He tried for a while to pretend that *The Dartmouth Review* did not exist. The policy was this: any alumnus who tried to reach the paper through the college switchboard was transferred to a dean's office, where he was told there was no such thing as *The Dartmouth Review*.

"The Dartmouth what?" the secretary would ask. "Are you sure you don't mean the *Alumni Magazine?*"

"No, I mean *The Dartmouth Review*," the alumnus would say.

"There's no *Dartmouth Review* here," the secretary would say. "Perhaps there was at one time, but it's long since out of business. Sorry."

Click.

This was a pathetic attempt to cut off alumni funding for the paper, and was seen as such by the faculty. In another attempt to win their respect, McLaughlin delivered a lame convocation address with the following insights: on Vietnam, he discussed "our involvement in a war of questionable merit"; on the genocide in Cambodia and Afghanistan, he benignly labeled evidence of "world political uncertainty," and in the same breath said "political unrest" in El Salvador and Poland was of a similar type. With pious genuflection he quoted the wisdom of his predecessor, John Kemeny.

On the same day, McLaughlin's name appeared in the *Boston Globe* with 40 other college presidents, including Kemeny, at the bottom of a letter to President Reagan, decrying "the catastrophe that major nuclear war would represent to the American people and all civilizations." In his address to the students he paraphrased the letter, stating, "We stand closer to the brink of potential nuclear catastrophe, because technology has seemingly outpaced man's capacity to excercise international statesmanship in a way that will further mutual welfare and promote peaceful and respectful coexistence."

The students appeared disgusted with McLaughlin's vacuous platitudes, especially when he urged students "to put themselves at risk as individuals" in the unfailing quest for truth and "moral courage."

The Dartmouth Review outraged official opinion by bringing in the Reverend Jerry Falwell to speak at Dartmouth. It is interesting to note that this small newspaper, with an annual budget of $100,000, in its three years of existence had brought to the campus more conservative speakers than had the college during the combined presidencies of Kemeny and McLaughlin, spanning 13 years.

McLaughlin declined the *Review*'s invitation to introduce Falwell, but did introduce the Soviet ambassador to the United Nations, Oleg Troyanovsky, who told a packed auditorium that "It's difficult to criticize the Soviet Union because our government's for the freeze." He went on to denounce U.S. militarism, imperialism, and obstructionism. President McLaughlin spoke in glowing terms of this agent of disinformation, calling him an "honored guest," and inviting him back to speak to the students any time.

President McLaughlin also announced a policy of backing draft registration resisters, saying that, although President Reagan, with the approval of Congress, will not grant low-interest loans for education to students who have not registered for the draft, similar loans will be guaranteed by Dartmouth College. McLaughlin said the law was "unconstitutional because it penalizes students who have not gone before a court." I consulted a number of legal scholars, who said they could find no precedent to support McLaughlin's claim; it seems Reagan's idea, that even people who have not appeared in court should be subject to the laws of the United States, is consistent with the Constitution.

President McLaughlin's second criticism of the law was that "It puts the college in the position of policeman." Never mind that Dartmouth employs a battalion of campus police to enforce state and local statutes and that he gleefully complies with federal Title IX and Affirmative Action regulations so the college can receive government money, including taxpayer-financed loans to students. (Is it fair that the janitors who clean up after the students also have to pay for those students' loans?)

McLaughlin said his decision to back the lawbreakers "has no political implications at all," although his announcement of the new loan program astounded most of the students, about 90 percent of whom had registered. He looked pleased with himself. He sensed that he was beginning to win the respect of the faculty. When asked about alumni reaction, President McLaughlin said, "If alumni knew the facts, they would go along," implying that alumni who disagreed with him didn't know the facts. The condescension in his voice was reminiscent of John Kemeny. President McLaughlin, the former football star, once a hero of the alumni, the man who would change Dartmouth into a serious academic institution, now distrusted them. "They just don't understand," he said. He was being transformed by the *ethos.*

Also instituted under McLaughlin was something called the "Interracial Awareness Council," which set up seminars on race awareness and put on parties with advertisements saying "Everyone Is Welcome!" implying that all races aren't welcome at fraternity parties. Featured at one of the seminars was Professor William Cole, who spoke on "Prospects of Racial Harmony at Dartmouth."

"Dartmouth is not unique," Cole told his audience. "I think almost all of the educational institutions in America are racist. There's no doubt about it . . . the institution is trying to perpetuate racism throughout its curriculum."

Now, there is nothing wrong with attempting to promote good relations between the races, but that wasn't the point of the Interracial Council. The point was for David McLaughlin, his administration, and the Dartmouth faculty to proclaim their virtue by setting up a forum where fanatics could denounce nonexistent campus bigotry—which the Dartmouth educational Establishment took tremendous delight in saying was "pervasive."

President McLaughlin did something that even John Kemeny would not have done. He announced that the Hovey Grill murals, portraying the founding of Dartmouth College, would be boarded over, more or less permanently, using nails, replacing Kemeny's hinged panels that could easily be removed. The murals, because they show Indians drinking rum with Eleazar Wheelock, Dartmouth's founder, were "offensive," according to John Heston, McLaughlin's director of communications. McLaughlin did say that the murals could be uncovered for special occasions, such as

248

class reunions, when wealthy alumni asked to see the paintings before giving their checks to omni-present fund raisers.

In noting McLaughlin's decision to break with America's tradition of free speech, it is worth reflecting on President Dwight D. Eisenhower's famous "book burning" address that he delivered in 1953 to Dartmouth's graduating seniors.

"Don't join the book burners," Eisenhower said. "Don't think you are going to conceal faults by concealing evidence that they ever existed." Eisenhower's specific reference was to communism, which by all accounts was more odious than the Hovey Grill murals.

"How will we defeat communism unless we know what it is, what it teaches? Why does it have such an appeal for men?"

"Now, we have to fight it with something better, not try to conceal the thinking of our own people . . . They are part of America, and even if they think ideas that are contrary to ours, they have the right to have them, and *a right to have them in places where they are accessible to others.* It is unquestioned, or it is not America."

In all likelihood, David McLaughlin, a junior at the time, heard Eisenhower's speech first hand, since many underclassmen attend commencement ceremonies. Apparently, he had forgotten the message.

President McLaughlin put Dartmouth once again in the national spotlight. The *Wall Street Journal* ran an editorial entitled "Dartmouth on Trial," in which the issue was—you guessed it—harassment of *The Dartmouth Review.* This time the target of the college was freshman reporter Teresa Polenz, who found herself charged by the college disciplinary committee with committing a serious crime. McLaughlin changed the committee's rules (as they had been applied during the Fossedal hearing) to prohibit any lawyer or advisor of the student from cross-examining witnesses if, in the judgment of the chairman, the questions were not germane to the case, or if such questioning would make the hearing unnecessarily long and drawn out. What young Miss Polenz had done was tape record a publicly advertised meeting of the Gay Students Association and then write a mild, eminently respectable article (without using members' names) explaining exactly what the homosexual group does with the money it gets from the college:

> REPORTER: What do you do with the money . . . Do you have functions:
> GAY STUDENT #1: We have parties. Wait until you see our parties!

This was about as racy as Polenz's article got, but the picture was clear. Polenz implicitly raised the point that it was not long ago that colleges were doing all they could to keep even heterosexual couples out of the bedroom. Now the college seemed to be encouraging, even promoting, deviant sexual activity. As one homosexual put it at the meeting Polenz attended, "Most heterosexuals are perverts," suggesting the values of the college had indeed changed over the last decade or so.

The new dean of the college, Edward Shanahan, accused the 18-year-old girl of having broken state laws by tape recording a public event and publishing the proceedings. Laurence Silberman, a Dartmouth alumnus and former deputy attorney general of the United States, said the charges against the student were frivolous and that Dartmouth has set itself up for a big harassment lawsuit. Silberman was so outraged by the college's treatment of the freshman that he flew up to Hanover, and decided to take on President McLaughlin's administration *pro bono*. The results of this case are not known as of this writing, but this was a hell of a way for an 18-year-old girl to be introduced to college life.

The college was not, in fact, concerned with Teresa Polenz's recording of an event. The outrage was over the *Review*'s reporting on the Gay Students Association, questioning college funding of its activities, and its academic merit. The same people who talk about "the importance of tolerance," "the need for diversity," and why "we must listen to other opinions," are usually astounded to discover that there actually is another opinion.

More strange things began to occur. *The Dartmouth Review* reported that David McLaughlin had forced the resignation of longtime athletic director Sever Peters. Peters was reportedly unhappy with Dartmouth's continued de-emphasis on athletics. It appeared, in fact, that Parkhurst Hall took a perverse pride in the fact that Dartmouth's men's teams were still at the bottom of the Ivy League. Alumni found this policy on the part of President McLaughlin surprising, since he had been such a great athlete himself.

But this was the new David McLaughlin, no longer the bronzed image of masculinity he once was. Physical deterioration had begun to set in. He had suffered a recent heart attack. He had also suffered the Dartmouth faculty. Before coming to Hanover, he was still chairman of the Toro lawnmower company, his home was famous for the Indian paraphernalia that decorated the interior. He could often be seen wearing an Indian necktie, and his daughter wore an Indianhead penny on her necklace. All that changed, however, after he became president of Dartmouth. He had taken, instead, to introducing Soviet propagandists to students, censoring art, and terrorizing freshmen reporters.

In another attempt to win faculty support, President McLaughlin issued the following statement regarding *The Dartmouth Review*:

> Without regard to the political ideology it may espouse, it is my opinion that the *Review* is not representative of the values held by the overwhelming majority of Dartmouth's students, faculty, and administrators... When freedom of expression is used relentlessly

251

to attack the integrity of individuals or segments of the community, it tests to the limit our commitment to that right.

But freedom of speech is a constitutional right. If Professor William Cole is free to speak, if agents of the Kremlin (who are unalterably opposed to free speech) are welcomed as speakers, students should be free to comment. That includes pointing out the imbalance in a lecture series, or questioning the misjudgments of people in authority.

President McLaughlin should have known that he would never win the respect of the Dartmouth faculty, because he never could have gone far enough for them. The former football star, head of a major corporation, president of his fraternity, the once vertebrate David McLaughlin, had been transformed into Silly Putty.

But the *ethos* is not confined to Dartmouth College. United Nations Ambassador Jeane Kirkpatrick, an anticommunist Democrat, was either shouted down, or told her security could not be assured, at Berkeley, Barnard, and Smith. Eldridge Cleaver, the former Black Panther, now a fierce opponent of communism after his experiences with the Castro government, was shouted down at the University of Wisconsin. After 90 minutes of din, Cleaver wrote on the blackboard, "I regret that the totalitarians have deprived us of our constitutional rights to free assembly and free speech. Down with communism! Long live democracy!" Cleaver said he would try to speak again, but didn't know when. William F. Buckley, Jr., was invited to speak at Vassar's commencement, but was warned that, if he appeared, he would be shouted down, and risk physical harm. He declined the invitation.

At Harvard, Secretary of Defense Caspar Wienberger tried to speak, but militants in the audience hurled insults at him, unfurled a banner calling him a "war criminal," and flung red paint at him that was supposed to symbolize the blood of the deaths they said he had caused in Central America. One member of the audience screamed, "How can we respect a mass murderer?" Weinberger was cut short because of the disturbances but at a reception later said most students were actually well behaved. It was a minority of militants who ruined the speech for everyone.

Bartlett Giamatti, president of Yale, at the request of the faculty, went after the *Yale Literary Magazine* for use of the Yale name. (Sound familiar?) Giamatti had taken his cue from Dartmouth, as *The Yale Lit*, edited by Andrei Navrosov, son of the dissident Russian émigré Lev Navrosov, evidentally was deemed antithetical to the values of Yale University. He also prohibited the Yale Glee Club from recording the Solidarity anthem "Let Poland Be Poland," to be broadcast over the Voice of America, saying the song was too political. But, Giamatti, in addresses to the students, had attacked repeatedly Jerry Falwell's Moral Majority as a threat to freedom in America and had taken stands in favor of continued federal aid to higher education. In addition, Yale's *Russian Chorus* has been making trips to the Soviet Union for years, which had been praised by Averell Harriman as "bridge building." Giamatti, evidently, did not consider these activities political.

I made the trip back to Hanover early in the fall of 1983 to visit some friends and attend a *Dartmouth Review* board meeting. I went into the Hanover Inn, where I found George Champion. Champion, the former chairman of the Chase Manhattan Bank, was also a *Review* board member. He was chatting with a number of very enthusiastic reporters from *The Dartmouth Review*. The staff, during its three years in existence, had grown to about 40, and Champion told the students how proud he was that they were not intimidated by the college.

David McLaughlin appeared in the lobby. He looked worn and seemed short of breath.

He glanced at the crowd of student editors and reporters who had joy and life in their faces. Then he saw George Champion, whom he had known as a business associate before coming to Dartmouth. Champion was to corporate America what Joe Dimaggio was to baseball. He also played on Dartmouth's national championship football team of '25. McLaughlin smiled momentarily, and his face was on the verge of lighting up as he walked toward Champion, his arm outstretched to shake hands. But then he must have thought better of it. The smile left his face, as he shuffled off to another room before Champion saw him. McLaughlin knew that his former business idol was unhappy about what had happed to Dartmouth. It was sad, in a way, because Champion had had such high hopes for McLaughlin.

Later that afternoon, I ran into a freshman arriving for his first day at Dartmouth. He was loaded down with bags. A tennis racket protruded from one of the leather side pockets.

"Where's South Fayerweather dorm?" he asked me.

"I'll show you," I said. "You look like you could use some help carrying those bags."

"Thanks," said the freshman, as he handed me a suitcase. "How do I get something to eat?"

"Thayer Dining Hall," I said. "It's right over there by the elm trees, across the Green."

"This place is really something," said the freshman.

"Have you got a roommate?" I asked.

"Yeah, I think his name is Norman Rudhauser. Haven't met him yet," said the freshman.

"This suitcase of yours is heavy," I said.

"It's full of books," said the freshman. "Can't wait to start reading 'em. There's Shakespeare, Chaucer, Homer, Joyce, Eliot. I think I've got the whole history of the world in that one suitcase." He was wide-eyed with enthusiasm. "I'll bet there are some great professors at this place," he said.

We arrived at South Fayerweather dorm. The freshman put his bags down for a moment, stood on the steps, looked at the campus, and listened as the bells from Baker Library boomed out the hour.

"Thanks a lot. I'll take it from here," said the freshman, as he picked up his bags and walked inside. But that's where this story began.